A SECOND LOOK

A SECOND LOOK

Reading the Bible Again for the First Time

Robert Smith Bader

VANTAGE PRESS
New York

FIRST EDITION

Published by Vantage Press, Inc.
516 West 34th Street, New York, New York 10001

Manufactured in the United States of America
ISBN: 0-533-12664-9

Library of Congress Catalog Card No.: 97- 91401

0 9 8 7 6 5 4 3 2 1

When I was a child, I spoke like a child, I thought like a child, I reasoned like a child; when I became an adult. . . .

—1 Corinthians 13:11

Contents

List of Figures

Preface

The Holy Bible—the Book of Books—is easily the most influential writing in the history of Western civilization. More importantly, it has traditionally been revered as the revealed "Word of God," the inspired canon that we swear upon literally and figuratively, our infallible guide to ethical behavior. Above all, its text locates precisely—in the cross hairs of eternal time and infinite space—the one, true, and living God. In vain, one searches for the true Deity in the Pyramid Texts of third millennium B.C.E. Egypt, the law codes of second millennium B.C.E. Babylonia, or the historical annals of first millennium B.C.E. Assyria. The living God, the God of history, is to be found in first millennium B.C.E. Israel, as described in the gilt-edged, leather-bound pages of the Holy Bible.

Not only is the Bible the most consequential literature in our culture but—as a text intended primarily for adults—it is conveyed to the young in an absolutely unique fashion. We may recall clearly enough our first encounter as adolescents with Hemingway or Shakespeare, and our eagerness to bring our immature criticisms to bear on the readings. But our "first look" at the Bible is lost forever in the mists of time. It is, in fact, impossible to remember that primordial period when we were totally innocent of biblical knowledge. This salient fact of our developmental years has produced a tendency to uncritical, even unconditional, acceptance—a process perhaps akin to that of "imprinting" in the avian world. Once the Inspired Word is firmly implanted in the immature, nondiscriminating mind, its authority can never be totally erased.

While the details may have faded, the social milieu in which we made our initial acquaintance with the Bible is reconstructed readily. Those venerable and awesome moral authorities—our parents, grandparents, Sunday school teachers, and ministers—

with a truly heroic effort, managed to maintain a semblance of order among their restless charges while imparting a modicum of practical ethics and seemingly impractical theology. With a "mystical" combination of love and discipline, these omniscient and omnipotent figures gave to us—or, if you will, imposed upon us—an elementary sense of cosmic purpose, meaning, and identity. Thus reinforced, our impressionistic young minds—like so many *tabulae rasae*—soaked up the supreme wisdom of the ages as it was proclaimed from the daunting pages of the Book.

Certainly we missed the nuances of the theological profundities that were dropped like so many pearls before us—though we could readily empathize with baby Moses in the bulrushes and infant Jesus in the manger. A few years later, we were soundly defeated by those exotic Old Testament (OT) names—from Amaziah and Azariah through Jehoahaz and Jehoiachin to Zedekiah and Zephaniah. Yes, we missed a good deal, but we did not miss the monumental fact that nothing—absolutely nothing—in our entire lives or this vast universe would ever rival in importance the eternal truths to be found in the august pages of the Holy Bible. In those tender years, we accepted cheerfully and passively the grand context, the metaphysical frame, within which our very lives were to be played out. In this "first look," the words of a popular Christian Sunday school song fused indissolubly the Book and the living Godhead: "Jesus loves me! This I know, for the Bible tells me so."

My personal faith journey is remarkable only for its ordinariness. Like millions of other families, mine took its biblically-based religion seriously but not as devoutly as those pious folk who attended church on Sunday evenings and Bible study on Wednesday. My inherited tradition is that of mainline Protestantism, specifically the Disciples of Christ and United Methodists. In both denominations, the Holy Bible is the cornerstone of the faith for the "priesthood of believers."

Originating in the early nineteenth century among dissident Presbyterians and Baptists, the Disciples affirm unequivocally the central authority of the Bible: "Where the Scriptures speak, we speak; where the Scriptures are silent, we are silent."[1] A founding father, Alexander Campbell, testified that as the basis of his faith, he took "the Bible, the whole Bible, and nothing but the Bible."[2] The eighteenth-century founder of Methodism, John Wesley, was a true son of the unadorned *sola scriptura* tradition of the Protestant Reformation. His five-volume biblical commentary had been carefully designed, he said, to give "the direct, literal meaning" of every sentence and to keep the reader's eye firmly fixed on the "naked Bible."[3]

Our more mature "second look" is consonant with the tradition that represents the Bible as "the true source of the knowledge of God."[4] Our interest coheres around the time-honored proposition that the character and purposes of God are revealed in Sacred Scripture. Unblinkingly we will examine the concepts and evidence presented in the text and draw only those conclusions that may be reasonably deduced therefrom. In this day and age, the public issue of religious credulity has shifted toward the question of *whether* one believes, a query that nearly all Americans answer in the affirmative. We intend to penetrate beyond that superficial datum and explore the character and designs of the scriptural Deity who is the object of such popular, but largely unexamined, belief. For more than a century, the standing of the Bible as "scientific" authority has been steadily and permanently eroded. The time is now propitious to inquire into its authority in the far more sensitive areas of ethics and morality, as revealed in the character of the scriptural God.

The facet of the divine character of primary interest is that of the "God of Justice" and the judicial system associated therewith. Of the several divine attributes, this dimension affords us an unexcelled opportunity to observe the systematic interaction between God and humankind. On this field, the great dramas of God and his subjects, in conflict, are played out. Of the two testaments, this dynamic receives a much more textured treatment in the OT—not surprisingly, since the OT, or Hebrew Bible, represents a historical-theological chronicle of the relationships between an ethnic people, their neighbors, and their God. In the NT, the historical God of Israel nearly disappears from view behind novel and imposing theological structures, being almost totally "superseded" by the Son.

As in the story line of a novel or biography, the biblical narrative delineates those distinctive qualities of its protagonist, God, that in the aggregate constitute what we know as "character." All that we may legitimately conclude regarding the moral attributes of the protagonist stems from his words and deeds. The consequential words and deeds of the God of Justice will be scrutinized in two different, but related, contexts. In the area of "foreign relations," God responds to the presence of the people in the nations surrounding Israel, the sometimes threatening but always Godless "other." In this setting, the elemental anthropological principle of "us-them" governs. In the more intimate "domestic" relationship between God and his people Israel, the dominant theme is fidelity to the covenantal laws. Within this framework, the retributional principle controls—what we have designated as the "Deuteronomic Hypothesis."

For over ninety percent of the nearly two-thousand-year history of the Bible, faith communities unquestioningly accepted it as the inspired Word of God. Those who seriously challenged the received tradition were promptly branded as heretics and consigned to hell. In the past century or so, but especially since the Second World War, an impressive and voluminous scholarship has yielded unprecedented insights into the manifold stages of formation of the Book. Of special significance has been the identification of the *Sitz im Leben* of the authors and their redactors, i.e., the immediate social, political, economic, and religious conditions that "inspired" them to set down in writing their most urgent concerns.

Utilizing the basic rationales of the scientific method, these historical and literacy studies have been primarily analytical in nature, necessarily resolving the whole into smaller and smaller subunits that receive ever more intensive scrutiny. As in many other fields of progressive academic endeavor, the trend is to say more and more about less and less. This course distances the relevant research ever further from the ken of the women and men in the pews. But for the Book to tell its overarching stories to both specialist and layperson, the pieces must be fitted once again into a synthetic whole—but now illuminated by the insights of the analytical work. Informed by these analyses, the present study reads the text holistically, rather than "atomistically," focusing on the "plain sense" that the canonical messages convey to the modern reader. In this manner, it may serve as a bridge between the more scholarly interests and those of the wider audience.

Firmly anchored in both text and scholarship, our God-seeking approach is rationalistic while appreciating that neither human beings nor their religious expressions can be completely captured in appeals to reason. Perhaps in a small way this study may serve as an antidote to the wave of irrationality that is sweeping across our turn-of-the-millennium scene. Not everyone will concur in the theological perspectives offered, but if thoughtful reflection is generated thereby, the primary objective will have been achieved. As Socrates might have said, "The unexamined Bible (or God) is not worth believing." Of course, anyone audacious enough to engage in serious God-talk should always bear in mind Lord Thomas Macaulay's sobering dictum that in matters of theology "the interval is small indeed between Aristotle and a child, between Archimedes and a naked savage."[5]

Chapter 1 sets the biblical portrayal of Israel and its God in a broad anthropological context with an emphasis on divine power and election. The next three chapters focus on the character of God as he responds to the surrounding peoples: chapter 2 analyzes the morality of the Conquest of Canaan; chapter 3 describes the relationships with the small nations on Israel's eastern and southern borders; chapter 4 takes up the vexed question of nationalism and universalism. The next three chapters deal with the relationship between the God of Justice and his people Israel. In chapter 5, the divinely-decreed principle of retribution (the "Deuteronomic Hypothesis") is examined; in chapter 6, dissidents of the concept have their day; in chapter 7, the development of the "afterlife solution" is outlined. In Chapter 8, the modern-day implications of the Marcionite heresy are explored.

For those less familiar with the history of Israel, Appendix A provides a chronological chart of the most momentous events. Appendix B is a brief excursus into theodicy that is tied closely to the character of God that emerges in the text. All biblical quotations are from the New Revised Standard Version (NRSV) unless otherwise specified. A few quotations are from the Revised Standard Version (RSV), the King James Version (KJV), or the translation of the Jewish Publication Society (JPS). The dates of the reigns of the Israelite kings are from the *Anchor Bible Dictionary,* volume 1, page 1,010. The dating sigla of B.C.E. ("Before the Common Era") and C.E. ("Common Era") replace the more triumphalist B.C. ("Before Christ") and A.D. ("Year of Our Lord").

Capitalization of deity follows the standard, "religiously correct" practice of honoring one's Own while deprecating the outlandish pretensions of the "other" and his "gods." The psychological impact of the capitalization differential is indeed striking as the following pair of lines illustrates:

> The God of Israel and the god of Moab were neighbors.
> The god of Israel and the God of Moab were neighbors.

Acknowledgment

For the many courtesies shown to me, my gratitude is extended to the librarians at the LeRoy, Kansas, public library and to the faculty of the Department of Religion, University of Kansas. Carole Larson, University of Nebraska-Omaha, also supplied useful bibliographic information. Eric Bader, Paul Beeching, John Peterson and Allan Sieffert read the complete manuscript and offered numerous useful suggestions. To my wife, Joan Larson Bader, I am indebted for her unwavering support, including the typing of the manuscript.

A SECOND LOOK

1
Divine Election

It is impossible to appreciate what the Bible has to say to us without an elementary understanding of the anthropological and theological world that preceded and surrounded it. For thousands of years before Israel became a gleam in the eye of God, innumerable human individuals and societies the world over had come and gone, lived and died. Like all communities before and since, ancient Israel inherited and subsequently modified the theological and ethnic concepts of its milieu. Therefore, we begin our biblical journey by considering briefly analogous patterns and principles found among the peoples of the Ancient Near East (ANE) and beyond. One of the most seminal and pervasive of these principles is divine election or chosenness. From this organizing doctrine flow other fundamental biblical concepts, such as power, covenant, justice, sacred names and space, and identity of in-group and out-group.

Ethnocentricity

Twentieth-century anthropologists have identified a few all-pervasive characteristics of traditional societies, recognizing that a good deal of variety in detail may occur within the common pattern of the species. The "primitive" nuclear community—the progenitor and functional analogue of our modern nation-states— is distinguished by its small size (typically a few to several hundred inhabitants), a high level of cultural and biological homogeneity resulting from endogamous marriage patterns, and a significant, though not total, isolation from its closest neighbors.

The functional unit (a village or several villages in proximity) maintained a pronounced degree of social, political, and religious "correctness"; that is, individual members shared a common world-view with little tolerance of "independent" thinking. The welfare of the individual tended to be subordinated to that of the community as understood from the tradition, making life for the ordinary man or woman a narrowly-constraining "one possibility thing." With its concern for ultimate meaning and numinous sources of power, religion played an unsurpassed role in the integration of society and the psychosocial identity of the individual. Given these basic characteristics—known or presumed in the thousands of such communities peppered across the face of the earth—a high degree of ethnic centeredness seems inevitable.[1]

The distinguished historian of religions Mircea Eliade has identified several pairs of bipolar opposites, or antithetical dyads, found universally in thought-patterns throughout humankind. These polarities include such fundamental concepts as right-left, male-female, life-death, sacred-profane, good-evil, and we-foreigners, or "us-them."[2] Thus, among the very most basic and universal of human perceptions, we find the sharp dichotomy of "us-them": the insider and the outsider, the known and the unknown, the loved and the feared, the personalized intimate and the undifferentiated other. Down through the millennia, this awareness undoubtedly conferred an adaptive, i.e., a survival, value on the individual societies. But as we come to confront each other in the global village on a shrinking planet, such "natural" predispositions increasingly appear to be maladaptive, even pathological.

The pioneering social scientist William G. Sumner produced the seminal work on what he called "ethnocentrism." Introducing the word to the world in 1906, he defined it as the view that "one's own group is the center of everything, and all others are scaled and rated with reference to it." Each group "nourishes its own pride and vanity, boasts itself superior, exalts its own divinities, and looks with contempt on outsiders." Sumner saw law and order within the us-group as partially a function of pressure from the hated outsider, so that the discipline and order generated thereby would enable the insiders to wage war successfully against the out-group. The more proximate and threatening the neighbors, the more intense the mutual enmity and the greater the control and discipline within each group.[3]

Another prominent social scientist, Erik H. Erikson, introduced the notion of *pseudospecies* to the field. Each religious and/or ethnic group tends to divide *Homo sapiens* into two very disparate "species": the in-group, small in number but large in merit and cosmic significance, and all the remainder of humanity, infinite in number but lacking in virtue and totally inconsequential in the Grand Design. The in-group, Erikson says, "has become *the* human species, considering all the others a freakish and gratuitous invention of some irrelevant deity. To reinforce the illusion of being chosen, every tribe recognizes a creation of its own, a mythology and later a history: thus was loyalty to a particular . . . morality secured." Other tribes served "as a screen of projection for the negative identities which were the necessary . . . counterpart of the positive ones. This projection, in conjunction with their territoriality, gave men a reason to slaughter one another in *majorem gloriam.*"[4]

The notion of subspeciation suggests that one may more readily abuse or oppress other human beings with moral impunity if they are considered as less human than ourselves—as immoral, or even amoral creatures incapable of moral choice. Sometimes the degradation of the "other" may be even more explicit. Anthropologist Rodney Needham reports that tribes from different parts of the world frequently "call themselves alone by the arrogant title 'man'," and refer to neighboring peoples as "monkeys or crocodiles or malign spirits." But, paradoxically, humans may relate favorably their own behavior to that of mere animals (e.g., brave as a lion; busy as a bee). However, Needham observed wistfully, "men have not on the whole put the observation of their fellow men to such didactic use. . . . That is, if men were perplexed about the meaning of existence, or the essential nature of their kind, or the right way of life, they were not immediately persuaded that the answers were to be found among foreigners."[5]

Among the manifold examples of ethnocentricity, we note

but a few, emphasizing those that relate to a particularly revealing element, the tribal or ethnic name. Among New World groups the designation frequently implies an exaltation above all others: The Pawnee Indians call themselves "Men of Men"; the Kiowa are the "real or principal people"; the Carib Indians declared to the European invaders that "We alone are people." The Lakota designate themselves as "the people," though known to others as Sioux ("the enemy"); the name of an Eskimo group means "real people," though outsiders refer to them by the more prosaic "eaters of raw flesh." The Navajo call themselves "the people," but their neighbors, the Hopi ("the Peaceful People"), refer to them as "thieves" and sometimes in even less endearing terms.[6]

Elsewhere, the San of the Kalahari Desert see themselves as "*the* human beings"; Egyptians considered themselves alone as true "men" and their language the only "human language"; the Greeks referred to those living in the hinterlands as "barbarians," a derogatory term derived from "bar-bar," the sound of a barking dog. The word "China" refers to its location as the "middle kingdom," felicitously positioned between heaven and the netherworld. Japanese Shinto claims that the sun god himself created the islands and its people for his particular glory and blessing. And finally, a personal note: in the spring of 1945, off Okinawa, my ship was hit by a Japanese kamikaze ("god's wind"), yet another claimant to divine election.[7]

Divine Power

The linchpin of community integration and identity is the deity, singular or plural—an unsurpassable centripetal force for unification and centeredness. No successful venture fails to obtain divine sponsorship; the hopes and fears of the community and those of its god are one. In its ultimate ethnocentric expression, the elect claim that their extinction would mean the loss of God for all humankind. The single attribute most essential for deity is power, i.e., control of his people, their neighbors, and ultimately the universe. Every ethnic group needs to feel proximate to, not derivative from, the divine and his all-encompassing power. From the creation myths and the ongoing human-divine dynamic to the eschatological expectations of the End-time, the deity controls events—past, present, and future.

The awesome power of deity may be concentrated in a physical object, which, when appropriated by "them," may wreak havoc among its usurpers. For example, the Philistines captured in battle a portable Israelite chest—the "Ark of the LORD"—a sacred object intimately associated with the Presence. But they quickly discovered that they had no ordinary war booty on their hands. Rather, "the hand of the LORD" was heavy upon them, inducing fatal tumors among the populace and causing the spontaneous disintegration of statues of their god. The panicked victims hastily fashioned golden figurines as "guilt offerings" and returned the terrifying Ark to its rightful owner (1 Sam. 4–6).

It is axiomatic that "our" god will designate "us" and/or our representatives as the elect among the nations, singling us out for divinely-commissioned work within the immediate society and beyond. These themes are expressed clearly in the famous eighteenth century B.C.E. law Code of Hammurabi, a Babylonian stela topped by the figure of the king receiving the laws from the "god of justice," Shamash. This theophany occurred some five hundred years before Moses was to receive the laws from his God at Mount Sinai. The Prologue to the Hammurabi Code begins as follows:

> When lofty Anum . . . (and) Enlil . . .
> determined for Marduk . . .
> the Enlil functions over all mankind . . .
> Called Babylon by its exalted name,
> made it supreme in the world,
> established for him in its midst an enduring kingship,
> whose foundations are as firm as heaven and earth—
> at that time Anum and Enlil named me
> to promote the welfare of the people,
> me, Hammurabi, the devout, god-fearing prince,
> to cause justice to prevail in the land,

to destroy the wicked and the evil,
that the strong might not oppress the weak,
to rise like the sun over the black-headed (people),
and to light up the land.[8]

Both the nationalistic and the universalistic dimensions of divine election shine forth from an inscription of the modest King Esarhaddon of Assyria (680–669 B.C.E.): "Property of Esarhaddon, great king, legitimate king, king of the world, king of Assyria, regent of Babylon, king of Sumer and Akkad, king of the four rims (of the earth), the true shepherd, favorite of the great gods, whom Ashur, Shamash, Bel and Nebo . . . have pronounced king of Assyria (ever) since he was a youngster."[9]

From the divine power equation (gods = power), we should expect the perceived strength of the deity to be closely correlated with the manifest welfare of his chosen people, and so it is. When the people flourish, the deity is simply demonstrating his providence. The problem arises from the cognitive dissonance generated by the brute fact that the elect often do not thrive, at times even experiencing a crushing defeat at the hands of their most despised neighbor and its god. Victory may have a thousand doting fathers, but a devastating defeat is a lonely orphan.

The vanquished and humiliated nation is vulnerable not only militarily but theologically. It is especially subject to the derisive cry of the nations roundabout, "Where is their God?" (Joel 2:17). God himself taunted an unfaithful Israel to save itself, if it could, by its hand-hewn wooden idols: "But where are your gods that you made for yourself? Let them come, if they can save you. . . . " (Jer. 2:28). Anxiety about an impotent god may also operate at the personal level. A desperately-ill psalmist raises his voice in anguish: "My tears have been my food day and night, while people say to me continually, 'Where is your God?' (Ps. 42:3)."

Must the vanquished perforce recognize the victor's god as the more controlling? Has the "defeated" god been exposed as impotent or, worse yet, as nonexistent? If that notion had become dominant, we would expect to find a volatile relationship between ethnic groups and their deities, but in fact over the centuries, we observe a great deal of stability. This holds true even in polytheistic societies, which typically exalt only one or a few major figures of the pantheon.

The solution to the power dilemma is elegant in its simplicity, the contribution of a religious genius whose identity remains shrouded in the eons of time. When an adverse situation requires a theological explanation, the god maintains his hegemony by withdrawing from the field ("hiding his face") or becoming "angry" and either taking direct action against his own sinful people or impressing into the divine service an unwitting "other" as an "instrument" of destruction and humiliation. Thus, for any given international issue, we must choose between two contradictory explanations: that of the victor in the salvation mode and that of the vanquished in the judgmental mode.

A modern scholar explains succinctly how Israel's God emerged as preeminent and maintained his sovereignty whether Israel's international fortunes waxed or waned: " . . . in the assembly of the gods, no one spoke with greater effect than Yahweh. If Israel proclaimed the legal preeminence of her god, it was because Israel found in her actual experiences adequate reason to trust Yahweh's effectiveness. And that effectiveness was not challenged by Israel's failures at war, for the divine judge was free to rule against as well as for his people. . . ."[10]

The dualistic explanation of historical events was not a late arrival on the theological scene. Some fifteen hundred years before the crushing defeats of the northern and southern kingdoms of Israel in the middle of the first millennium B.C.E., Mesopotamian theologians had employed the rationale to explain the fall of one of its leading cities. A legendary account written in the late third millennium B.C.E., *The Curse of Agade,* combines historical fact with a thorough-going theological rationale of those facts. Founded in the twenty-fourth century B.C.E. in the upper Tigris-Euphrates valley, Agade (=Akkad) remained the capital of the first great Mesopotamian empire until its destruction some two hundred years later. Enlil, the chief god of the pantheon, "chose" King Sargon of Agade as the sovereign of all Mesopotamia. The great goddess Inanna came to reside in Agade, assuring the continued prosperity and authority of the capital city. But ominous clouds loomed on the horizon as the city grew into a mature metropolis.

Inanna abandoned the city because a suitable temple had not been built for her. The grandson of Sargon, King Naramsin, turned impatient and surly, refusing to bow to the divine will. In an ultimate act of defiance, he plundered the temple of Enlil in the southern city of Nippur. Enraged, Enlil employed adjacent nomads, the barbarian Guti (who, the legend claims, had "human instinct but canine intelligence and monkeys' features"), as his human "instrument" to ravage the land. Eventually "a long, unique and terrible" divine curse was directed at Agade and—due to the unforgivable sins of Naramsin—it fell in utter ruin.[11]

Theological explanations of historical events and fervent appeals for divine relief became commonplace in the ANE (Ancient Near East). National troubles tended to collect around one or more of five nodes: famine, plague, meteorological phenomena (usually drought or flood), rebellion from within, and military attack from without.[12] A prayer by the beleaguered Hittite king Mursilis II (circa late fourteenth century B.C.E.) begged relief from two of the five troubles, giving us some notion of the human-divine interaction at this time and place. The fortunes of this Hatti kingdom in Asia Minor had begun to wane under Mursilis and it would become completely extinct early in the twelfth century B.C.E. In his prayer the king strikes notes of mercy, idolatry, faithlessness, judgment, and divine pride— all of which would become commonplace in the OT.

> O gods, take ye pity again on the Hatti land! On the one hand it is afflicted with a plague, on the other hand it is afflicted with hostility. The protectorates beyond the frontier . . . each one has rebelled; they do not acknowledge the gods and have broken the oaths of the gods. . . . Let the gods take an interest therein again! Send ye the plague, hostility, famine (and) evil fever into the Mitanni land and the Arzawa land! Rested are the rebellious countries, but the Hatti Land is a weary land. Unhitch the weary, but the rested harness! . . . O god, bring not thy name into disrepute![13]

An especially revealing story of the confounding of the historical and the theological is found in the Babylonian inscriptions of the aforementioned King Esarhaddon of Assyria. His father, King Sennacherib (704–681 B.C.E.), captured Babylon in 689, later boasting that he had "looted, burnt and destroyed" the city and had carted off to Assyria the statue of its chief god, Marduk. Upon his ascension to the throne just ten years later, Esarhaddon inaugurated an enlightened policy of reconciliation and reconstruction, rebuilding the city and Marduk's temple and arranging for the return of the icon of the deity from Assyria.

Though memories of his father's brutality must have remained vivid among the oppressed populace, Esarhaddon nonetheless rendered an account of the late unpleasantness that flew directly in the face of history. His inscription makes no mention at all of Sennacherib and his merciless legions; rather, it ascribes the city's destruction to a divinely-induced flood of the Euphrates River! In this version, the people had sinned grievously by lying, dishonoring their parents, and failing to worship in a proper manner. In response to such waywardness, Marduk became "angry" deciding to destroy the land and its people. The river overflowed, the city became a swampland, and the citizens were forced to flee for their lives. Subsequently, under the benign Esarhaddon, the gods became "reconciled," orthodox cultic practices were reestablished and Babylon once again came to occupy "an honored place among nations."[14] The causation of the destruction had shifted from international aggressor to divinely-directed, natural catastrophe. The historical event is captured by the theological explanation, a not uncommon occurrence in the OT.

Election of Israel

As we have seen, the concept of election is universal; every X submits claims that no non-X honors. Not surprisingly, the notion of the election of Israel arises in Israel. God chose Israel, the rabbinic scholar Solomon Schechter commented, "but indeed

God's choice invariably coincides with the wishes of Israel."[15] Israel's version fits comfortably within the broad anthropological concept of chosenness that we have sketched for humankind in general. A people is formed who enjoy a special relationship with the cosmic power as they understand it. This relationship, mediated by a "covenant" and divine "promises," will govern both cultic and moral behavior within the ethnic group, and the interaction between the group and the "other." Unremarkable in its essence, Israelite election, nonetheless, has impacted the world's culture to a far greater extent than that of any other.

The notion of divine chosenness is prominent in Gen. 12:1–3, the very first discourse between God and the father of the Israelites, Abraham. God informs Abraham that from him will spring "a great nation," that his name will be made "great," and that "in you all the families of the earth shall be blessed." This key promise is repeated to Abraham in Chapters 15 and 17 and to his son, Isaac, in chapter 26 and to Isaac's son, Jacob, in chapter 28. Only later, especially in the Book of Deuteronomy, is the idea expanded and made more explicit. The classical locus is Deut. 7:6: "For you are a people holy to the LORD your God; the LORD your God has chosen you out of all the peoples on earth to be his people, his treasured possession." The idea of a special vocation for Israel—a kingdom of priests for the entire world—is introduced by God in Exod. 19:5–6: "Indeed, the whole earth is mine, but you shall be for me a priestly kingdom and a holy nation."

God makes it clear that the Israelites were not chosen because of their numerical strength: "It was not because you were more numerous than any other people that the LORD set his heart on you and chose you—for you were the fewest of all peoples" (Deut. 7:7). Nor for their moral superiority: "Know, then, that the LORD your God is not giving you this good land to occupy because of your righteousness; for you are a stubborn people" (Deut. 9:6). Passages such as these have encouraged modern defenders to portray election as primarily requiring suffering and sacrifice rather than connoting privilege or superiority.[16]

If the Israelites were not selected because of any special merit, then why did God choose them? The closest we come to an answer is found in Deuteronomy: "It was because the LORD loved you and kept the oath that he swore to your ancestors. . . ."(7:8); "the LORD set his heart in love on your ancestors alone and chose you . . . out of all the peoples" (10:15). The text doesn't take us behind the original, "random" preference for the ancestors, though anthropologists would not find the choice puzzling. Some theologians have argued for a "logic" of election and some have claimed "historical proof" of Jewish chosenness because Israel introduced to the world the idea of one God. Here again anthropology and theology would part company.[17]

Election implies specialness, and specialness, separation; therefore, many passages deal explicitly with the separation of Israel from "the nations." At Mount Sinai, Moses beseeched the LORD to accompany the assemblage as they struggled toward the promised land: "In this way, we shall be distinct . . . from every people on the face of the earth" (Exod. 33:16). The Mesopotamian seer, Balaam, speaks of Israel: "here is a people living alone, and not reckoning itself among the nations!" (Num 23:9). The classical locus is Lev. 20:26: "You shall be holy to me; for I the LORD am holy, and I have separated you from the other peoples to be mine."

The notion of an unbridgeable, "natural" chasm between Israel and the nations, between "us" and "them," continued through the biblical period into the Common Era. As Jewish legend has it, just as God has set natural bounds between day and night, "so also has He separated Israel from the other nations. . . . " If one could eliminate the boundary between light and darkness, "then only can you remove the boundary of separation between Israel and the rest, but not otherwise."[18]

Inevitably chosenness impacts the self-image of the segregated and their manner of relating to the "unchosen." This relationship will be explored in detail in later chapters; for now we may note only the intimate connection between election of the few and their perception of the many. In Deuteronomy we may locate a progressive development from the more to the less subtle: in 26:18–19, the "treasured people" are set "high above all nations that he has made"; in 28:10: "All the peoples of the earth shall see that you are called by the name of the LORD, and they shall be afraid of you"; and in 33:29, the so-called blessing of Moses:

> Happy are you, O Israel! Who is like you,
> a people saved by the LORD,
> the shield of your help,
> and the sword of your triumph!
> Your enemies shall come fawning to you,
> and you shall tread on their backs.

Sacred Names

"Special" ethnic groups could be expected to bear distinctive names of their gods and themselves. Names in the ANE carried a particular importance as signifiers of being, identity and character. Knowing the name of a person or thing offered the opportunity to understand, to communicate, to draw near, possibly even to possess. No name presented the challenge and opportunity of that of the eternal mystery, God. Throughout the Semitic world, the generic name for God was El (plural Elohim), occurring some 2,700 times in the OT. The word also may be used as a proper noun and appears commonly as an element in theophoric names, i.e., compounds bearing a divine name or epithet. Some examples include Elijah, Immanuel, Ishmael, Ezekiel, Joel, Michael, and Israel itself ("one who struggles with God").

In addition to generic terms for deity, the several "elected" groups worshiped national gods who bore distinctive, personal names generally not recognized across political boundaries. Among Israel's near neighbors, the Ammonites worshiped Milcom; the Moabites, Chemosh; the Edomites, Qaus; the Philistines, Dagon; the Canaanites, Baal. The personal name of the God of the Israelites is Yahweh ("I am who I am" [Exod. 3:14]), appearing in the vowelless early text as the tetragrammaton "yhwh."

"Yahweh" has yielded a host of theophoric names, including some of the most prominent in the OT: Joshua, Jonathan, Jehoshaphat, Elijah, Jehoram, Isaiah, Hezekiah, Josiah, Jeremiah, Obadiah, Joel, Zephaniah, amd Zechariah. For Christians, the most important example is Jesus, a Greek form of Joshua meaning "Yahweh is salvation" or "Yahweh saves."

Given the centrality of the personal name, it is curious that one hears God's most intimate designation so seldom in the public square or the house of worship. At least two major reasons for this anomaly may be identified. The sacred name began to be considered ineffable in Judaism sometime in the second temple era, as a corollary of the general proposition that relates inversely the degree of holiness with the distance from the Holy. Since no human being could possibly possess the purity necessary to speak God's most intimate name, it was argued, Adonai ("Lord") was pronounced in its stead.

In both Jewish and Christian Bibles, "LORD"—fully capitalized—substitutes for, but does not translate, the holy tetragrammaton, *yhwh.* The preface to the NRSV states that "careful readers" may notice the word LORD "here and there" in the OT. It turns out that "here and there" translates into no less than 6,490 occurrences! A really "careful reader" would note the difference between passages such as Gen. 2:4b in which we find "LORD God" (from Yahweh Elohim) and those such as Ezek. 28:25, where we read "Lord GOD" (from Adonai Yahweh). This sort of confusion is compounded by the fact that both Yahweh and Jesus are referred to as "Lord" in the NT (possibly confusing passages include Matt. 22:44; Mark 1:1–3; Rom. 10:12–13; 1 Cor 1:29–31). In addition, the chief competitor of "the LORD" in Israel is the Canaanite god, Baal, which, of course, means "Lord." And finally, we have the common secular usage as in "lord of the manor."

In addition to the sacredness argument, an absolutist monotheism has been advanced as a reason to avoid the divine personal name. The editors of the NRSV continue to use the all-purpose LORD, they say, because "The use of any proper name for the one and only God, as though there were other gods from whom the true God had to be distinguished . . . is inappropriate for the universal faith of the Christian Church."

In the late middle ages, Christian ignorance of Judaic cultic practices regarding the non-use of the sacred name produced the mongrel word *Jehovah,* still in wide circulation in this century. Jewish priests had attached the vowel signs from "Adonai" to the tetragrammaton as a purely mnemonic device to ensure that the ineffable word was always read as *Lord*, not *Yahweh*. But in the sixteenth century *C.E.*, Vatican scholars combined the consonants of *Yhwh* with the vowels of *Adonai* to yield the "impossible" neologism, *Jehovah*.[19]

The first human being to use the sacred name was Eve, the biblical mother of us all, gratefully acknowledging the help of Yahweh in the first birth recorded in the Book for the species (Gen. 4:1). Although the scriptural God subsequently manifests his displeasure at a myriad of human moral deficiencies, he never frowns on the use of his personal name rather than a more "vanilla" substitute. Modern Judaism continues to distance itself from the sacred name, and that tradition should certainly be respected. For others, a reevaluation may be in order.

A goal, if not *the* goal, of human life—"few of days and full of trouble"—is to seek a greater knowledge of and a more intimate relationship with God. After centuries of neglect of the personal divine name and the wrong-headed popularity of the usurper "Jehovah," reversal of the trend is overdue. After all, as a rabbi—with a twinkle in his eye—once said, "Yahweh is God's Christian name!"

Sacred Space

The final dimension of the principle of divine election that we shall consider is that of sacred space. If the universe revolves around "us" and "our" god, then surely the lands that we occupy cannot be ordinary real estate. In traditional societies we find the geographical equivalent of the concept of pseudospeciation: our god-given territory represents the sacred cosmos, "the world"; everything outside constitutes an unknown, unorganized and chaotic space populated by ghosts, devils, and foreigners. Traditional mankind saw its sacred abode as the "center of the world," with the cosmos stretching out in more or less symmetrical fashion from this central point. In many tribes the notion is further developed by an *axis mundi*, a symbolic sacred pole that rests on the netherworld below and serves to connect and support the earth and heaven above.

Facilitating communication with heaven, this cosmic axis may be represented by a pillar or pole (e.g., among natives of British Columbia), a ladder (e.g., Jacob's) or a mountain (e.g., Mount Gerizim, the sacred mountain of the Samaritans). Assimilating their temple to the cosmic mountain, Babylonians called their sanctuaries "House of the Mountain of all Lands" and "Link between Heaven and Earth." The name Babylon itself translates as "gate of god." Since the sacred mountain, "the navel of the earth," is the conduit to heaven, it and its surrounding territory are often perceived by the inhabitants as the highest point in the world. From this perspective, the early rabbis reasoned that the Noahide Flood did not inundate Israel.[20]

Through the centuries, as empires arose in bloody succession to engulf the surrounding peoples and lands, the notion of the cosmic centrality of the homeland of the conqueror became easy to sustain. In their day, the Nile and the Tigris-Euphrates valleys served as central organizing forces for the entire "known" world. The idea has continued down to the present day in the form of the principal city of the dominant culture: Athens, Rome, Lisbon, Paris, London, New York.

As did the surrounding societies of the ANE, Israel developed as an extremely "place-oriented" ethnic/religious community. The correspondence of the sacred and the spatial was perfect. The holy people had erected the holy building in the holy city in the holy land. Needless to say, the total destruction of the building, city, and nation in 586 B.C.E. and 70 C.E. precipitated theological crises of the first order.

Ezek. 5:5 sets the dominant theme: "Thus says the Lord GOD [Adonai Yahweh]: This is Jerusalem; I have set her in the center of the nations, with countries all around her." In Ezek. 38:12, the Israelites are said to "live at the center [or navel] of the earth." In Jubilees 8:19 (an intertestamental Jewish writing), Mount Zion is declared to be "in the midst of the navel of the earth." Even after destruction of the second temple in 70 C.E.,the rabbis doggedly asserted that the bare rock on which the temple had stood constituted the "foundation" upon which the entire world is set.

God had originated all creation from its navel, Jerusalem—more specifically, the navel of the navel, the temple altar.[21]

By the first centuries of the Common Era, the rabbis had produced a "cultic map" of the world based on the practices of the second temple. These were, in turn, premised on the principle of inverse correlation between holiness and distance from the Divine. The cultic map distinguished some twelve zones that radiated out in concentric rings centered on the temple. The zones advanced in purity from the outermost "lands of the gentiles"—deemed to be thoroughly unclean and defiling—to the innermost "Holy of Holies," the most inaccessible room in the temple, wherein dwelt the Sacred Presence.

In ascending degrees of holiness, one locates the land of Israel, the city of Jerusalem, the temple precinct. Gentiles could approach no nearer than the outermost temple court upon penalty of death "without appeal," a warning posted in several languages at regular intervals along the wall of the inner court. Next, we find the "court of women," though menstruant women were forbidden from even approaching the temple area. Next is the so-called "court of the Israelites," misnamed since it limited access to Israelite males. Finally, we arrive at a series of areas available only to priests, requiring a progressive stringency of purification. The ordered sequence culminates in the *sanctum sanctorum*—entered only on the Day of Atonement only by the High Priest and then only after special rites of purification.[22]

When Israel struck an agreement with Yahweh at Mount Sinai, after being liberated from Egyptian bondage, the first order of business was to conquer and settle the sacred land, "the land of milk and honey." How it said it did so, and what moral problems this poses for us today, is taken up in chapter 2.

2

Conquest of the Promised Land

A major theme of OT historiography—some would say *the* theme—centers on the land: its promise, conquest, settlement, loss, and restoration. After the Hebrews had endured some four hundred years of bondage in Egypt, Yahweh remembered his covenant with them, acknowledged their suffering, and dramatically led them to freedom. Down through the centuries, the anguished cry, "Let my people go!" has resonated among the marginalized and the oppressed, in recent decades most especially among those in the Third World. The former slaves covenanted with Yahweh at Mount Sinai and obediently (more or less) received his laws. The moral eye is unclouded; virtue had found a home among the people Israel.

According to the text, the incipient nation had formed without a homeland to call its own! Anthropologists might question whether that has a known precedent or is even possible. But the Bible tells us that it happened that way, so we accept it, at least provisionally. The new nation is headed toward a land "promised" to them by their God, one of whose chief attributes is "justice." The moral eye begins to cloud when we learn that the "promised land" teems with a large, well-established, nonaggressive population of men, women, and children. Dare we call them the "children of God"?

What of the elementary morality of this usurpation? Does the divine "promise" to the randomly selected "chosen" override bare bones justice to the "unchosen"? Were the inhabitants so "wicked" that they forfeited all moral and legal claim to their land? Can a modern reader interpret these events as anything other than unprovoked aggression, religious intolerance, and unpardonable genocide? And exactly what role did God play in this invasion? Curiously, the moral problem is scarcely addressed in the Bible itself or by modern theologians.[1] But before we take up these questions, we will survey briefly current ideas of how Israel actually came into being.

Archaeology

The "hottest" area in biblical archaeology is that of the origin of Israel. The salient facts include a rather rapid appearance of small settlements in the central hill country of Canaan beginning around 1200 B.C.E. (Early Iron Age) and the victory stele of Mernepth, a pharaoh of Egypt, dated to 1207 B.C.E., declaring that "Israel is laid waste, his seed is not." The settlements are generally taken to be Israelite, but the evidence rarely is ethnic-specific. Four different models of the origin of Israel are currently being debated by archaeologists and historians.

Earlier generations of archaeologists understood the available evidence as confirming, at least in major outline, the account in the Book of Joshua of a rapid "blitzkrieg" conquest of the land of Canaan. With Yahweh in the van, the Israelites attack, the walls come tumbling down, the natives are dispatched to their eternal reward, and the aggressors get on with their lives. However, this traditional "Conquest" model has fallen radically from favor in recent decades. A leading archaeologist recently pronounced the last rites over it, declaring unequivocally that "there isn't a single reputable professional archaeologist . . . who espouses the conquest model in Israel, Europe or America."[2] Nevertheless, it continues to receive attention as the classical paradigm of the origin of Israel, if for no other reason.

A second model, of German ancestry, is that of "peaceful infiltration." The proto-Israelites are viewed as pastoral nomads of the desert who gradually entered Canaan and settled down in the less desirable sites. These shepherds-cum-farmers are seen as being responsible for the settlements in the hill country, but this development was devoid of significant violence.

A more radical model, from America, is that of the "peasant revolt" or "social revolution." This paradigm, most fully developed by Norman Gottwald, suggests that an ethnic hodge-podge of lower class, dispossessed Canaanites revolted from their urban overlords and took to the hills. There they developed a society characterized by its economic, social, and political egalitarianism. This model has been particularly attractive to Christians in Third World countries.

A fourth model is that of peaceful development within Canaan, sometimes referred to as the "symbiosis" model. Here the early Israelites are pictured as living harmoniously alongside the Canaanites for some considerable period before they undergo a radical divergence. In this model—indeed, in all of them save the traditional—the Exodus story is disregarded or considered of minimal historical importance. In fact, the historicity of the Exodus, in its own right, has been seriously questioned in recent years. Most exponents of a non-traditional model leave it hanging by a slender reed, though the NRSV reassures us that "there can be little doubt that the story rests upon actual historical occurrences."[3]

Of the four hypotheses, two bring the Israelites in from the outside, two from the inside; two are accompanied by violence, and two are not. Some archaeological evidence can be marshaled to support each of the models, and no evidence absolutely rules out any theory. Indeed, it is somewhat startling to discover how much the "objective" archaeologists and historians still rely on the Genesis-Kings biblical account in their reconstruction of a "scientific" history of Israel. The archeological dispute will, no doubt, continue for decades to come, though the trend is clearly toward some version of *in situ* development. But, for the modern reader of the Bible, the key questions are much less antiquarian than ethical-theological. That is, the morality of the Conquest as presented in the text and the light that it sheds on the character of God should be of much greater interest to us than the factual early history of Israel.

Biblical Rationales

The biblical rationales for the Conquest fall into two broad categories: the gift of the God of Israel and the reprehensible religious and sexual practices of the inhabitants. The concept of the divine grant of territory is well-known from the ANE and elsewhere.[4] The gift of land by a god is at once a "no-reason" and an unassailable mandate depending upon whether one is enrolled with "them" or "us." The divine gift to the homeless Israelites is clearly the more dominant and fundamental of the two proffered explanations. That is, even if the natives had been as virtuous as Job, the chosen would have replaced the unchosen.

From the outset, God bound together in a single indissoluble package the promises of election, covenant, and land. The first words with which Yahweh greets Abraham upon his arrival in Canaan concern the future disposition of the land: "To your offspring I will give this land" (Gen. 12:7). God repeats the promises to Abraham in Gen. 13 and 15, and in 17:7–8, he pledges an apparently unconditional covenant in one breath and the land of Canaan in the next: "I will establish my covenant between me and you, and your offspring after you throughout their generations, for an everlasting covenant . . . And I will give to you, and to your offspring after you, the land where you are now an alien, all the land of Canaan, for a perpetual holding; and I will be their God."

The promise is repeated to Isaac (26:3–4) and Jacob (28:3–4), and with almost monotonous regularity thereafter, most especially in Deuteronomy, before we reach the actual Conquest in the Book of Joshua. A subtle shift from the centrality of the gift itself to the promise or "oath" that God "swore" to the patriarchs can be detected—as though a promise kept was more important than the grant itself.[5] For example, Deut. 9:5 asserts that Israel will gain the land "in order to fulfill the promise that the LORD made on oath to your ancestors, to Abraham, to Isaac, and to Jacob."

The theme of promise fulfilled can be followed into the post-Conquest period. After the dust and Israel had settled in the land, Joshua forcefully reminds the people of Yahweh's eternal fidelity to his promises. The aging leader, "about to go the way of all the earth," tells the assembled conquerors "that not one thing has failed of all the good things that the LORD your God promised concerning you; all have come to pass for you, not one of them has failed" (Josh. 23:14).

Within the theme of "gift," we may identify sub-themes. The "Promised Land" (surprisingly, a phrase not found in the Bible) is no ordinary land, but "a good and broad land, a land flowing with milk and honey. . . ." (Exod. 3:8). The idea is expanded in Deut. 8:7–9: "a land with flowing streams, with springs and underground waters . . . a land of wheat and barley, of vines and fig trees and pomegranates, a land . . . where you will lack nothing. . . ." And, most critically, "a land that the LORD your God looks after. The eyes of the LORD your God are always on it, from the beginning of the year to the end of the year" (Deut. 11:11).

Another sub-theme is that of the hereditary possession of the newly gained territory, implying an occupation that will continue in perpetuity. Yahweh gave the land as "your possession" (Deut. 4:21), as "an inheritance" (Deut. 19:10) and as "an inheritance to possess" (Deut. 25:19). Subsequently, Joshua distributed the land to Israel "according to their tribal allotments" (Josh. 11:23; 13–19).

The secondary rationale for the Conquest sounds a more ominous note. Promising, giving, inheriting, and allotting the land of milk and honey sound benign enough. But, as the tone turns more grim, we are once again reminded that living, breathing human beings were peacefully going about their daily lives in their land. Before the gift can be awarded to the chosen, it must first be wrested from the unchosen. Toward this end, we encounter a series of hostile terms in Deuteronomy, such as *dispossess, subdue, drive out, blot out, demolish, destroy* and *devour.*[6] The object of the verbs is the Canaanites, the inhabitants whose practices and behaviors constitute the second God-inspired rationale for usurpation.

Although we will employ the generic term *Canaanite* for the natives, several passages list a number of generally obscure ethnic groups. These lists of "nations" vary from one (Gen. 12:6), to two (Gen. 34:30), to five (e.g., Exod. 13:5), to six (e.g., Exod. 33:2), to a maximum of ten (Gen. 15:19). The standard, or stereotypical, list is found at Deut. 7:1: the Hittites, Girgashites, Amorites, Canaanites, Perizzites, Hivites, and Jebusites.[7] For our purposes, these "nations" will all be assimilated to "Canaanite."

The principal charges against the Canaanites are religious and sexual. The core of the religious accusation is not that they are atheists, but that they are idolaters, i.e., they worship gods other than the God of Israel ("You have seen their detestable things, the filthy idols of wood and stone. . . . " [Deut. 29:17]). Yet no passage suggests that the Canaanites had the slightest prior acquaintance with the God of Israel or his predilections. Nevertheless, they paid the ultimate price—total extinction as a culture—as if they had broken a divine covenant with malice aforethought.

Actually, to say that the Canaanites stood accused of idolatry is not quite accurate. Their practices were deemed idolatrous, but that was a problem only for the Israelites. The natives and their "abominations" had to be removed from the scene to eliminate temptation from the eyes of the chosen. The text treats the unchosen in a mechanical, dismissive fashion—as cardboard foils incapable of moral choices. God capsulizes his attitude toward "them" in his cold, deterministic explanation for the long delay between the covenant with Abraham and the conquest of the land: "the iniquity of the Amorites is not yet complete" (Gen. 15:16). Evidently it took another five hundred years to run its wicked course. In his numerous encounters with "them" of whatever ethnicity, the xenophobic God of Israel often strips them of their basic human attributes; i.e., in the divine equation, they become wicked "constants" rather than moral "variables."

Poised on the plains of Moab preparing for the attack, the Israelites receive a crash course in the "demonization" of the enemy. With regard to the most sacred sites of the natives—the abominable "high places"—Moses commands his forces to "demolish completely all the places where the nations whom you are about to dispossess served their gods, on the mountain heights, on the hills, and under every leafy tree. Break down their altars, smash their pillars, burn their sacred poles with fire, and hew down the idols of their gods, and thus blot out their name from their places" (Deut. 12:2–3). Among such exhortations directed at the "strangers" who occupy the land, we discover one of the Bible's greatest nonconformities. At Deut. 10, amid genocidal passages brimming with hatred toward "the other," the God of the Conquest claims to "love strangers" and urges the Israelites to follow his example!

Fear of the seductive power of the locals' young people and their religious practices produced an uncompromising stand against intermarriage. Yahweh warned that "when the Canaanites prostitute themselves to their gods and sacrifice to their gods, someone among them will invite you, and you will eat of the sacrifice. And you will take wives from among their daughters for your sons, and their daughters who prostitute themselves to their gods will make your sons also prostitute themselves to their gods" (Exod. 34:15–16).

There were yet other "abhorrent" religious practices of the "host" nation that especially concerned the LORD, traditions that tapped alternative sources of knowledge regarding the supernatural. These competitors would remain worrisome to the Israelite priesthood for centuries to come. Via Moses, Yahweh warned that "no one shall be found among you who . . . practices divination, or is a soothsayer, or an augur, or a sorcerer, or one who casts spells, or who consults ghosts and spirits, or who seeks oracles from the dead" (Deut. 18:10–11).

Sexual offenses constituted a second major indictment against the Canaanites, overlapping the religious in the area of cultic prostitution. The sexual charges may echo the "curse of Canaan" stemming from the time of the humiliation of the drunken Noah: "Cursed be Canaan; lowest of slaves shall he be to his brothers" (Gen. 9:25). Leviticus 18 itemizes the Canaanite crimes to be avoided by the Israelites. A dozen types of incest are listed, all from the male perspective. Surprisingly, no specific father-daughter prohibition is found, though it may be presumed under the granddaughter provision. In addition, adultery, homosexuality, bestiality, and approaching a woman sexually "while she is in her menstrual uncleanness" are proscribed. In Leviticus 20, specific penalties are assigned to the transgressions of Leviticus 18. Several carry the death penalty, including adultery, homosexuality, and bestiality. The punishment for lying with a woman "having her sickness" is that both partners shall be "cut off from their people."

These sanctions are not to be mistaken for simple moral exercises in which individuals will be punished for their sins without regard to the impact on the collective. With respect to their religious practices, the Canaanites had to be removed, not as punishment for idolatry, but to eliminate Israelite temptation. But, regarding the cause-and-effect relationship between sexual transgression and loss of the land, the text is very clear. The LORD states flatly that "by all these practices the nations I am casting out before you have defiled themselves. Thus the land became defiled; and I punished it for its iniquity, and the land vomited out its inhabitants" (Lev. 18:24–25; repeated in 18:27 and 20:22–23).

Then the LORD drops a bombshell on a perhaps too-smug Israel: "But you shall keep my statutes and my ordinances and commit none of these abominations . . . otherwise the land will vomit you out for defiling it, as it vomited out the nation that was before you" (Lev. 18:26,28). The unsettling thought recurs in the NT though in radically different circumstances. The apostle Paul utilizes it in his famous olive tree metaphor. As a newly grafted branch replacing the cut-off branches of Jewish unbelief, Christians should avoid becoming proud and boastful lest "you also will be cut off" (Rom. 11:17–22).

The Invasion

In turning from the rationales to the actual invasion, we confront one of the most difficult concepts for the modern reader to accept, the ban (*herem*) or ideology of "holy war." Since it combines the concept of holiness with ritual slaughter on a massive scale, the subject is said to induce among moderns "gnashing of teeth, chills of the spine, and head-scratching bewilderment." The ban entails the total "dedication" to the victor's god of the possessions and population of the enemy. The goods and people "devoted to destruction" may be viewed as sacrificial offerings to

Yahweh or a necessary product of the demands of Yahweh's justice. In theory, it is God's war, the human participants being merely his tools. Scholars debate the precise dimensions and implications of the ban and the extent to which it was actually employed in Israel but do agree that it has numerous ANE precedents.[8]

In anticipation of the Conquest, Deuteronomy 20 details for the Israelites the rules of engagement for dealing with the enemy. If a non-Canaanite town surrenders, its citizens shall be reduced merely to "forced labor." But if it offers resistance, "You shall put all its males to the sword" and take the women, children, and livestock as "your booty." But, for the Canaanite cities, the full-fledged ban is prescribed. Here, nothing that breathes should be allowed to continue to do so. "You shall annihilate them . . . just as the LORD your God has commanded, so that they may not teach you to do all the abhorrent things that they do for their gods, and you thus sin against the LORD your God."[9]

After the walls came tumbling down at Jericho, the first town to fall to the Israelites, the invaders moved into the city and captured it. "Then they devoted to destruction by the edge of the sword all in the city, both men and women, young and old, oxen, sheep and donkeys" (Josh. 6:20–21). The next stop was Ai where they did take booty but only after Joshua "had utterly destroyed all the inhabitants" (Josh. 8:26). In a summation passage, Joshua is said to have "defeated the whole land . . . he left no one remaining, but utterly destroyed all that breathed, as the LORD God [Yahweh Elohim] of Israel commanded" (Josh. 10:40).

The true God is no passive bystander to these proceedings, nor is Israel a renegade nation defying the humane dictates of its Deity. Yahweh is fully engaged, leading the hosts in spirit and in truth. He "fights" for Israel; "hands over" the Canaanites and "blots out" their name; sends "pestilence," divine "terror," "the hornet," and a "devouring fire" to clear the way; produces "great panic" among the enemy; and "harden[s] their hearts" so that they may be "utterly destroyed" and "receive no mercy."[10]

The magnitude of the opposition and the might of its arms are irrelevant so long as "the LORD your God is with you" (Deut. 20:1). As the triumphant Joshua reminded his compatriots, "One of you puts to flight a thousand, since it is the LORD your God who fights for you, as he promised you" (Josh. 23:10). Of course, in fact, this enterprise must be a cooperative venture between unequal partners. The Eternal gives but the mortal must take. The collaborative nature of the relationship is implied in verses such as Deut. 15:4: " . . . the land the LORD your God is giving you as a possession to occupy." [11]

A passage from the "Song of Moses," recited to the Israelites while still gathered on the Plains of Moab, summarizes Yahweh's mood and intent toward "them":

> For I lift up my hand to heaven,
> and swear: As I live forever,
> When I whet my flashing sword,
> and my hand takes hold on judgment;
> I will take vengeance on my adversaries,
> and will repay those who hate me.
> I will make my arrows drunk with blood,
> and my sword shall devour flesh. . . .
>
> —Deut. 32:40–42a

Whatever the facts on the historical ground, the biblical story of the Conquest is straightforward and devoid of internal moral ambivalence. The patriarchs are repeatedly portrayed as "aliens" in the land of Canaan. All but one of Abraham's twelve sons are born in northern Mesopotamia (Aramea) (Gen. 35:16–26), and they all die in Egypt (Exod. 1:1–6). As he bargains for a burial site after the death of his wife Sarah, Abraham describes himself to the locals as "a stranger and sojourner with you" (Gen. 23:4, KJV). Burial grounds were apparently the only permanent holdings that the Israelites possessed in Israel in the pre-Egyptian era.

The text offers none of the rationales for conquest that we have come to expect from conquerors. The Israelites are not recapturing formerly held territory, the grounds for Douglas

MacArthur's famous cry, "I shall return." No irredentist claim for even a small political hegemony in Canaan is made before or after the descent into Egypt; in fact, the Israelites attained nationhood only after they left Canaan. In a cultic ceremony, they confess that "A wandering Aramean was my ancestor; he went down into Egypt and lived there as an alien, few in number, and there he became a great nation, mighty and populous" (Deut. 26:5). The land is not empty; the Canaanites have neither "invited" the Israelites in nor provoked them in any way, unless their mere existence be provocation. Yet, then, as now, brute force must be replaced by reasons more acceptable to a "civilized" world. From the Akkadian Emperor, Sargon I, in the third millennium B.C.E. through Nebuchadnezzar II of Babylonia and Alexander the Great of Macedonia to Napoleon Bonaparte and Saddam Hussein, a skeptical world records "official" explanations of the aggressor.

As rationale for the Conquest, the biblical text offers divine gift and iniquity of the endemic population, with a greater emphasis on the former. It caricatures the inhabitants as the incorrigibly wicked "them," a moral contagion that must be eliminated at all costs. We are left with the "Divine Right" of the chosen to a land held in peace by others. Struggle as we might with the conclusion, it seems impossible to avoid the label of "naked aggression" for the biblically described Conquest, an act of infamy and injustice led by the one, true, and just God.

Responses to the Biblical Account

We can only surmise how the Canaanites might have reacted to Yahweh's declaration of the "gift" of their land, assuming that they had an inkling. Given the theological landscape of the ANE, the best guess is that they would only have given a prosaic shrug. As we saw in the "power equation" of chapter 1, the gods control events, including international events. No nation would dare to travel or attack without the blessing of its god or pantheon. If the news is bad, we may presume that the god was "angry"—an unfortunate truth that we perceive only after the fact. In the eyes of the Canaanites, it would simply be Baal against Yahweh, and the devil take the hindmost.

Although we may be in some doubt as to the Canaanites' reaction to the Conquest rationales, we are on firmer ground with respect to modern commentators. The most common response by theologians is to ignore entirely the embarrassing ethical implications of the aggression. When direct reference is made, typically it is in bland and euphemistic terms that manage to sidestep entirely the moral quagmire and the blood-letting. We read of "a homeland . . . acquired"; the "establishment of the nation in Canaan"; the Israelites leaving Egypt "to settle back in Canaan"; the "settlement in ancestral lands"; and "the Great Settlement in the Promised Land" (the Capitalization Solution).[12] The land "represented their future"; lay "waiting and open to them"; and offered an opportunity "to build their national home in the land of their fathers."[13]

These references manage to avoid mention of the inhabitants altogether. They reappear with the theologian who complains that the Israelites had to build their nation "in the face of the constant encroachment by alien elements," by which, of course, he means the native Canaanites. Another expresses a "moral" principle that would surely make an entire congregation of "them" tremble: "to insure the survival of cherished values may require wholesale slaughter."[14]

A leading Jewish activist and philosopher, Hayim Greenberg (1889–1953), grappled bravely, but unsuccessfully, with the moral nexus of election, conquest, superiority, and justice. Jewish history, he argued, presents "the picture of a patrician in the midst of a plebeian world." The "belief in their own superiority" didn't entitle Jews to "specific rights and privileges of an economic or political nature." Their claim to Canaan wasn't "based on any special rights to land . . . granted to God's favorite. True, God had pledged to give Canaan to Abraham . . . but there was no element of *privilege* in His promise. Canaan was the legitimate 'heritage' of the Jews. . . . " A legitimate heritage based on a promise devoid of privilege. One wonders if the Canaanites would have appreciated the subtlety of the argument.

As for the natives themselves, Greenberg maintains that

the "primitive hate" of the Israelites toward the inhabitants included "no racial motivation." The indigenous population "presented a danger" to the invaders since the natives had "claims" on the land that God promised to the Israelites. In evaluating the relative merit of the conflicting claims, the Israelites felt that they had "moral and religious" justification to dismiss the "pretensions" of the natives as "unwarranted." To have lived peacefully in the land with the Canaanites would have meant "to tolerate the polluting presence of great numbers of pagans."[15]

Most liberal Christians openly acknowledge the rank injustice inherent in the European conquest of the "New World." But they shun that characterization of the biblical paradigm that inspired it. Christians have rationalized the Conquest of Canaan as a necessary vehicle for the realization of "God's purpose."[16] A typical "Christian" expression can be found in the writings of the British theologian W.S. Bruce. Although he wrote in the early twentieth century, the mind-set that he reveals remains widespread today. Bruce concluded that "moral surgery" on the Canaanites was justified because of "the heinousness of a sensual idolatry." And what of the God of Justice? Admittedly, some critics might perceive the received morality as compromising "the gracious character of Jehovah." But, everything considered, it was "one of those hard necessities to which the God of redemption condescended."[17]

Although moderns have been hesitant to come to grips with Conquest morality, some of the ancients were not so reluctant. Our first evidence comes from the Bible itself. The OT contains two parallel histories of the period from creation to the destruction of Jerusalem in 586 B.C.E. The "primary" history is contained in Genesis-Kings, the "secondary" history in the Books of Chronicles. Probably writing in the fourth century B.C.E., the "Chronicler" drew especially on the Books of Kings, though he modified, deleted, and added to the earlier writings.

In the Chronicler's "alternative" view, the first historical event of moment is the reign of King Saul, which occurred shortly before 1000 B.C.E. This event appears in 1 Chron. 10, the first nine chapters being filled with genealogies from Adam forward. For our purposes, the salient and startling fact is that the

Conquest and the Exodus have been totally omitted from the narrative! In this bowdlerized version, the Israelites are present and thriving in the land in a continuous sequence from Jacob forward to Saul and David.[18] No Exodus, no wilderness, no Canaanites. In Chronicles, "inheritance of the land" refers to continuous possession rather than to conquest.[19]

When Israel significantly expanded its territorial limits in the second century B.C.E., it didn't unfurl the biblical banners of "conquest" and "annihilation." The Maccabean revolt against the Seleucid Greeks, which began in 167 B.C.E., led to the reestablishment of full sovereignty for Israel for the first time since 586 B.C.E. The resulting Hasmonean dynasty expanded the boundaries to approximately those of the kingdom of David. But as Simon the Hasmonean told the Seleucid King: "We have neither taken foreign land nor seized foreign property, but only the inheritance of our ancestors, which at one time had been unjustly taken by our enemies" (1 Macc. 15:33). Throughout their campaigns, the Hasmoneans "neither mentioned or implemented the ancient laws concerning the conquest of the lands."[20]

Jewish literature early in the Common Era also reflects a certain moral ambivalence, a rethinking of the harsh doctrines of the Conquest. The rabbis put forward a number of alternative explanations for Israelite presence in the land, some flatly contradicting the biblical text and/or each other. One view held that the land was empty and desolate, totally deserted by the time Israel arrived. In another version, God had "provisionally" granted the land to the Canaanites until such time as the "rightful owners" should appear. Although Gen. 10:15–19 assigns the land to Canaan, son of Ham, son of Noah, some rabbis claimed that the Canaanites had stolen the land from Shem, the progenitor of the Semites, including Israel, to whom it was originally assigned. In still another reading, the "reasonable" Canaanites voluntarily leave the land upon learning that Israel is en route from Egypt.

Other "rewrites" go even further in softening the biblical picture. The Talmud states that the Torah had been inscribed on stones in seventy languages and had the pagans accepted it, they would not have been dispossessed. Some rabbinic sources portray Joshua as entering into humane negotiation with the Canaanites, i.e., offering them an opportunity to either leave or make peace, rather than subjecting them to the harsh measures of the ban. This account clearly contradicts the rules of engagement for the ban as spelled out in Deut. 20 but was in accord with contemporary standards of legality and morality. We also find the notion that Israel will refrain from annihilating the natives if they will but "repent." This idea found its way into the Bible at Wis. 12:10 though prospects for a metamorphosis of the incorrigible are not hopeful.[21]

Not all the latter-day Jewish reflections on the Conquest and the conquered softened the traditional view. The Qumran sect that produced the Dead Sea Scrolls around the turn of the era evidently felt quite comfortable with the harsh strictures of the ban.[22] The prominent eleventh-century rabbi Rashi endorsed theological fatalism as the solution to the "us-them" problem. Since the earth belonged to the "Holy One Blessed be He" he could assign all or parts of it as he saw fit. Originally he had given the land to the Canaanites, but later, for no apparent reason, "He took it from them and gave it to us."[23] A midrash leaves us with a final Jewish characterization of the Canaanites and an imaginative variation on Lev. 19:18, the celebrated "love your neighbor" passage. In his "last will and testament," Canaan is said to have addressed his children as follows: "Speak not the truth; hold not yourselves aloof from theft; lead a dissolute life; hate your master [Israel] with an exceeding great hate; and love one another."[24]

A few of the early Church Fathers also contemplated the Conquest though most did not find it a congenial topic. Writing in the third-century C.E., the influential Origen of Alexandria brought his considerable talents to bear on the Book of Joshua. Origen's principal mode of text interpretation was the allegorical, wherein the literal sense is rejected in favor of a more "spiritual" meaning or "deeper truth." The hidden meaning is available only to the dedicated exegete, not the "simple believer." Some zealous Christian devotees of allegory even maintained that "evil angels" had induced the Jews to understand the text in its literal or historical sense.[25]

The first feature of Joshua that caught Origen's eye was the name of the conqueror, which translates into Greek as the equivalent of *Jesus.* Joshua represented "Jesus, my Lord," who came to pronounce the end of the Mosaic Law and announce the entry of the "new Israel" into the promised "spiritual land." The king of the city of Ai is the Devil; the Canaanites as a group are identified with "diabolical races of inimical powers."A true Christian understanding of Joshua will reveal only God's "goodness," Origen claimed. When the Jews read the more sanguinary Conquest passages, they become "cruel and thirst for human blood." But in the allegorical understanding, these texts refer only to the slaying of our "guilty passions." Contrary to the Jewish literal reading, with its emphasis on ethnic history, the stories of holy war actually teach of a "peace" that is offered to us by a benevolent God. [26]

Baal-Bashing

The clear-cut account of the triumphant extermination of the Canaanites in the Book of Joshua is flatly contradicted in the Book of Judges. In the latter, the Israelites continued to struggle with the pesky Canaanites on all fronts. Some Canaanites survived as God's instrument, both to test the conquerors' fidelity and to furnish cannon fodder for successive generations of Israelites who otherwise would not "know war."[27] Joshua had warned his compatriots that any natives whom they allowed to remain in the land would become "a snare and a trap for you, a scourge on your sides, and thorns in your eyes. . . . " (Josh. 23:13). The greatest "snare" of all was the worship of other gods, the most potent being the widely revered storm god, Baal. "Baal-bashing" in the mid-ninth century B.C.E.—a direct legacy of Conquest theology—can be traced in a dramatic sequence of events involving some of the Bible's most memorable characters.[28]

In the northern kingdom of Israel, the economy waxed but piety waned. The apostate king, Ahab, and his notorious queen, Jezebel, sat on the throne; almost single-handedly that "troubler of Israel," the prophet Elijah, carried the banner for the LORD.

With Baalism in the ascendancy over a beleaguered Yahwism, the zealous Elijah felt compelled to resort to desperate measures. Since the contending parties both claimed that their god controlled the weather, Elijah proposed a unique showdown on Mount Carmel before "all Israel." These "high noon" dramatics were intended to bring an end to a disastrous drought, now in its third year, and to demonstrate once and for all the supremacy of Yahweh over his popular rival.

Each side prepared a "barbecue" of bull meat over an unlighted fire and then called down the Power from heaven to ignite the tinder. Though no fewer than four hundred and fifty Baal prophets "limped" around the altar and called on the name of Baal from morning until noon, their entreaties brought "no voice, no answer and no response." Elijah then petitioned the God of Abraham, Isaac, and Jacob, who promptly responded with a fire from heaven and a drought-busting deluge.

Convinced by these wondrous acts, the electrified crowd prostrated itself and rent the air with repeated shouts of "The LORD [Yahweh] indeed is God [Elohim]." Although one might suppose that all but the most obtuse of the Baalists would have been ripe for conversion, Elijah would have none of that. He ordered them seized, making certain to "not let one of them escape." The pious prophet marched them down to a nearby stream and put all four hundred and fifty to the sword, a veritable human sacrifice to the LORD. Joshua would have been proud.

When a vengeful Jezebel vowed to take his life, Elijah fled to Mount Horeb (Sinai), where he heard the "still small voice" (KJV) of the LORD. Its message was far more important than its celebrated volume. The small voice gave the prophet a large mission that included both domestic and international dimensions. The three-fold task was to anoint Hazael as king of Aram (Syria), Jehu as king of Israel, and Elisha as prophet "in your place." The thin sound concluded on a chilling note: "Whoever escapes from the sword of Hazael, Jehu shall kill; and whoever escapes from the sword of Jehu, Elisha shall kill."[29]

Soon thereafter, God translated the blessed Elijah directly to heaven, his mantle falling, as decreed, on Elisha. He proceeded to anoint Hazael king of Aram so that, as Yahweh's "instrument," he would punish the idolatrous Israelites—a sacred mission the prophet carried out with grave misgivings. "Why does my lord weep? a bemused Hazael asked. "Because I know the evil that you will do to the people of Israel," the troubled, but faithful, Elisha responded; "you will kill their young men with the sword, dash into pieces their little ones, and rip up their pregnant women" (2 Kings 8:12; cf Hos. 13:16).

Everything that the "small voice" commanded came to pass, but the career of the "religious reformer," Jehu, had the most profound impact on the subsequent history of Israel.[30] Following his anointment as king, Jehu (842–814) launched a frenzied campaign in the service of the LORD.[31] He set an ANE record by killing two kings in a single day—Ahab's son, Joram, king of Israel, and Ahaziah, king of Judah. He directed the killing of the "cursed woman," Queen Jezebel, whose body was eaten by dogs as prophesied by Elijah. He next arranged for the grisly slaughter of the seventy sons of Ahab, whose bloody heads were delivered to him in baskets. In a mopping-up operation, he eliminated everyone left in the house of Ahab, "all his leaders, close friends, and priests, until he left him no survivor." Finally, for good measure, he slaughtered forty-two princes of the house of King Ahaziah of Judah; "he spared none of them."

With those preliminaries out of the way, Jehu was now free to go directly to the heart of the problem. Acting with great "cunning," he called for a grand assembly of the Baalists—their prophets, priests, and ordinary worshipers—at which the king himself would offer sacrifices to Baal. So many excited and unsuspecting devotees responded to the king's proclamation from the far corners of the realm that the temple was filled "from wall to wall." As he finished the solemn cultic offerings before the congregation of the faithful, Jehu suddenly turned and ordered eighty of his henchmen to "come in and kill them; let no one escape." Elijah would have been proud. Following the slaughter, they utterly destroyed the Baalist temple and "made it a latrine to this day." The tireless servant of the LORD had literally "wiped out Baal from Israel."

Since the archaeological record of Israel is full of gaping holes, we are fortunate to have preserved the words of the true

God in evaluation of the busy career of Jehu. As recorded in 2 Kings 10:30: "The LORD said to Jehu, 'Because you have done well in carrying out what I consider right, and in accordance with all that was in my heart have dealt with the house of Ahab, your sons of the fourth generation shall sit on the throne of Israel.'" The only blemish noted on Jehu's otherwise sterling record was his failure to destroy the "golden calves" at the shrines at Dan and Bethel in the northern kingdom, a common shortcoming of northern kings. Despite that defect, Jehu reigned for twenty-eight years and his four-king dynasty for nearly one hundred years, the longest and most prosperous in the history of the northern kingdom.[32]

The Canaanites and their Baalist faith remained "a snare and a trap" down to the destruction of the southern kingdom in 586 B.C.E., though with ever-decreasing vitality. Eventually, they would be absorbed by Yahwism and become extinct as a religion, a culture, and a people. Israel's neighbors on its eastern flank also posed a continuing religious and occasional military threat to the chosen people. It is to them that we now turn.

3
The Neighbors

Nations having significant intercourse with Israel within the biblical time-frame can be divided into three groups. The superpowers—Egypt, Assyria, Babylonia, Persia, Greece, and Rome—dominated the ANE in successive waves from the late second millennium B.C.E. into the Common Era. In their heyday, these imperial powers could have their way militarily with a vastly overmatched Israel. Understandably, the memory of the devastation wrought by these international bullies left an indelible mark in the minds of their victims and their God.

A second group of nations—Philistia, Phoenicia, and Aram (Syria)—maintained a fluctuating parity with Israel over the centuries. Fortunes waxed and waned from era to era, but no nation in this group dominated its neighbors for an extended period of time. Hostility marks these relationships for the most part as well, though it is not as intense or long-lasting as that toward the superpowers.

A third group of small Transjordanian states—Ammon, Moab, Edom, and Amalek—occupied the territory east and south of the Dead Sea largely in what is the modern state of Jordan. Israel and the superpowers generally dominated these weaker states and not infrequently reduced them to a vassalage status. On occasion, these neighbors could become an irritant on the eastern and southern flanks, but at no time did they pose a serious threat to Israel's existence. We will explore this relationship in order to observe the attitude of the God of Israel toward these marginal peoples. It is here that we might expect Yahweh to be his most understanding and gracious. Archaeology and history will set the frame, but the focus will be on the theological dimension—the character of the one, true, and living God.

Ammon and Moab

According to the biblical text, Ammon and Moab were established kingdoms when Israel first appeared in the Transjordan en route to Canaan. Ammon occupied a somewhat indeterminate region northeast of the Dead Sea bordered by the Jabbok River and its tributaries on the west and north and by the Syrian desert on the east. Moab was its neighbor on the south (Fig. 1). Outside the Bible, the earliest written evidence of Ammon is from Assyrian inscriptions of the eighth century B.C.E., but archaeological remains indicate a considerably greater antiquity. The capital city, Rabbath-Ammon, was a regional power as early as the eighteenth century B.C.E., though how early the Ammonite kingdom appeared is not precisely known.

The Ammonites lived a hardscrabble existence in a harsh unforgiving environment not unlike that of their Transjordanian neighbors. The soil was thin, much of it not arable, and rainfall was constantly in short supply. They herded sheep and goats on the uplands, and farmed the thin, more fertile strips along the stream courses. To a limited extent, they profited from the trade facilitated by the north–south highway ("The King's Highway") that traversed the Transjordan. All in all, it was a weak and marginal land frequently subjugated by its more powerful neighbors, perhaps as much from a desire for domination as significant economic gain.[1]

Hostilities broke out between Israel and Ammon during the period of the Judges (Judges 10–11). Because Israel had been worshiping Baal and other deities, an angry Yahweh "sold" them into the hands of the Ammonites who are said to have "oppressed" them in the Transjordan for eighteen years. When Israel repented of its "evil" ways, Yahweh raised up the judge Jephthah to save the day. The Ammonite king and Jephthah exchanged belligerent messages, the king getting one biblical verse to tell his side of the story, Jephthah getting fourteen. Subsequently, Jephthah inflicted "a massive defeat" on the Ammonites, though in its aftermath, he had to sacrifice his own daughter in order to fulfill an earlier vow to the LORD.

Early in the tenth century B.C.E., Ammon lost its independ-

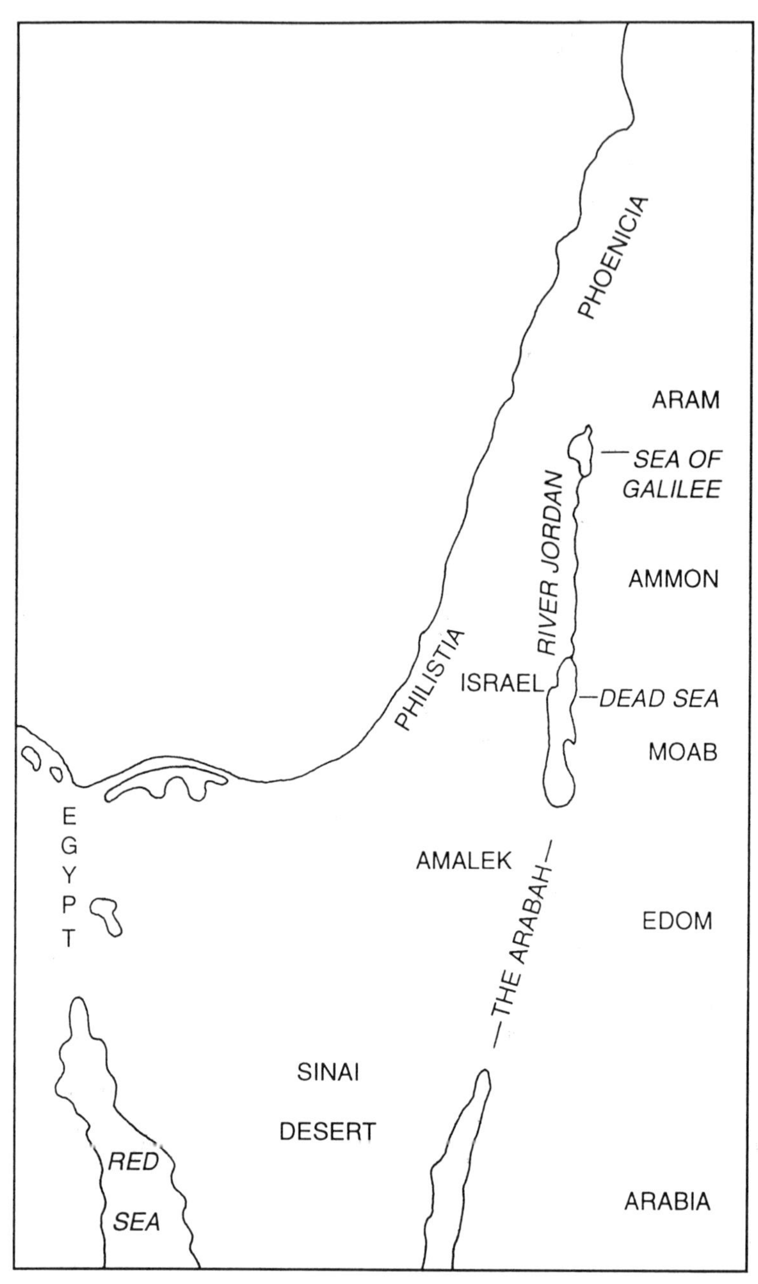

FIGURE 1. MAP OF ISRAEL AND ITS NEIGHBORS, CIRCA 1000 B. C. E.

ence to the conquests of the ambitious King David as did most of the surrounding nations. David captured the capital city, and with it, a magnificent jeweled crown, and set the natives to work with "saws and iron picks and iron axes, or sent them to the brickworks" (2 Sam. 12:31). Ammon remained in subjugation to Israel through the reigns of David and his son, Solomon. The schism in Solomon's kingdom and the rising power of Aram to the north encouraged them to throw off their Israelite bonds toward the end of the tenth century B.C.E.

During the reign of King Jehoshaphat (873–849 B.C.E.), a coalition of Ammonites, Moabites, and Edomites came up against Judah in a battle so memorable that it is celebrated in song, even to this day, as a paradigm of the LORD's power (2 Chron. 20). Although he possessed an army said to be in excess of one million, Jehoshaphat lamented that it was "powerless" against such a "great multitude" and called on God to "execute judgment" upon them. At the critical confrontational hour, the Levitical singers burst into worshipful song, causing the enemy to attack and destroy one another. Their abundant corpses littered the ground, for "no one had escaped." Jehu would have been proud. The "fear of God" came upon all the countries round about when they learned that "the LORD had fought against the enemies of Israel."

A century later, Judah collected tribute from Ammon during the reigns of King Uzziah (783–742 B.C.E.) and his son Jotham (742–735 B.C.E.).[2] But the Assyrian expansion, which began in the mid-eighth century, dominated the region for the remainder of the century and most of the next. The Ammonites and their Transjordanian neighbors paid taxes and tributes, contributed corvee labor, and furnished military support to the Assyrian overlords. In return, they received some protection from the menacing desert tribes on the east whose strength increased during the period. Ironically, the economies of the vassals flourished during much of the Assyrian period.

When the Babylonians destroyed the Assyrian capital, Nineveh, in 612 B.C.E., a new power cast its dark, menacing shadow over the entire ANE. The Babylonians evidently forced the cooperation of the Ammonites, Moabites, and Arameans in the suppression of the rebellion of King Jehoiakim of Judah, circa 600 B.C.E. (2 Kings 24:1–2). However, in 594 the Ammonites, along with others, participated in an abortive plot to overthrow the Babylonians (Jer. 27:3). During the eighteen-month siege of Jerusalem, which capitulated in 586, the Ammonites remained firmly anti-Babylonian. However, Ammon was completely subjugated by 582. Arabian tribes from the east continued to increase their pressure, so that by the latter part of the sixth century B.C.E. Ammon had ceased to exist as a distinct culture or people. Later references to "Ammon" are to an imperial administrative unit only.

Moab occupied the high plateau south of Ammon, east of the Dead Sea. Straddling the River Arnon, it extended to the Brook Zered at the southeast corner of the Dead Sea (Fig. 1). In broad outline, its history paralleled that of its ally, Ammon. An established kingdom when the Israelites arrived, Moab lost its independence during the united monarchy of David and Solomon. It regained it early in the divided kingdom, only to lose it again to the Israelites for a few decades in the ninth century. It, too, fell victim to the Assyrian and Babylonian dominations of the eighth to sixth centuries. By the end of the sixth century, it had become extinct as a distinct people and polity, though for centuries the term continued to be used for the region.[3]

In the era of the Judges, the Israelites had once again evoked the wrath of Yahweh by whoring after foreign gods. As punishment, the LORD "strengthened" the king of Moab as an "instrument" against Israel. In alliance with the Ammonites and Amalekites, the Moabites took control of the region around Jericho, which they maintained for eighteen years. Eventually moved by the anguished cries of his people, Yahweh raised up their deliverer, Ehud. Through a subterfuge, Ehud killed the Moabite king and led the Israelites to a resounding defeat of the enemy. On that day, they killed ten thousand Moabites, "all strong, able-bodied men; no one escaped."[4] Jehoshaphat would have been proud.

When the fugitive David was on the run from the Israelite king Saul, he felt sufficiently comfortable with the Moabites and their king to leave his parents with them for safekeeping. But as king, in direction of the expansion of the empire, David did not hesitate to subdue the Moabites. He measured out "two lengths of cord" for those who were to be slaughtered and "one length" for those who were to be spared.[5] Ehud would not have approved.

We need constantly to keep in mind that though the biblical text is incomplete enough, it stands in sharp contrast to the muteness of the Transjordanian record. To this day, we receive a one-sided account of most every interaction between the Israelites and their "Godless" neighbors. A major archeological discovery in 1868—the Moabite Stone or Mesha Inscription—affords a welcome glimpse of how the Moabites viewed international affairs, both militarily and theologically. The mid–ninth century B.C.E. memorial stela recounts the events leading to the successful Moabite rebellion against the Israelites during the reigns of Omri (882–871) and his son Ahab (871–852), events that are alluded to in several biblical passages.[6]

King Mesha dedicated the stela to the Moabite god, Chemosh, who, he said, "caused me to triumph over all who opposed me." He then turned to relations with Israel:

> Omri, king of Israel, oppressed Moab for
> many years, because Chemosh was angry
> with his land.
> When his son succeeded him, he too said, "I
> shall oppress Moab." In my days he spoke
> this way,
> but I triumphed over him and his house, and
> Israel was utterly destroyed forever. Omri
> took possession of the entire land
> of Medeba, and [Israel] lived there during his
> days and half the days of his son—forty
> years; but
> Chemosh restored it in my days. . . .
> Then Chemosh said to me,
> "Go capture Nebo from Israel!" . . . I captured
> it and slew them all—seven thousand men,
> boys, women, girls,
> and maidservants—for I had devoted it to Ashtar-
> Chemosh. I took from there the utensils of Yahweh,
> dragging them before Chemosh . . . .[7]

In these few words, we may identify several themes common to the Bible, though they are presented as the opposite of our usual perspective. Like the historians of Israel, King Mesha confounds history and theology. The divine "power equation" is in full view, but it is now Chemosh, not Yahweh, who controls the flow of events. Chemosh "restored" the oppressed land to the Moabites; his "anger" explains their defeats. The boast that Israel is "utterly destroyed forever" is a common type of braggadocio found in the Bible and throughout the ANE. The "devotion" of the victims at Nebo to the triumphant god—the ban—echoes the Conquest theology of the Books of Deuteronomy and Joshua. In another common biblical motif, the humiliation of the vanquished is completed by defiling or destroying objects ("utensils," "vessels" in some translations) intimately associated with its god.

A final point of comparison is worthy of our attention. The statements that King Omri and his son "oppressed Moab" are more rare grammatical constructions than one might suppose. In the nearly six hundred thousand words of the OT, not a single sentence has Israel or its representative as the subject, *oppress* as the verb, and a foreign nation as the object.[8] Yet, on the Moabite Stone of some five hundred words, the expression occurs twice. This disparity is another sobering reminder of the biased nature of the biblical lens through which the descriptions of international events are filtered.

The biblical text often groups Ammon and Moab together in its more ideological pronouncements. The origin of the two peoples as depicted in the folk story in Gen. 19:30–38 is a case in point. After the cataclysmic destruction of Sodom and Gomorrah, all that remained of the family of Lot, Abraham's nephew, was the father and his two daughters. In order to perpetuate the lineage, the women schemed to induce the elderly Lot to become intoxicated and to seduce them. And so it came to pass: the firstborn was named Moab and the second Ben-ammi, the eponymous ancestors of their respective nations. It may be doubted that the peoples so named adopted for themselves this genetic tale of drunken incest.

When Israel moved up through the Transjordan on its way to attack Canaan, Yahweh warned it not to "harass" or "engage in battle" the Ammonites, Moabites, or Edomites because he had "given" their land to them as a possession. This is the first suggestion that Yahweh was claiming specific providence over the neighboring peoples and their land.[9] But the protective posture melted away as the relationship turned sour over the centuries.

The most unkind cut of all is delivered in Deut. 23:3. In addition to those "blemished" Israelites who have crushed testicles or lack a penis or are born of an illicit union, no Ammonite or Moabite of any stripe could be admitted to the assembly of the LORD "even to the tenth generation." The rabbis later altered this harsh injunction, limiting the prohibition to males—a modification influenced no doubt by the Moabite ancestry of David and the Ammonite parentage of his grandson, Rehoboam. Still later, they dropped the restriction altogether, reasoning, in effect, that intermixing among the Transjordanian peoples had so attenuated the polluting influence of the primary DNA that it no longer carried its original theological potency.[10]

The Ammonites and Moabites also did not fare well in the oracles of the Israelite prophets, often being vilified more for an "attitude" than for concrete action. Among the many examples, a passage from the late seventh-century prophet, Zephaniah, conveys the typically ominous tone. The LORD speaks of the future of the unchosen:

> I have heard the taunts of Moab
> and the revilings of the Ammonites,
> how they have taunted my people
> and made boasts against their territory.
> Therefore, as I live, says the LORD of hosts,
> the God of Israel,
> Moab shall become like Sodom
> and the Ammonites like Gomorrah,
> a land possessed by nettles and salt pits,
> and a waste forever.

The remnant of my people shall plunder them,
    and the survivors of my nation shall possess them.
This shall be their lot in return for their pride,
    because they scoffed and boasted
    against the people of the LORD of hosts.[11]

Edom

Israel's "brother," Edom, occupied the land that stretched south from the Brook Zered for some one hundred miles to the north shore of the Gulf of Aqaba. On the north, it straddled the Wadi Arabah, making a border as the "land of Seir" with the Negeb ("dry south country") in southern Judah, though its heartland lay to the east of the Arabah. A poorly defined eastern border graded into the Arabian desert (Fig. 1). Several inaccessible mountain retreats, or "rock fortresses," dotted the rugged landscape. Archeological evidence of human habitation in the area spans a period of up to one-half million years.

Especially in its southern reaches, Edom was a more impoverished and less well-watered land than its neighbors to the north or Israel. Today the average annual rainfall ranges from sixteen inches in the north to less than ten inches in the south. The population engaged chiefly in subsistence farming and sheep and goat rearing. The economic value to outsiders of this arid, marginal plateau lay principally in copper deposits and the "King's Highway," the north-south trade route that moved goods from the gulf seaport of Elath to northern Edom, Israel, Aram, and the Mediterranean coast.[12]

The historical outline of Edom approximates that of Ammon and Moab. The Bible states that Edom existed as an organized kingdom when the Israelites first arrived, though some scholars have challenged this view. Circa 990 B.C.E., David conquered Edom, killing "eighteen thousand" in the process, a predetermined outcome inasmuch as the LORD "gave victory to David wherever he went." His field commander, Joab, who stayed on for six more months, theoretically "cleansed" the group permanently, since he is said to have "eliminated every male" in the nation.[13]

Judah dominated Edom from the Davidic conquest to the reign of King Jehoram (846–843 B.C.E.), when it regained its full independence. It maintained that status for more than a century though Judah represented an ever-present threat on the west. In the 730s, Assyria began extracting tribute, a vassalage that continued until near the close of the seventh century. When Assyrian power waned, Edom again enjoyed a brief period of sovereignty before it fell under the yoke of Babylon. In the sixth century, under Arabian pressure from the eastern desert, Edom expanded its territory west of the Arabah, even encroaching on some southern Judean territory. As a distinct political and cultural entity, Edom had disappeared by at least the fifth century B.C.E., being absorbed into Judea as Idumea on the south and into the Arabian nation of Nabatea on the east.[14]

The long, difficult relationship between Edom and Israel has often been likened to that of hostile brothers. Much is expected of the "proximate other," but little that is elevating is forthcoming from either side. The celebrated story of the birth and maturation of the eponymous twins—Esau/Edom and Jacob/Israel—anticipates much of later political history. The identification of Edom with Esau probably dates from the time of Edom's revolt in the ninth century B.C.E.[15]

Religious ideology serves not only to integrate "us" but to exclude "them." The lengthy genealogies of Noah's descendants in Gen. 10-11 progressively winnow the grain from the chaff, the holy line from the discarded dross. The text points as an arrow to the lineage of Abraham, Isaac and Jacob; the last of the unchosen to be shucked off is Esau/Edom. Although "brotherhood" implies a biological and psychological, even political, intimacy, the theological chasm that separates the twins is fully as great as that between Israel and any other foreign nation.

As related in Gen. 25–36, the God of Israel orchestrates the fraternal relationship from start to finish. He grants Isaac's prayer that his barren wife Rebekah conceive. While yet pregnant, Rebekah learns from the LORD that two nations are in her womb and that "the elder shall serve the younger." As an adult, the readily duped Esau sells his birthright to Jacob for a pot of stew. Through trickery, Jacob also obtains Isaac's death-bed "blessing," an echo of the nationalistic promise to Abraham in Gen. 12:3a: "Let peoples serve you, and nations bow down to you. . . . Cursed be everyone who curses you, and blessed be everyone who blesses you!" (Gen. 27:29)

To prevent him from marrying a Canaanite and distance him from his irate brother, Jacob's anxious parents send him back to Rebekah's family in northern Mesopotamia to search for an ethnically suitable spouse. On the journey, the LORD repeats to him his earlier covenantal promises to Abraham and Isaac of land, a great name and multitudinous offspring. "Know that I am with you" said the LORD, "and will keep you wherever you go. . . . "

In Mesopotamia, the LORD oversees the births of Jacob's eleven sons and one daughter, facilitates the impressive growth of his wealth in sheep, and tempers the behavior of his chief antagonist, his uncle, Laban. God chooses the time for the return trip to Canaan: "Return to the land of your ancestors and to your kindred, and I will be with you." The night before his dreaded reunion with Esau after a twenty-year separation, Jacob experienced a numinous encounter with the Almighty that changed both his persona and his name. All night long he struggled "face to face" with God who renamed him "Israel," a divine act that fortified him for his meeting with a possibly still-enraged brother.

Meanwhile, in a futile attempt to please his parents, Esau had married a half-dozen local women, some of whom had "made life bitter" for their in-laws, Rebekah and Isaac.[16] At one time, Esau had been angry enough to contemplate killing his twin, but the years had so dampened his ire that he gracefully welcomed back his peripatetic kin. As the tale moves to its divinely-ordained conclusion, a stark theological fact intrudes itself: never, ever, does the true God make the slightest overture to the unchosen Esau—but then, that is what chosenness is all about. Even so, centuries later, the author of the Book of Hebrews blames the victim, warning that no one should become like Esau, "an immoral and godless person" (12:16).

In the wake of the satisfying meeting with his brother, the relieved and grateful Jacob instructed his household to put away their "foreign gods" and travel with him to Bethel where they would erect an altar to the God "who answered me in the day of my distress and has been with me wherever I have gone." From that touching scene, we turn and take leave of the God-forsaken Esau. Amid impenetrable genealogical lists, a short, prosaic note reports that he and his are off to the barren wilderness of Edom, a country not to be mistaken for a "land of milk and honey." No birthright, no blessing, no election, no covenant, no God.[17]

The issues of divine choice, power, and justice raised by the Esau-Jacob tale attracted the attention of the apostle Paul (Rom. 9:6–24). Did the differential treatment of Jacob and Esau mean that a grave injustice had been perpetuated by the One who proclaims loudly that he "love[s] justice" (Isa. 61:8)? "By no means!" exclaims Paul, who proceeds to give "power" answers to "justice" questions. The un-choice of Esau *in utero,* came from an omnipotent Deity who may bless or curse "whomever he chooses." But, some may ask how the God of Justice can still "find fault" with the unchosen. In response, Paul continues to shift the focus from justice to power: "But who indeed are you, a human being, to argue with God? Will what is molded say to the one who molds it, 'Why have you made me like this?' " God made "objects of wrath" for destruction in order to reveal to the "objects of mercy" his "power" and the "riches of his glory." For Paul and his followers, an end that blesses the few Jacobs fully justifies the means that damn the many Esaus.

There remain a few intriguing passages that suggest that Israel perceived Edom in a somewhat different light than its other neighbors. While the god of Ammon, Milcom, and the god of Moab, Chemosh, are routinely condemned as "abominations," the god or gods of Edom are neither named nor condemned. Some scholars have suggested that initially the Edomites may have worshiped Yahweh and subsequently adopted Quas, a god known only from archaeological inscriptions of the seventh century and later.[18] This hypothesis is supported by biblical passages, such as Judges 5:4, that portray Yahweh as approaching Israel from the southeast: "LORD, when you went out from Seir, when you marched from the region of Edom." The hypothesis is questioned by others and is not supported by the Esau-Jacob account.[19]

The Deuteronomist stressed brotherhood: "You shall not abhor any of the Edomites, for they are your kin" (23:7). He described the Israelites in their wilderness trek as passing peacefully through the territory of "your kindred, the descendants of Esau." These lands, along with those of Ammon and Moab, were inviolate because they had been assigned to the neighbors by Yahweh. In contrast to the Ammonites and Moabites, who were denied entry forever into the cult of Israel, the Edomites (and Egyptians) had only to endure a purgatorial period of three generations before their admittance into the sacred assembly.[20]

The Israelite attitude toward Edom shifts radically in the prophetic literature of the sixth century and later. A full-blown "Damn-Edom" theology unfolds in the prophetic Books of Isaiah, Jeremiah, Ezekiel, Amos, Joel, and Malachi.[21] Obadiah, the shortest book in the Bible, devotes its twenty-one verses entirely to condemning Edom. The hostility stems from Edom's transgressions, real or imagined, in connection with its "settlement" in southern Judea and its behavior at the time of the Babylonian conquest in the early sixth century.

The archaeological evidence is abundant that beginning in the seventh century Israelites and Edomites intermingled extensively in the region southwest of the Dead Sea. How to interpret this evidence remains an unresolved problem. Possible explanations include commercial trade, a residual population of Edomites, peaceful infiltration, and Edomite conquest. The shifting settlement pattern continued over an extended period and would, perhaps, have caused less concern in Israel if the Babylonian destruction had not shaken the foundation of its society to its very roots.[22]

Direct evidence regarding the activities of the Edomites in the events surrounding 586 is scanty in the extreme. Edom is not listed as one of the nations joining Babylon in quelling the rebellion of Israel circa 600. It is named as joining in the plot against Babylon in 594. Israelite refugees of the Babylonian depredations fled to Edom (and to Ammon and Moab as well). Numerous biblical passages attribute the destruction solely to King Nebuchadnezzar II and his army, as the appointed instruments of Yahweh.[23]

But several biblical passages bring serious, though generalized, charges against the Edomites. They are said to have "looted," "acted revengefully," "shed innocent blood," and given Israel over "to the power of the sword at the time of their calamity." The most explicit charge came some three hundred years after the fact when, it is claimed, they "burned" the temple (1 Esd. 4:45).[24] Other charges are more attitudinal than behavioral. The Edomites are said to have "gloated," "boasted," "rejoiced," "stood aside," and behaved "like one of them." They "cherished an ancient enmity" while screaming "tear it down!" as Jerusalem was reduced to ruins.[25]

Some interpreters, unrestrained by the biased source and paucity of the evidence, have unhesitatingly branded Edom as "perfidious," "insidious," and "despicable," and gleefully applauded its latter demise as "the calamity he has deserved, for his old sins." For these apologists, the biblical charges alone are sufficient to make it "clearly evident" that the Edomites participated with "a fury and a vindicative spirit."[26] But a leading student of Edomite history, John R. Bartlett, attributes the "ancient enmity" to Judah's "hatred" of Edom, which traces back to the Davidic conquest and Edom's rebellion, hostilities that left in their wake a "legacy of bitterness." Bartlett argues that Edom has been "falsely maligned" and "played no direct part" in the fall of Jerusalem.[27]

Giving the biblical charges more credence, Beth Glazier-McDonald strikes a more realistic note. That Edom survived 586, at least for a few years, argues for its accommodation with Babylon in the service of its self-interest. As an impoverished country, it probably joined in the looting and, aware of Judah's vulnerability, accelerated its settlement of the southern reaches of Judea. She notes that the two countries seemed to have reached a "rapprochement" in the seventh century based on their mutual interests in the commercial trade that flowed from Arabia to the Philistine coast. In 586, any untoward behavior by Edom, regardless of its magnitude, would have been perceived by Judah as rank treachery by a trusted "brother."[28] We may be certain only that Edom acted in what it saw as its national interest, as all peoples are wont to do.

Whatever the facts on the ground, in the Bible Edom stands guilty as charged. Embittered exiles call on the LORD to punish the hated Edomites and Babylonians by dashing their "little ones" against the rocks (Ps. 137:7–9). Yahweh is pitiless in his denunciations—threatening humiliation, desolation, depopulation, and loss of the "little ones":

> For by myself I have sworn, says the LORD, that Bozrah [i.e., Edom] shall become an object of horror and ridicule, a waste, and an object of cursing; and all her towns shall be perpetual wastes. . . . As when Sodom and Gomorrah and their neighbors were overthrown, says the LORD, no one shall live there, nor shall anyone settle in it. . . . Therefore hear the plan that the LORD has made against Edom. . . . Surely the little ones of the flock shall be dragged away; surely their fold shall be appalled at their fate.[29]

In certain post-exilic passages, a new development appears that we did not encounter in the literature concerning Ammon or Moab. Edom becomes transformed from *an* enemy to *the* enemy, i.e., a "type" of the enemy nation for all times and all occasions. It came to symbolize the hostile world that stands in unmitigated opposition to the God of Israel and the Israel of God. The metamorphosis is complete when Edom is portrayed as the eschatological (End-time) foe who must be destroyed before cosmic order is restored and Israel can return to Zion.[30] The restoration of Zion in Isa. 35 follows these verses from chapter 34, which depict the annihilation of Edom as a symbol of all nations:

> Draw near, O nations, to hear;
> O Peoples, give heed! . . .
> For the LORD is enraged against all the nations,
>   and furious against all their hordes;
>   he has doomed them, has given
>   them over for slaughter . . . .
> When my sword has drunk its fill
>   in the heavens

lo, it will descend upon Edom,
upon the people I have doomed to judgment.
The LORD has a sword; it is sated with blood,
it is gorged with fat,
with the blood of lambs and goats,
with the fat of the kidneys of rams.
For the LORD has a sacrifice in Bozrah,
a great slaughter in the land of Edom. . . .
For the LORD has a day of vengeance,
a year of vindication by Zion's cause.[31]

In extra-biblical writings from the turn-of-the-era and beyond, Edom continued to represent the quintessence of evil. In the "War Scroll," one of the celebrated Dead Sea Scrolls, the "sons of light" launch a preemptory strike against the "sons of darkness," against "Edom and . . . Moab and . . . Ammon. . . ."[32] In later Jewish legend, embellishment of the Esau-Jacob tale becomes a favorite literary activity, revealing something of the psychological needs of the originative community. Jacob was destined to be born first, it is said, but Esau threatened to kill their mother if he didn't get precedence. Jacob was born "clean and sweet of body," bearing the sign of the covenant, "a rare distinction." In stark contrast, his evil twin bore a congenital mark in the form of a serpent, "the symbol of all that is wicked and hated of God."[33]

In other Jewish legends, Esau's "guardian angel," Sammael, is identified with "the evil inclination" and, in turn, with Satan and the serpent in the Garden of Eden. By imaginative expansion of the biblical text, Esau is found guilty of theft, rape, and murder. The land of Edom becomes the place wherein "wicked plans are concocted against God." A continuing sensitivity to the morality of the Conquest generates the claim that Esau lost his rights to the Promised Land with the sale of his birthright to Jacob. In the early Common Era literature, Edom, Esau, and Seir began to appear as symbols for the despised oppressor, Rome, a substitution facilitated by the fact that the unpopular King Herod (37–4 B.C.E.) was an Idumean. After Rome adopted Christianity, the same symbols were transferred to it. And when may we expect God to restore Israel to its holy land and return to his holy temple? Only after he has "requited wicked Edom."[34]

The last word on Edom is reserved for the one, true, and loving God, in an oracle in the half-forgotten Book of Malachi. Written by a "minor prophet" of the fifth century B.C.E., the book has been known chiefly for its strategic position as the last book of the OT and for its claim that Elijah's return will herald the coming of the Messiah. But Malachi also includes the final and absolutely unambiguous divine word on the men, women, and children who constituted the late, great nation of Edom. The oracle's message bring us back full circle to the fraternal tale in Genesis and the questions of divine choice, power, and justice:

> I have loved you, says the LORD [to Israel]. But you say, 'How have you loved us?' Is not Esau Jacob's brother? says the LORD. Yet I have loved Jacob but I have hated Esau; I have made his hill country a desolation and his heritage a desert for jackals. If Edom says, 'We are shattered but we will rebuild the ruins,' the LORD of hosts says: They may build, but I will tear down, until they are called the wicked country, the people with whom the LORD is angry forever.[35]

Amalek

Our final ethnic group, Amalek, hardly qualifies as a "nation" and scarcely has a history; yet it has left an indelible mark on the history and theology of Israel. Unknown outside the Bible and with no certain archaeological remains, the Amalekites apparently lived as bedouins over a vast, largely desert, territory that stretched from the western Sinai to northwest Arabia (Fig. l). With camels as their chief mode of transportation, their rag-tag lifestyle featured mobility and the constant threat of shortages of food and water. Compared to their more sedentary contemporaries, they would have been noted for their impoverished diet, bad teeth, high morbidity and low life expectancy. Their precarious existence on the margin of the margin ended during the reign of David, in the tenth century B.C.E.

Though the Amalekites ranged as far north as Samaria, their traditional heartland centered on the western fringe of Edom and the adjacent southern Negeb. Indeed, the biblical account of their origin identifies them with Edom. The eponymous ancestor, Amalek, is said to be the son of Eliphaz, son of Esau, and his concubine, Timna; i.e., Amalek is the grandson of Esau (Gen. 36:12). From this relationship, Amalek becomes the first cousin once removed of the children of Jacob, the twelve patriarchs of Israel. But no whiff of "brotherhood" taints the relationship of Amalek and Israel. Always portrayed in the context of warfare, Amalek became the pure, unadulterated arch-enemy of the true God and his people.[36]

Their first encounter is dramatic and has had reverberations down to the present day. Following its escape from Egypt, the Israelite party met opposition for the first time at an indeterminate spot in the Sinai wilderness. The Amalek "came and fought with Israel" (Exod. 17:8). Though the action of Amalek is often depicted by non-Amalekites as "unprovoked," even "treacherous," the sudden, threatening presence of a horde of homeless "foreigners" would have been provocation enough to the established bedouin populations of the region.[37]

The ebb-and-flow of the historic battle was regulated in a unique manner. Though Joshua was the field commander, Moses, holding the "staff of God," actually controlled the battlefield from the top of an adjacent hill. When he stretched out his arms, Israel's fortunes waxed; when his arms fell to his side, they waned. Since his arms understandably grew weary as the day progressed, two associates helped hold them up, eventually delivering the victory to the Israelites. The author of the Epistle of Barnabas, a Christian work incorporated into some early versions of the NT, saw in the stark figure of Moses on the hill a vivid prefiguration of the cross of Jesus the Christ.[38]

Following the victory, a grateful Moses built an altar on the site and announced that the LORD would wage war with Amalek "from generation to generation." For his part, an enraged Yahweh declared that he would henceforth "utterly blot out the remembrance of Amalek from under heaven" (Exod. 17:14–16). Several hundred years later—centuries after the Amalekites had passed from the scene—the Deuteronomist added new details of the battle to a reminder to Israel never to forget: "Remember . . . how he attacked you on the way, when you were faint and weary, and struck down all who lagged behind you; he did not fear God. Therefore . . . you shall blot out the remembrance of Amalek from under heaven; do not forget" (Deut. 25:17–19). The reminder not to forget "the evil done by Amalek" became one of the 613 *mitzvot* (commandments) that are to be eternally observed by Jews. Further reminders to "blot out" the memory of the arch-enemy are provided to this day on Shabbat Zakhor ("Sabbath of Remembrance") and the festival of Purim.[39]

Amalek obtained a measure of revenge for its defeat when the Israelites moved toward Canaan and contemplated invading it from the south. Moses sent out twelve spies to make a full report on the land and its people. The majority report described the inhabitants as "strong," the towns as "fortified and very large," and the Amalekites as among the peoples blocking the way. The "stiff-necked" people decided to attack even though Moses had warned that "the LORD is not with you." As could be predicted from the divine power equation, the Amalekites and their allies easily routed the Godless Israelites.[40]

Approximately two hundred years later, the LORD directed his newly anointed King Saul (ca. 1025–1005), through the prophet Samuel, to apply the complete ban to Amalek in punishment for its opposition to Israel in the Sinai. "Now go and attack Amalek," said the LORD, "and utterly destroy all that they have; do not spare them, but kill both man and woman, child and infant, ox and sheep, camel and donkey" (1 Sam. 15:3). As a modern commentary so coldbloodedly expresses it, this divine directive afforded Saul a golden opportunity "to demonstrate his allegiance to the LORD by obedience in this assigned task."[41] Dutifully Saul proceeded to invoke the ban and "utterly destroyed all the people with the edge of the sword." But he took King Agag alive and saved some of the better livestock for what he claimed would be a "sacrifice to the LORD" (1 Sam. 15:7–9,15).

Samuel was furious with Saul for this lapse, piously lecturing the king that "stubbornness is like iniquity and idolatry." The prophet promptly corrected Saul's omission and "hewed

Agag in pieces before the LORD." The true God said that he bitterly regretted having ever made Saul king for he had not "carried out my commands." Samuel informed Saul that on "this very day" the LORD had "torn the kingdom of Israel from you" and handed it over to David, "who is better than you." In most circles, that substitution would qualify as a change of mind. But in the next breath, the text assures us that God does not change his mind, "for he is not a mortal, that he should change his mind."[42]

Although Amalek became extinct in the tenth century B.C.E., the core idea of a totally wicked person or population has thrived in both the biblical and extra-biblical literature. In the Book of Esther, a novella of the fourth century B.C.E., the villain Haman, who plots the destruction of the Jews, is said to be a descendant of King Agag (Esther 3:1). Jewish legend teaches that Agag became Haman's progenitor during the short interval in which he was spared by Saul. Haman stands first in a long line, both deserving and undeserving, who have been assimilated to Amalek: Antiochus IV, Titus, Hadrian, Eichmann, Hitler, and Romans, Arabs, and Native Americans, inter alia.[43]

In the imaginative Jewish midrashim of the early Common Era, a "totally evil" Amalek symbolized the lowest level of moral degradation that the "other" could ever attain. The sages declared that God had sent Amalek as a scourge to punish Israel for its sins. Israel could only proceed successfully against Amalek if it first asked repentance for its own transgressions. Serious though those sins might be, they couldn't begin to compare with the iniquities of the arch-enemy, so heinous that its very name had to be "blotted out" from memory.

What were the specific sins of Amalek—a people who, "like a dog, came to lick up Israel's blood"? A partial list conveys the range and gravity: pederasty, castration, the most obscene forms of blasphemy, destruction of Torah scrolls, reduction of the temple to its foundation, incitement of other nations to attack Israel. No proselyte could ever originate from the ranks of Amalek, for it was beyond redemption. So long as Amalek endures in the world, God's face will remain hidden, his throne will not be "whole," his name will not be "complete." Only when the "seed of Amalek" perishes from this earth will these manifestations of the LORD once again become perfect.[44]

Historians and archaeologists reconstruct historical events insofar as the extant evidence permits, but that evidence can never resolve questions of faith and morality. God is to be located in the Book, not the ground. For members of the biblically based communities of faith, the moral "should be" ought to eclipse in importance the antiquarian "what was." The character of the scriptural God, as revealed in his intercourse with the "other," should be profoundly troubling. "Hard" passages such as 1 Sam. 15:3, in which God commands the extermination of not only all the adult Amalekites but their "infants and sucklings" (JPS) as well, are especially difficult. They are not rendered less so by the protestation that the ban was an ubiquitous practice in the ANE or that it was never fully implemented or that what we have here is only the morality of the "primitive" Israelites.

What we do have here is a text in the name of the true God that states unambiguously an unacceptable ethic for dealing with the unchosen. Texts such as these taste just the same when you bite them as those speaking of "love," "grace," and "salvation." Most readers would like to agree with the theologian Martin Buber that in 1 Sam. 15 the prophet Samuel simply "misunderstood" the divine message.[45] That suggestion would be more persuasive if the divine message didn't stand in need of "misunderstanding" so often.

A prominent Jewish scholar, Irving Greenberg, has searched diligently for firm theological ground in the light of the fires that devoured the children at Auschwitz. He has proposed, as a "working principle," that no theological proposition be considered valid that "would not be credible in the presence of the burning children." Certainly that is an appropriate and practical criterion of universal morality. Unfortunately, the OT would fail that test at 1 Sam. 15 and numerous other pericopes.[46]

Although we moderns may quail before the "us-them" morality of the OT, our forefathers had no such qualms. In their unprovoked invasion of what they called the "New Canaan," the New England Puritans freely cited the Deuteronomist and the prophets for moral justification. Over twenty-five hundred years after the events depicted in Exod. 17 and 1 Sam. 15, the "New Israel of God" eagerly adopted the biblical paradigm, though anxious not to repeat Saul's mistake. The celebrated Puritan divine Cotton Mather described the Native Americans as "a treacherous and barbarous enemy" and urged his fellow colonists to subdue ruthlessly the "Amalek annoying Israel in the wilderness."[47]

Over the centuries, many "well-meaning" spiritual leaders have jettisoned their elemental sense of compassion and justice to adopt tortured and inhumane rationalizations in order to salvage the integrity of the genocidal God. A parade example is John Wesley, the founder of Methodism. A decent man of deep spirituality, Wesley, nonetheless, accepted fully the traditional view that the Amalekites and their ilk were moral ciphers to be manipulated at will by the God of Israel. In his commentary on 1 Sam. 15:3, Wesley declared that the slaying of the Amalekites was "not unjust" because the Lord of life can "require his own when he pleases." And since all infants are "born in sin," they are "liable to God's wrath." So far, so good—an Amalekite baby appears to be at no greater risk than an infant of the true believer.

But Wesley shifts to reasoning that can only be applied to the morally impenetrable "other": "Their [the infants'] death also was rather a mercy than a curse, as being the occasion of preventing their sin and punishment."[48] In this "Christian" solution to the problem, Wesley proposes that the babies of the Amalekites are better off being slaughtered in infancy than growing up in (Christian-defined) idolatry and paying the dire consequences! The most disquieting aspect of this sentiment is that it represents a perfectly logical extension of the thoughts and actions of the God of Israel as portrayed in the sacred Scriptures.

4
Nationalism and Universalism

In this chapter we widen our angle of vision to encompass the relationships between Israel and all the nations, both those interactions that manifest "nationalism" and those said to demonstrate "universalism." These international relationships, developing after the settlement in the land, offer a prime opportunity to explore further the character of the God of Israel. Passages on point are scattered widely throughout the OT canon, including the three major prophets, nearly all of the twelve minor prophets, and the Books of Lamentations, Daniel, and Psalms. Nations from all three categories (chapter 3) are included as well as the catch-all generic, "nations." Exclusive of the primary history (Genesis-Kings), well over one thousand verses may be identified with nationalistic and/or universalistic themes.

Nationalism

Though the two categories overlap one another to some degree, we define as nationalistic those passages in which the God of Israel addresses one or more nations in a condemnatory mode without direct reference to a more inclusive or universalistic dominion. The nucleus of the nationalistic message is found in the so-called "Oracles Against the Nations" (OAN) in the major prophets—three blocks of passages encompassing the twenty-five chapters of Isa. 13–23, Jer. 46–51, and Ezek. 25–32. If the question relates to the attitude of the true God toward the Gentile nations in the aggregate, the answer should be sought first of all in the 540 verses of these oracles.[1]

A number of suggestions have been made as to the role and purpose of the OAN in their original settings: oracles before battles to strengthen resolve; cultic or ritual curses on the enemy; indirect condemnation of Israel for reliance on foreign alliances rather than solely on Yahweh; moral instruction of Israel in the consequences of pride, idolatry and oppression as demonstrated by their heathenish neighbors; reassurance to the Israelites that regardless of the circumstances, Yahweh will prevail. That the oracles were intended for domestic consumption rather than spoken or written in anticipation of a response from the enemy is generally agreed. Though the nations are in the foreground, the OAN function primarily to advance the welfare of Israel and its divinely ordained purposes.

Scholarly attempts to isolate historical events that inspired the oracles have sometimes proven successful though they often result in frustration or rank speculation. Specific accusations are typically lacking; indeed, a number of oracles lack a particular indictment altogether. Although details vary somewhat from group to group, the pagan, Godless nations share a common, predetermined fate, as one would expect in descriptions of the "undifferentiated other."[2]

Whatever the original purpose or *Sitz im Leben* of the oracles, the divine message remains uniform, repetitive, and unequivocal: the pagans are to be visited by calamity, to be broken, humiliated, and destroyed for their attitudes and/or actions—or for no particular reason at all. If the "Hate-Edom" label was appropriate for the literature directed at that nation, then certainly the OAN can be described as "Hate-the-Nations" writings. The xenophobic God of Israel introduces himself to the great unwashed mass of humanity as a grim, sometimes even gloating, agent of doom. No expectation of redemption or invitation to repentance emanates from the LORD. The morally impregnable heathens are nothing if not cardboard objects of divine wrath and scorn who worship "no-gods"—hardly flesh-and-blood subjects of caring and concern. If we accept the modern notion of hell as a state of separation from God, the nations, like Esau, led a "hellish" existence. The OAN represent a classic anthropological example of us-versus-them social typology.

Among the many possible examples, we select a few of the OAN to demonstrate the range of themes that can result in a common outcome. In Jer. 49, an exuberant Yahweh addresses an anguished Damascus, capital of Syria, circa 600 B.C.E.:

> Damascus has become feeble, she
> turned to flee,
> and panic seized her;
> anguish and sorrows have taken
> hold of her,
> as of a woman in labor.
> How the famous city is forsaken,
> the joyful town!
> Therefore her young men shall fall
> in her squares,
> and all her soldiers shall be
> destroyed in that day,
> says the LORD of hosts.
>
> —Jer. 49:24–27

In Ezek. 29, the failure of Egypt to relieve the Babylonian siege against Jerusalem in 588 B.C.E. evoked the wrath of the LORD, the first of four consecutive hostile chapters directed toward Israel's ancient antagonist. Reliance on foreign alliances rather than solely on Yahweh's mighty arm is Israel's sin, but pagan Egypt must also bear the consequences. A prideful Yahweh vows to humiliate the superpower on the Nile:

> Therefore, thus says the Lord GOD: I will bring a sword upon you, and will cut off from you human being and animal; and the land of Egypt shall be a desolation and a waste. Then they shall know that I am the LORD. . . . It shall be the most lowly of kingdoms, and never again exalt itself above the nations; and I will make them so small that they will never again rule over the nations. The Egyptians shall never again be the reliance of the house of Israel; they will recall their iniquity, when they turned to them for aid. Then they shall know that I am the Lord GOD.
>
> —Ezek. 29:8–9,15–16

An oracle against Elam, a nation east of Babylon, is vintage

OAN, an afterthought in the final verse striking a limp note of restoration after the nation has been destroyed:

> Thus says the LORD of hosts: I am going to break the bow of Elam, the mainstay of their might; and I will bring upon Elam the four winds from the four quarters of heaven; and I will scatter them to all these winds, and there shall be no nation to which the exiles from Elam shall not come. I will terrify Elam before their enemies, and before those who seek their life; I will bring disaster upon them, my fierce anger, says the LORD. I will send the sword after them, until I have consumed them; and I will set my throne in Elam, and destroy their king and officials, says the LORD.
>
> But in the latter days I will restore the fortunes of Elam, says the LORD.
>
> —Jer. 49:35–39

On occasion, the target of judgment is not a specific nation but the entire inhabited planet, the all-inclusive "them." In a section of Jeremiah, originally associated with the OAN, the LORD sends a "cup of the wine of wrath" to all nations. Since Israel was being punished, "how can [they] possibly avoid punishment?" The LORD commands "them" to "drink, get drunk and vomit, fall and rise no more, because of the sword that I am sending among you." Those who fall by that sword "shall extend from one end of the earth to the other. They shall not be lamented, or gathered, or buried; they shall become dung on the surface of the ground" (25:15,27,29,33).

A number of oracles outside the OAN of the three major prophets deliver a similar message of divinely directed doom. The oldest may be in Amos 1–2, where the charges are more specific than in many oracles, though still so vague and undatable that they cannot be identified historically. In a few passages, a nation is castigated for transgressions against a neighbor other than Israel. This has led some scholars to posit an international standard of behavior in the ANE derived from "natural law" or convention rather than Yahwist theology.[3]

The stereotypical nature of the oracles is highlighted in Amos by successive verses that bring identical charges and punishments in almost identical language against two pagan cities belonging to two distinct ethnic groups, Philistia (Gaza) and Phoenicia (Tyre). When confronting the "undifferentiated other," the parts are readily interchangeable:

> Thus says the LORD:
> For three transgressions of Gaza,
> and for four, I will not revoke
> the punishment;
> because they carried into exile
> entire communities,
> to hand them over to Edom.
> So I will send a fire on the wall
> of Gaza,
> fire that shall devour its
> strongholds. . . .
> Thus says the LORD:
> For three transgressions of Tyre
> and for four, I will not revoke
> the punishment;
> because they delivered entire
> communities over to Edom,
> and did not remember the
> covenant of kinship.
> So I will send a fire on the wall
> of Tyre,
> fire that shall devour its strongholds.
>
> —Amos 1:6–7, 9–10

Given the disposition of their God toward the heathenish nations, the chosen people often beseeched him to dispose of their enemies, which, of course, were his as well. The Psalms contain a rich lode of invective against the unchosen, usually in the form of a group lament or "prayers for deliverance from national enemies." In 60:11–12, the petitioners recognize that the aid of mere mortals will not extricate them from their plight:

> O grant us help against the foe,
> for human help is worthless.
> With God we shall do valiantly;
> it is he who will tread down
> our foes.

In Ps. 79, a devastated people cry out in anguish and call for sevenfold vengeance on the enemy for its hostile attitudes:

How long, O LORD? Will you be
Angry forever?
Will your jealous wrath burn
like fire?
Pour out your anger on the
nations
that do not know you,
and on the kingdoms
that do not call on your name. . . .
Return sevenfold into the bosom
of our neighbors
the taunts with which they
taunted you, O Lord!

79:5–6,12

In Ps. 83, the people of God call on the LORD for vengeance against no less than ten of their pagan neighbors who had conspired against them, closing the petition on a universalistic note:

O God, do not keep silence;
do not hold your peace or be
still, O God!
Even now your enemies are in
tumult;
those who hate you have raised
their heads. . . .
They conspire with one accord;
against you they make a
covenant—
the tents of Edom and the
Ishmaelites,
Moab and the Hagrites,[4]
Gebal[4] and Ammon and Amalek,
Philistia with the inhabitants of
Tyre;
Assyria also has joined them;
they are the strong arm of the
children of Lot. . . .

Let them be put to shame and
dismayed forever;
let them perish in disgrace.
Let them know that you alone,
whose name is the LORD,
are the Most High over all the
earth.

83:1–2, 5–8, 17–18

Open hostility to outsiders continued to be expressed in the OT until the close of the canon in the first century C.E. Although direct communications from the LORD had largely ceased, his supplicants implored him to intervene violently against the un-Godly, a sentiment that they had reason to believe would be favorably received. Writing around 180 B.C.E., Jesus Ben Sirach (Ecclesiasticus) ironically calls on the God "of all" to flex his divine muscles and wreak havoc indiscriminately on the "foreign nations" in much the style, spirit, and letter of the earlier "us-them" literature.

Have mercy upon us, O God of all,
and put all the nations in fear of you.
Lift up your hand against foreign nations
and let them see your might.
As you have used us to show your
holiness to them,
so use them to show your glory to us.
Then they will know, as we have known
that there is no God but you, O Lord. . . .
Rouse your anger and pour out your wrath;
destroy the adversary and wipe out the enemy.

36:1–5, 8–9

The late-first-century B.C.E. author of The Wisdom of Solomon kept the spirit alive, and even took a significant step beyond what had, heretofore, been accepted implicitly as the limit in the thriving business of castigating the pagans. He portrays "them" as not just ordinarily wicked, in the garden-variety sort of way, but as creatures whose evilness was genetic or "inborn," confronting us four-square with a bald, unblinking racism. He reflects upon events that had transpired over a millennium before, back to the time of the Conquest and the original inhabitants of the land. God had "hated" the Canaanites for their "detestable practices" and willed their destruction so that the land "most precious" to him might receive "a worthy colony of the servants of God" (12:7). But the Almighty decided to grant temporary mercy to the undeserving idolaters, opting to destroy them bit by bit:

> But judging them little by little
> you gave them an
> an opportunity to repent,
> though you were not unaware that
> their origin [or nature] was evil
> and their wickedness inborn,
> and that their way of thinking
> would never change.
> For they were an accursed race
> from the beginning. . . .
>
> 12:10–11

Passages that warn of calamity for the nations may serve not only a vengeful function, but also as a pre-condition for the salvation of Israel. In a type of deadly "zero-sum" game, the destruction of the "other" brings in its wake the salvation of Israel. At the macro-literary level, the linkage of doom for the nations with hope for Israel can be observed most clearly in the three major prophets and Zephaniah. A section of judgment on Israel is followed by the OAN which, in turn, are capped by a section of salvation for Israel. For example, in Ezekiel, the OAN (chapters 25–32) link the oracles of warning for Israel (1–24) with oracles of its salvation (33–46).[5] In the interests of symmetry, if nothing else, we should expect a section of salvation for the nations. That hypothetical section is noticeable only by its absence.

The association of doom for "them" and hope for "us" may also be identified in smaller units of only one or a few verses. The "hate Esau-love Jacob" motif in Mal. 1:1–4 obviously falls in this category. In the following we note the intimate union of the two themes and how easily the focus shifts from one to the other:

In fury you trod the earth,
in anger you trampled nations.
You came forth to save your people,
to save your anointed.

—Hab. 3:12–13

For I am with you, says the LORD,
to save you;
I will make an end of all the nations
among which I scattered you,
but of you I will not make an end.

—Jer. 30:11

The punishment of your iniquity,
O daughter Zion, is accomplished,
he will keep you in exile no longer;
but your iniquity, O daughter
Edom, he will punish,
he will uncover your sins.

—Lam. 4:22

Lastly, we consider Psalm 149 (a "hymn to accompany a festival dance") and note that the change in mood from festive to hostile occurs in mid-phrase:

Praise the LORD!
Sing to the LORD a new song,
his praise in the assembly of the faithful. . . .
Let them praise his name with dancing,
making melody to him with
tambourine and lyre. . . .
Let the high praises of God be in
their throats
and two-edged swords in their
hands,
to execute vengeance on the nations
and punishment on the peoples . . .
to execute on them the judgment decreed.
This is glory for all his faithful ones.
Praise the LORD!

149:1,3,6–7,9

Modern Response to the Pagan

God may frequently move in mysterious ways, but his dismissive and denunciatory attitude toward the nations is one of the OT's most unequivocal messages. No trace of the sentiment of Matthew 25 ("as you did it to one of the least of these. . . . ") corrupts the response of either biblical or modern authors to the plight of the despised Godless pagan. Taking their clue from the biblical posture, latter-day theologians often defame these "not-us" nations as a matter of course. With no survivors of the extinct cultures to say them nay, commentators enjoy an open season on the defenseless victims. The underlying and unexamined assumption is that the Israelite side of the story is sufficiently close to the unvarnished truth that one may make valid moral judgments about peoples who remain largely mute. This despite the well-documented and universal recognition that ethnic communities are notoriously biased in their reporting of hostile encounters with the "other." Like dead men, dead nations do not talk, at least not very loudly.

"Objective" scholars report that the Philistines were "a warlike people"; the Amalekites "a fierce desert tribe"; Mesha, King of Moab, "a petty tyrant"; the Moabites, a "callous, pitiless" people of "bovine" intelligence whose country was a "bad place" filled with "wicked people."[6] King Agag of Amalek is described repeatedly as "murderous," while the murderous King Jehu is sanitized as a "religious reformer."[7] Israel is said to be surrounded by "greedy," "ill-natured," and "hostile and envious" neighbors whose calamitous fates, as recorded in the OAN, are "surely deserved."[8] Even in the most straightforward historical accounts, unconscious bias can creep in. In a recent summation of the pre-exilic hostilities between Aram and Israel, we read of the "aggression," "domination," "oppression," "atrocity," "plunder and pillage," and "unleashed power" of Aram; but for Israel, we learn only of benign "victories," "reclaimed" land, and the "capture" of enemy holdings.[9]

The "wickedness" of the biblically-unchosen frequently appears in modern as well as ancient writings as the quintessence of evil. Ironically, their despised status—which includes equating them with the Devil—is essentially the same as that of "the Jews" in the Gospels which modern scholars have roundly and appropriately condemned. The "immoral" behavior of the non-elect is understood as the logical consequence of not "fearing God"—as if they could have, given that the God of Israel chose not to introduce himself, at least not on favorable terms.[10] Though our understanding of the religions of the ANE has increased enormously in this century, fatuous comparisons between the God of Israel and those of the ANE remain popular. A theological work widely used by college-level teachers makes claims that can only bring dishonor to its cause. Whereas the "will, purpose, and nature" of the ANE gods can only be "inferred," it says, these same characteristics of the God of the OT are "a matter of public record provided by Yahweh."[11]

Since the end of the Second World War, leading figures of the German fascist regime have been equated with the biblical "other." Adolf Eichmann has been assimilated to King Agag; Adolf Hitler to the Amalekites; the Nazis, in toto, to the Egyptians of the Exodus.[12] Such comparisons seem unnecessary and grossly unfair to the ancient peoples. The Nazi atrocities are among the most completely documented mega-events in human history. The Amalekites and the Egyptians of the Exodus are known only from the Bible, legendary figures whose very historicity has been challenged. Given our ignorance of the facts on and in the ground, is it necessary to make such a reach for a standard of unsurpassable evil? Isn't that why God invented the Devil?

The peoples of the ANE have hardly received a fair hearing from either Jewish or Christian theologians or from the God of Israel. A mere one hundred or so generations ago, these roundly-excoriated human beings sought the intimacy and guidance of the Divine according to their lights, captives as they were of their time and place, as are we all. They struggled through brief, difficult lives—devoutly seeking a seminal story to live by, a numinous encounter with deity, answers to the unanswerable, and a small glimpse of the Grand Design before their inevitable curtains fall. They assuredly confirm Thomas Hobbes's observation that the lives of the great unwashed mass of humanity have always been "poor, nasty, brutish, and short." And, we should add, according to the Bible—Godless.

It is seldom remarked that if Yahweh is the one, true and living God, the ANE peoples paid a huge price for his Israelite "experiment." Apologetes insist that the God of Israel was benevolently disposed towards the heathenish pagans, but the OT contradicts that sentiment flatly. If he brought intimacy, justice, and salvation to the chosen, his Providence meant only bemusement, misery, and alienation for those accursed souls who found themselves on the "outside" looking in. Expressed in terms of the modern vernacular: as the basketball coach of, say, Team Edom with an upcoming game with Team Israel, how would one feel upon learning that the referee would be Yahweh, the universal "God of Justice"?

One of the more remarkable manifestations of the Western spirit has been its congenital inability to perceive ANE merit in any sphere but the profane. The pioneering excellence of the ANE civilizations has been honored in agriculture, architecture, art, ceramics, commerce, engineering, language, law, literature, medicine, seafaring, and science, inter alia. But in matters of religious moment, we are told these hopeless heathens know not "their right hand from their left."[13]

More respect should be paid, not only to the religions and peoples of the extinct cultures, but to the phenomenon of extinction itself, given that God has made it so pervasive. If he has been concerned principally to effect salvation for humankind, the evidence suggests that he has failed miserably in the effort. In the fullness of time, a people and its unique culture will certainly disappear, just as surely as will the individual person. Over three-quarters of all mammalian genera are now extinct, the great majority before the advent of man. The United Nations' membership currently numbers fewer than two hundred, the result of literally thousands of human cultures having disappeared over the millennia. The ghostly roll-call runs from the Arawak of the Caribbean, the Bena Bena of New Guinea, and the Comanche of the American plains to the Xhosa of southern Africa, the Yahi of California, and the Zenaga of Morocco. As the cemetery epitaph whispers in its "still small voice" to individual and group alike: "As I am now, you soon will be."

That the nationalistic river ran wide and deep in Israel is undeniable, though we must not suppose that the current generated thereby flowed with any greater power than those of its ANE neighbors. Apologetes tend to be uncomfortable or embarrassed by the nationalistic thrust, though its prominence in the millennial-long history of a people is natural enough. Pervasive though OT nationalism may be, it is said to be more than offset by its "universalistic" sentiments. It is to the latter that we now turn.

Universalism

The principle of universality has been a central concern of both Jews and Christians for centuries. For Judaism, universalism is important, though not absolutely essential, for its self-understanding as a "priestly kingdom and holy nation" whose vocation will bring blessings to the world. For traditional Christianity, universalism is absolutely critical, for unless the God of Israel is perceived as reaching out to the Gentiles on felicitous terms, all is lost. Transforming the xenophobic and ethnocentric Deity into one to whom the Gentiles can relate has been a major and unfinished task of Christian theologians for two millennia. For both religions, nationalism and universalism have come to acquire a very value-laden status. The former is offensive to the modern spirit, especially in its more blatant manifestations; the latter is much to be desired, implying as it does in its fullest expression an open-minded and loving concern for the entire human race. But this simplistic dichotomy ignores the adaptive value of ethnocentrism in ancient cultures and the imperialistic dimensions of universalism. Before taking up specific texts, we shall examine more closely the concept of universalism and its component elements.

Since the word "universalism" does not appear in the OT, we must impose on the text our own biases and preconceptions. Two basic elements of the concept may be identified: the output, or target audience and the input, or source group. To be taken seriously as a universalistic proposition, the target audience should theoretically include all humankind. To qualify in this minimal sense, one need only to proclaim confidently that the proposition in question applies to all men, women, and children, the beasts of the field and the fishes in the sea. We have no difficulty in identifying such statements; they were common in the ANE and biblical Israel. Indeed, the roster of the world's most sincere universalists would have to include such imperialists as Alexander the Great, Julius Caesar, Genghis Khan, Napoleon Bonaparte, Adolf Hitler, and Joseph Stalin.

The second element of "input" represents a more difficult hurdle to clear. Most theological propositions have emanated from a single ethnic group, or more precisely, from one or a few representatives of the group. We call this unilateral or "narrow" universalism, the few speaking to the many. Biblical claims of universality clearly fall under this rubric. A second, more uncommon, type of input is multilateral or "broad," the many speaking to the many. The Olympics, United Nations, ecumenical religious movements, and international conferences on disarmament and the environment fall in this category. The type specimen is the United Nations' "Universal Declaration of Human Rights." If we substitute "Universal" for "Human," we have the "Universal Declaration of Universal Rights," the many speaking to the many. In the twenty-first century, optimists claim, "broad" universalism may become more important than the traditional "narrow" type, perhaps even in the ultra-sensitive area of religion.

Universalism and Israel are linked early in the biblical story. In their first meeting, God declared to Abraham that "in you all the families of the earth shall be blessed" (Gen. 12:3b). This translation in the passive voice has met with resistance from those scholars who prefer a reflexive rendering: "by you all the families of the earth shall bless themselves." One accepts with reluctance the premise that God's communication with his children turns significantly on such grammatical niceties, especially since Israel remains the elected centerpiece in both renditions. But one scholar, of a poetic bent, insists that "the meaning is clearly passive and the implications for OT biblical theology are massive!"[14] Forgotten in this linguistical contretemps is the ultra-nationalistic message of the first part of the very same verse (12:3a): "I will bless those who bless you, and the one who curses you I will curse."

Although the idea was present at Israel's scriptural birth, universalism didn't reach its full flower until hundreds of years later with the advent of "Second Isaiah," the great prophet of the restoration that followed the Exile. During the pre-exilic era, the religious ideas and practices of the Canaanites attracted many an Israelite heart as well as the scorn and ridicule of the ever-vigilant prophets. In this period of full engagement with the Baalists, declarations concerning the providence of Yahweh tended to the abbreviated and anemic rather than the protracted and full-blooded. For example, in his showdown at Mount Carmel with the Baalists, the beleaguered Elijah beseeched Yahweh to demonstrate only that he was God "in Israel" (1 Kings 18:36). A sequence of textual statements of increasing complexity may be traced without any suggestion of strict linearity or chronological development.

We begin modestly and comparatively with Deut. 32:31: "Indeed their rock is not like our Rock; our enemies are fools." And quickly move to the superlative: "In days to come, the mountain of the LORDs house shall be established as the highest of mountains . . . " (Mic 4:1). The first commandment, given at Sinai, makes no monotheistic claims, saying only that "you shall have no other gods before [besides] me" (Exod. 20:3). But on the plains of Moab, Moses is more explicit, telling the Israelites that the "terrifying displays of power" in Egypt should have convinced them that "the LORD is God; there is no other besides him" (Deut. 4:34-35).

Testimony with a universalistic flavor also came from outside the elect, the more persuasive because of that origin. Impressed with Yahweh's engineering of the escape from Egypt, Moses' father-in- law, Jethro, declared that "now I know that the LORD is greater than all gods" (Exod. 18:11). The Canaanite traitor of the Conquest, Rahab, threw in her lot with Israel after watching her countrymen "melt in fear" upon learning of the mighty exploits of the invaders' God. Yahweh, she said, "is indeed God in heaven above and on earth below" (Josh. 2:11). Some time after the settlement in the land, the prophet Elisha effected a miraculous cure of the leprosy of Naaman, the commander of the army of Aram (Syria). In gratitude, the general enthusiastically declared: "Now I know that there is no God in all the earth except in Israel." But he continued to harbor some doubt as to the universal providence of this Deity of the neighboring land. He requested "two mule-loads" of Israelite dirt to be hauled back to Aram so that the newly-discovered God could be worshiped on his native soil (2 Kings 5).

Early in the biblical story, brief, undeveloped assertions of world dominion may be found, as in Exod. 19:5 where Yahweh himself declares that "the whole earth is mine." But most passages on point adopt an ad hoc position, Yahweh exercising cautiously circumscribed hegemony as the occasion required. "Did I not bring Israel up from the land of Egypt," he asks in Amos 9:7, "and the Philistines from Caphtor and the Arameans from Kir?" As we saw in Chapter 3, the LORD claimed to have allotted to Ammon, Moab, and Edom their Transjordanian homelands (Deut. 2:4–5,9,18–22). Of course, the OAN of the three major prophets demonstrate convincingly the increasing prowess of Yahweh in the region.

Yahweh himself may be visualized as "ruling" the nations (e.g., in Pss. 22; 82) and often his earthly surrogate, the king of Israel, is portrayed as dominating the world. Thus are the theological and the political fused in the primitive nationalistic-universalistic bond. Anticipating a common post-exilic theme, Ps. 2 essentially offers "them" the alternatives of "submit, convert or die." Peoples who had been subjugated by Israel plan rebellion, but God in heaven "laughs" at their presumption. To the newly-crowned Israelite king—God's "begotten son"—the LORD gives the nations as a "heritage," the "ends of the earth" as a "possession." If the rebellious leaders do not "serve the LORD with fear, and with trembling kiss his feet," he will become very angry, "for his wrath is quickly kindled" (2:4,7–8,11–12).

In Ps. 18, King David gives thanks to the God of "salvation" who exalted him above all his adversaries among the nations. The hapless enemies "cried for help, but there was no one to save them; they cried to the LORD, but he did not answer them" (v.41). The psalmist skillfully interweaves the hymn of thanksgiving to the LORD with naked imperialism:

> You delivered me from strife with
>   the peoples;
>   you made me head of the
>   nations;
>   people whom I had not known
>   served me.
> As soon as they heard of me they
>   obeyed me;
>   foreigners came cringing to me.
> Foreigners lost heart,
>   and came trembling out of their
>   strongholds.
>
> vv. 43–45

The subjugation-domination theme is reprised in Ps. 72, a psalm said by modern interpreters to describe Israel's "ideal universal empire" (NRSV) whose "divine blessing" via the king saturates Israel and "overflows to other nations"[15]:

> May he [the king] have dominion from sea
>   to sea,
>   and from the [Euphrates] River to the ends
>   of the earth.
> May his foes bow down before
>   him,
>   and his enemies lick the dust. . . .
> May all kings fall down before him,
>   all nations give him service.
>
> vv. 8–9,11

In Amos 1–2, Yahweh punished transgressor nations for offenses against their non-Israelite neighbors. From this stage, it is but a small step to the concept of the foreign "instrument," a non-Israelite agent who unknowingly carries out Yahweh's purposes against the designated sinner, either another nation or, ironically, Israel. Yahweh's "universal" providence has now extended specifically to the superpowers. In 605 B.C.E., an Egyptian army rushed to meet Babylon in battle at Carchemish on the upper Euphrates River in a desperate attempt to fill the power vacuum created by the fall of Assyria. Jer. 46:2-12 credits Yahweh with the crushing defeat of Egypt: "For the Lord GOD of hosts holds a sacrifice in the land of the north by the river Euphrates." And he made additional plans that the victor would fulfill with enthusiasm in the foreseeable future.

The notion of instrument developed some intriguing ramifications in the realm of "divine politics" among Israel and the super-powers. Within the frame of the divine "power equation," the gods of both the victor and the vanquished endorse the victor's leader as the ruler of the world, though for diametrically-opposed reasons. For example, in the eighth century B.C.E., Assyria came to dominate the ANE under the auspices of its principal god, Ashur. But in Yahweh's eyes, the control center remained firmly anchored in Jerusalem: "Ah, Assyria, the rod of my anger—the club in their hands is my fury!" (Isa. 10:5). In the late seventh century, sanctioned by his god Marduk, King Nebuchadnezzar II of Babylonia succeeded Assyria as the prevailing force in the "known" world. But Yahweh decreed that as creator of the earth (Gen. 1:1) "I give it to whomever I please." And it now pleased him to give it to Nebuchadnezzar, "my servant," to whom "I have given . . . even the wild animals of the field to serve him" (Jer. 27:5–6).

Matters became more complex in the sixth century with the advent of Cyrus II, the emperor of Persia. Cyrus became popular with his victims due to his tolerant policy toward local customs and gods, so long as no sign of rebellion spoiled the arrangement. In addition to carrying the expected endorsement of the Persian god, Ahura-Mazda, he became a favorite instrument of Yahweh. The LORD volunteered to march before the emperor to "level the mountains" in his path and took the unprecedented step of referring to the pagan king as his "anointed," i.e., the Messiah (Isa. 45:1–2). The widely admired Cyrus gained divine support from Babylon and Greece as well. So the Persian Emperor, "ruler of all the world," became the instrument of at least four prominent national deities: Ahura-Mazda, Yahweh, Marduk, and Zeus.[16]

But pagan instruments could receive their comeuppance after being "used" by the LORD for his holy purposes. In the eighth century, he had "whistled" for the king of Assyria to march against Israel, "a godless nation," the "people of my wrath" for alleged injustices. The royal assignment was "to take spoil and seize plunder, and to tread them down like the mire of the streets." But the heathen king deigned to take all the credit, announcing that "By the strength of my hand I have done it." Yahweh scoffed at this "arrogant boasting," declaring that it was as if "a rod should raise the one who lifts it up." Bent on reprisal, Yahweh threatened to destroy Assyria "both soul and body," a promise fulfilled a century later by another instrument.[17]

Following his destruction of Jerusalem as God's agent, King Nebuchadnezzar was put on notice that he could expect a sharp reversal of fortune: "many nations and great kings shall make him their slave" (Jer. 27:7). Although Cyrus would eventually bring that to pass, the Babylonian king remained in the LORD's good graces for a remarkably long time, considering the fact that he and his army were responsible for the single greatest catastrophe in the history of Israel.

Inexplicitly, the LORD promised the Phoenician city of Tyre to Nebuchadnezzar who took up the siege shortly after Jerusalem fell in 586. Yahweh predicted the reduction of the island fortress to "a bare rock," which would "never again" be rebuilt and the consignment of its people to "a dreadful end" in the netherworld of Sheol. But the combined effort of the Babylonian tyrant and the Israelite God failed to capture the city even after a brutal thirteen-year siege. In 571, to make amends for his failed promise, the LORD gave to the disappointed despot an ancient enemy of them both—the land of Egypt. The LORD directed the king to "carry off its wealth and despoil it and plunder it" and to consider the booty "wages" for his army, which had "labor[ed] hard" but futilely against Tyre. That economic arrangement seemed fitting enough since, as the universal Lord GOD said, "they worked for me."[18]

The anonymous author of Isa. 40–55, "Second Isaiah," wrote circa 540 B.C.E., i.e., near the end of the Babylonian captivity, as the victories of Cyrus II began to bring a renewed hope to the exiled community. To appreciate fully the purposes, accomplishments, and nationalism/universalism of the prophet, we must first locate him in his historical context. Apparently, he had been taken to Babylon sometime after the fall of Jerusalem along with thousands of other political, professional, and religious elite. After nearly fifty years in captivity, the exiled community was rent by uncertainty, alienation, and apostasy. Many exiles had decided to settle permanently in Babylon, one of the most progressive and exciting places on the globe. Without question, the calamity of 586 and its aftermath, had produced the darkest, most perilous hour in the history of Judaism, a religion whose very survival hung in the balance.

From its inception, Judaism had been a very place-oriented religion. The "promised land" had been an integral part of God's covenant with Abraham and his descendants. The homeland was sacred soil, not to be equated with, or exchanged for, any other place on the face of the earth. Since the Deuteronomic reforms of King Josiah circa 621 B.C.E., all worship and sacrifice had been centralized in or near the holy building, the temple. Of all the places in the universe, God had concentrated his Presence most intensely in the temple's inner sanctum, the Holy of Holies with its winged cherubim and Ark of the Covenant. The Almighty himself had solemnly guaranteed the continuity in perpetuity of the Davidic royal lineage (2 Sam. 7). But now, nation, city, and temple lay in ruins, and for the first time in over four hundred years, no member of the House of David sat on the throne of Israel.

The traditional theological explanation of military defeat and devastation had been the malediction of the "defeated" god on his sinful people, a solution that dated to at least the third millennium B.C.E. (chapter 1). The prophets Jeremiah and Ezekiel had emphasized sin-and-punishment as the divinely inspired interpretation of the tragedy, as did almost all of those who followed them. Second Isaiah fully accepted this theodicy, but above all else, he offered hope, healing, and restoration. The opening words of the "Prophet of Consolation" set the tone: "Comfort, O comfort my people, says your God" (40:1). The severity of the catastrophe of 586 called not merely for an ad hoc explanation of the proximate events, but a root-and-branch defense of the viability, even existence, of the God of Israel. Not since Elijah confronted the Baal prophets at Mount Carmel had the central question of divine control been so starkly drawn between "us" and "them."

In chapter after chapter of brilliant poetry, Second Isaiah contrasts the all-encompassing power of the ascendant Yahweh with the pitiful impotency of the pagan pseudo-gods. A full-throated monotheism, which implies universalism, leaves no doubt in the readers' mind concerning the celestial head-count: "I am the first and I am the last; besides me there is no god. . . .Is there any god besides me? There is no other rock; I know not one" (44:6,8).[19] In turn, monotheism implied creatorship: "I am the LORD who made all things, who alone stretched out the heavens, who by myself spread out the earth" (44:24).

The poet drew extensively on the well-springs of a centuries-old tradition that had linked so intimately the people and their God. "Remember the former things of old," said the LORD; "Look to the rock from which you were hewn. . . . Look to Abraham your father and to Sarah who bore you; for he was but one when I called him, but I blessed him and made him many." A new God-led exodus to the Promised Land awaited the people of hope: "In the wilderness prepare the way of the LORD, make straight in the desert a highway for our God."[20]

The most critical test of the authenticity of the true God lay in his ability to predict the course of history. In the cosmic courtroom, the LORD challenged the gods of the nations to "tell us what is to come hereafter, that we may know that you are gods." But the no-gods proved to be no more effectual in this arena than they had been at Mount Carmel. The God of Israel both announced the future and brought it to fruition: "The former things I declared long ago, they went out from my mouth and I made them known; then suddenly I did them and they came to pass."[21]

Second Isaiah's single-mindedness of national purpose shines through the numerous passages that are aimed at reassuring the anxious exilic community and restoring the nation to its former glory. The LORD admitted that "for a brief moment" he had indeed "abandoned" Israel; but, he assured, he would once again gather it to his bosom with "great compassion." Skeptics might claim that Zion had been totally forsaken, but, the LORD asks rhetorically, "Can a woman forget her nursing child, or show no compassion for the child of her womb?" In an echo of Gen. 12:3a—in which all other peoples are judged by their behavior toward Israel—the nation is promised that "those who strive against you shall be as nothing and shall perish."[22]

In the grand strategy of restoration, humiliation of the "other" is as necessary and effectual as the elevation of the holy people. In the celestial court, Yahweh declares that the work of the gods is as "nothing at all" and that whoever worships these ciphers is "an abomination" (Isa. 41:24). Within a pericope that has been called the "greatest hymn" to monotheism, Second Isaiah declares that "All the nations are as nothing before him; they are accounted by him as less than nothing and emptiness."[23] The relative value to the LORD of the holy nation and the "undifferentiated other" is brutally contrasted in a ransom scene: "Because you are precious in my sight, and honored, and I love you, I give people in return for you, nations in exchange for your life."[24] In this cynical trade, "people" and "nations" become merely inanimate objects offered in exchange for the beloved chosen.

In Isa. 44:9–20, Second Isaiah presents a classic satire of the use of idols by the pagan peoples. His underlying premise is that the worshipers see in their graven images the actual deity rather than its symbol or representation. The distinguished scholar, Jon D. Levenson, has concluded that the prophet's sarcastic portrayal of the origin and function of the icons is so "highly polemical and grossly unfair," that it would be unlikely that the worshipers would have "recognized their religion in his parody of it." Why would Second Isaiah deliberately distort the religion of the "other"? To draw the line more sharply between "us" and "them." As Levenson develops the argument, the gods of the ANE who are "spiritual, creative, loyal to their worshipers, intent on punishing wickedness and rewarding goodness, insistent upon the establishment of justice and equity and upon the prevention of the victimization of the weak—these gods stand too close to YHWH."[25]

The expressions in Second Isaiah that have been most frequently cited as universalistic are imbedded in a thick matrix of hard-core nationalism. One of the most celebrated verses, cited twice in the NT, conveys a clear message of religious imperialism: "To me every knee shall bow, every tongue shall swear" (Isa. 45:23).[26] In that same chapter, the universal LORD condemns the nations to a future of servitude, deprivation, and coerced conversion that only terminal masochists would choose for themselves. He assures Israel that the wealth of Egypt, Ethiopia, and Arabia "shall come over to you and be yours . . . they shall come over in chains and bow down to you. . . . saying 'God is with you alone, and there is no other; there is no god besides him' " (v. 14). In verses 16–17, the pagan idolaters are "put to shame and confounded," but the LORD promises Israel "everlasting salvation; you shall not be put to shame or confounded to all eternity."

Chapter 49 of Isaiah includes a famous universalistic passage that has sparked a missionary interest through the centuries. In verse 6, the LORD tells the Servant, presumably the nation Israel, that since it is "too light a thing" that he should merely restore the House of Jacob, "I will give you as a light to the nations, that my salvation may reach to the end of the earth." But a few verses later (22–23), the LORD promises Israel that he shall soon force "the peoples" to return its exiled sons and daughters, and that pagan royalty "with their faces to the ground . . . shall bow down to you, and lick the dust of your feet." The chapter concludes (v. 26) on an even more bloodthirsty and power-hungry note: "I will make your oppressors eat their own flesh, and they shall be drunk with their own blood as with wine. Then all flesh shall know that I am the LORD your Savior, and your Redeemer, the Mighty One of Jacob."

Moving beyond Second Isaiah into the post-exilic period, the theme of domination-subjugation continues to be prominent. We hear in the voice of "an oppressed and resentful people" the fantasy of a sudden reversal of fortune that will bring the ubiquitous and undeserving "other" into total subjugation to "us" and our God.[27] (Centuries later, Christians fantasized that the Jewish fantasy of universal domination pointed directly to them.) In this imaginary world of cosmic dominion, the amoral pagan may be induced, more often coerced, to acknowledge the universal hegemony of the true God.

In some passages, the humiliation of the nations is effected without any suggestion at all of the possibility of conversion, even forced conversion. In Mic. 7:16–17, a post-exilic addition, it is said that the nations "shall see and be ashamed of all their might . . . they shall lick dust like a snake, like the crawling things of the earth." As prophesied in Gen. 12:3a, the LORD may link the fate of the pagan to his attitude toward Israel:

> Your gates shall always be open . . .
> so that nations shall bring you their wealth. . . .
> For the nation and kingdom
>   that will not serve you shall perish;
>   those nations shall be utterly laid waste. . . .
> You shall suck the milk of nations,
>   you shall suck the breasts of kings;
>   and you shall know that I, the
>   LORD, am your savior. . . .
>
> —Isa. 60:11–12,16

In other pericopes, the fantasy finds the people of the world barely containing their enthusiasm for worshiping at the altar of the God of Israel. In a vision of the messianic era granted to the post-exilic prophet Zechariah, the LORD promises that "many peoples and strong nations" shall stream in to seek his divine "favor." Indeed, so great is the magnetic pull of Jerusalem that ten men from every nationality shall grasp the coat of a single Jew and beg to be taken to the holy city "for we have heard that God is with you" (Zech. 8:20–23).

But the LORD frequently flexed his imperialistic muscles to convey to the nations the more potent message of "submit, convert or die."[28] Outside Second Isaiah, the most widely-cited example of bona fide universalism is Isa. 19:24–25, one of the OAN with post-exilic redactions. "On that day," it declared, "Israel will be the third with Egypt and Assyria . . . whom the LORD of hosts has blessed, saying, 'Blessed be Egypt my people, and

Assyria the work of my hands, and Israel my heritage.' " On its face, this sentiment does seem to take us a generous step beyond the more hostile passages that we have been reviewing. But to appreciate fully the nuances of the passage, we must look at the tone and thrust of the full chapter, of which it is the culmination.

The contextual verses reveal the undisguised intention of the God of Israel to wreak havoc on the social, political, economic, and religious aspects of Egyptian life. Riding in from the east on a "swift cloud," Yahweh brushes aside the Egyptian no-gods, foments social revolution across the land, and places over the confused natives a "hard master," a "fierce king." The Savior of Egypt causes the waters of the Nile to dry up, resulting in widespread suffering due to the loss of food, fiber, and jobs. The Pharaoh's confounded political advisers now give such "stupid" counsel that the once-proud nation flails and flounders as "a drunkard staggers around in vomit." "On that day" the Egyptians tremble in fear "like women" before the true God because of "the plan" that he devises "against them." In such a manner did the LORD "make himself known" to the Egyptians. For their part, the bullied victims—anxious to return to their livelihoods and their life-long addiction to eating—offer burnt offerings and make unspecified "vows" to the LORD.

The concluding passage (vv. 24–25) appears to be an attempt to vault tiny Israel into the heady company of the superpowers, Egypt and Assyria. Despite its context of naked religious despotism, apologetes salute the passage as "remarkable in its universal breadth."[29] The Christian theologian H.G. May rhapsodized that in such "great passages . . . Old Testament religion reaches its zenith and . . . we find the crown of biblical theology."[30] In truth, such tributes reveal something about the poverty of OT "universalism." But the evidence exists to be read and evaluated; the reader should take a "second look" for herself.

In both name and deed, Yahweh "Lorded it over" the unwashed pagans of the surrounding cultures. In a late passage in the Book of Jeremiah, the LORD declares that if "my evil neighbors" would only "learn the ways of my people, to swear by my name . . . as they taught my people to swear by Baal," they would be "built up in the midst of my people." But if any nation proves reluctant to repudiate its traditional allegiance, "then I will completely uproot it and destroy it," says the LORD (12:14,16–17).

The conclusion of the eschatological vision of Zech. 14 vividly expands on the theme, introducing the notion of the forced observance of Israelite religious holidays. In this "early apocalyptic" fantasy, Jerusalem is assured that "never again shall it be doomed to destruction"; it shall continue to abide "in security." But a "great panic" shall seize Jerusalem's enemies, as the LORD strikes them with the mother of all plagues, an affliction in which their flesh, eyes, and tongues shall "rot." The wealth of the surrounding nations—in the form of gold, silver, and clothing—shall be brought to Jerusalem and a plague shall afflict even their domestic animals. All "the families of the earth"—that is, all those who manage to survive Yahweh's depredations—are forced to go up to Jerusalem to worship the LORD and "keep the festival of booths." Failure to do so will result in a drought and a special plague that the LORD reserves for those nations that "do not go up to keep the festival of booths" (14:11–19).

Another early apocalypse caps the Book of Isaiah (Chapter 66) with its imperialistic, eschatological message. "Rejoice with Jerusalem," said the LORD, "I will extend prosperity to her like a river, and the wealth of the nations like an overflowing stream." But from the holy mountain comes a voice roaring in judgment of the nations, of the entire human race: "For by fire will the LORD execute judgment, and by his sword, on all flesh; and those slain by the LORD shall be many." In the End-time, a righteous remnant, possibly including both Jews and Gentiles, shall enjoy "the new heavens and the new earth" and "all flesh shall come to worship before me," says the LORD (66:10–23).

The final scene has inspired those of later generations who have felt compelled to fill in the details of an uncongenial afterlife. The LORD invited the righteous to participate in what the early Church called the "abominable fancy," the uplifting notion that part of the joy of being saved lay in viewing the agonies of the wicked.[31] The LORD directed the righteous to look on "the dead bodies of the people who have rebelled against me; for their worm shall not die, their fire shall not be quenched, and they shall be an abhorrence to all flesh" (66:24).[32] Centuries later, Jesus alluded to this verse in his warning to the sinful of the infelicity that awaited them in hell (Mark 9:48).

Enthusiasts of OT universalism are fond of offering as prime exhibits the post-exilic Books of Ruth and Jonah. In the second temple period, community leaders had severely chastised the Israelites for miscegenation with pagans, most especially their women, as described in the Books of Ezra and Nehemiah.[33] Numerous scholars have suggested that the authors of Ruth and Jonah wrote in not-so-subtle reaction to this hard "nationalistic" line by offering a more inviting, "universalistic" alternative.

Down through the centuries, both Jews and Christians have lauded the "lovingly loyal behavior" of the convert Ruth, the Moabite, and have doted on 1:16 in which she confesses to her Israelite mother-in-law, Naomi, that "your people shall be my people, and your God my God."[34] Recently, a scholar has suggested that the author was "possibly" Moabite, that the two nations enjoyed "mutually tolerant and even supportive" relations, and that the story served a "rehabilitating" function for the tarnished image of Moabite women.[35] All of which implies some degree of religious tolerance and respect across the cultural and political divide.

But approaching the book from the "us-them" angle of vision yields a surprising result. The text produces only two isolated facts, one of which must be inferred, about the "other" country, which we will dub "nation X." We infer that nation X must be convenient for immigration by distressed Israelites and from 1:15, we learn that the inhabitants are polytheistic. Beyond that, we discover absolutely nothing about nation X—its people, their hopes and fears, or Israel's attitude toward them. In any event, it is difficult to imagine a Moabite author who would perceive conversion to Yahwism as "rehabilitating" for the image of his women.

Of course, any of Israel's neighbors could have met readily the two criteria for nation X. As we have seen, when dealing with the "other" as literary foil, the parts are readily interchangeable. As for universalism, the text focuses on the conditions under which "others" may be accepted into an inflexible Yahwism, nothing more "warm and fuzzy" than that. Ruth is acceptable—in person and in the canon—only because she discards completely her relatives, religion, and country to embrace the Israelite ethos. The text fails utterly to acknowledge Moab as a viable society to be respected and prized by a "universal" God for its own sake. The book has nothing at all to do with Moab; it has everything to do with Israel and its religious praxis.

The Book of Jonah was cut from the same nationalistic/universalistic cloth as the Book of Ruth. But in it, the conversionary focus shifts from the individual to the national group, in order to demonstrate once again Yahweh's prowess beyond the borders of Israel. Here we encounter a broad burlesque of the "foxhole" conversion of the clueless, with an additional comic touch that is rare in the Bible. During a violent storm at sea, terrified pagan sailors each "cried to his god"; but as the wind continued to threaten, they decided to call "to the LORD" with nothing less than the spectacular results that Elijah obtained at Mount Carmel. In our last view of the newly converted, they "feared the LORD even more" and—like the coerced Egyptians in Isa. 19—they offered "a sacrifice to the LORD and made vows."[36]

Approximately a nanosecond after hearing Jonah, a total stranger of a foreign culture, announce the impending destruction of their fair city by his God, the credulous citizens of Nineveh "proclaimed a fast, and everyone, great and small, put on sackcloth." The Assyrian king promptly ordered the Ninnies and their beasts—the latter now also resplendent in sackcloth—to "cry mightily to God" and repent "their evil ways" on the outside chance that Yahweh might "turn from his fierce anger" before it was too late. As the curtain falls, the LORD explains to a pouting Jonah his concern for Nineveh, "that great city" of over one hundred thousand souls, all now basking in the sunshine of salvation. But as a reminder of the continuing status of the Mesopotamian converts as "not-us," the last line informs us that they still "do not know their right hand from their left."[37]

Summary

Even those who give the universalistic passages of the OT the most friendly reading are forced to acknowledge that they are but small ships afloat in a vast nationalistic sea. The responses to this self-imposed "dilemma" have been varied in the extreme. It has been suggested that the offending nationalistic passages simply be ignored or deleted, that they should be read metamorphically as the product of "poetic exuberance," or read as yet another example of the "incomprehensibility" of God, that ultimate refuge of the theological scoundrel. To account for this "conflict" within Second Isaiah, theologians have proposed that perhaps he didn't fully comprehend the implications of his own "revolutionary" idea; that he changed his mind during the course of his ministry, i.e., he received a second message from God; or that he patronized his fellow exiles with "out of harmony" nationalistic passages since "the higher truth" had fallen on such deaf ears.[38]

Though in a minority, other interpreters have taken a more realistic position, acknowledging the *Sitz im Leben* of Second Isaiah and his successors. Norman H. Snaith has stated flatly that Second Isaiah was "a convinced, persistent and consistent nationalist." Joseph Blenkinsopp has characterized the dreams of Israelite world domination as the "fantasy of the oppressed." It is "strange," he writes, that this mode of thought "should be mistaken for universalism."[39] The distinguished Jewish scholar, Harry M. Orlinsky, who has written extensively on the subject, chides his more traditional colleagues for reading their prejudices into the text (eisegesis) rather than extracting the authors' original intent (exegesis). Of course, no one sits in splendid "objectivity," he admits, but students of the Bible should bring to Scripture the mind-set and methodology of those more dispassionate souls who study the ancient texts of the ANE, Greece, and Rome.[40]

Orlinsky adopts wholeheartedly the "us-them" perspective and makes a critical distinction between a "universal" God and an "international" one. He argues that the God of Israel is simultaneously a national God and the Sovereign of the universe without being accepted as the "international" God of any pagan nation: "the *natural* God of biblical Israel is a *universal* God, but not an *international* God."[41] Translated into the terminology introduced earlier, the universalism of the scriptural God falls into the "narrow" rather than the "broad" input category. This uncompromising, imperialistic view of the world is not unlike that of modern transnational corporations such as McDonald's and Coca-Cola. A company (nation) sells its unmodified product (religion) to a world (pagan) without regard or respect for local customs and behaviors. Not even in the most universalistic OT passages, Orlinsky points out, can one identify "a single aspect of the beliefs and practices of any people in the world except Israel . . . that was worthy of the slightest consideration for incorporation into God's *torah.*"[42]

To perceive a major tension between nationalistic and universalistic themes in the passages we have reviewed is wrongheaded. Rather, the tension resides in the minds of interpreters who attempt to impose modern theological coordinates on the ancient text. For the biblical authors, their redactors, and their audiences, these passages were all of a piece. Second Isaiah lived during the most critical period of his nation's history; with great skill and urgency, he wrote to save Israel, not the world. He and his successors crafted their message of religious imperialism to bolster the faltering interest of their compatriots in their traditional religion, to integrate the second temple community against the perceived hostility of the world and, most critical of all, to restore confidence in the potency of the ostensibly-defeated, historical God. As a sane and sober genius, he would have been more surprised than anyone to see the nations of the world suddenly "bow and swear" to Yahweh.

For the biblical authors, universalism was placed in the service of nationalism; indeed, nationalism and "narrow" universalism spring from the same particularistic fount. "Particularism" is a more appropriate descriptor than "nationalism" since it is ethnocentrism, not nationhood status, that is relevant. Traditionally, nationalism and universalism have been viewed as a binary pair at opposite poles of the spectrum. For the twenty-first century, the spectrum should be reoriented, locating particularism—represented by ethnocentrism, nationalism, and narrow universalism—at one pole and broad universalism at the other. In this delineation, the apparently conflicting views on proselytism of Ezra-Nehemiah and Ruth-Jonah are both located at or near the particularistic pole. In either approach, the "us-them" wall of Israel remains high, strong, and fiercely defended. Of course, a passionate determination to persevere under the most adverse circumstances enabled Israel to adapt and survive, while one by one its neighbors became forever assimilated into the dominant cultures.

Heretofore, interest in OT universalism has been focused on the degree and manner of acceptance of Gentiles into Judaism. Indeed, a "great universalist" has been defined as an Israelite who "welcomes the Gentiles" on terms that go beyond "benevolent colonialism."[43] In the future, as devotees of the world's religions rub elbows far more often than ever before, universalism must be envisioned as something more catholic than the establishment of parameters for the conversion of "them" to "us." As painful and contrary to human nature as it may seem, we must come to recognize and nurture the idea that, even in religious matters, "they" have something meaningful to say to "us."

5
The Deuteronomic Hypothesis

Of the many characteristics attributed to the scriptural God, all, save one, are beyond human influence. God is said to be both immanent and transcendent—omnipresent, omniscient, and omnipotent. He is creator, law-giver, warrior, rescuer, and king of heaven and earth. The God of love, grace, mercy, and salvation who is at once jealous, zealous, and mysterious. The Voice, the Father, the Shield, the Rock, the Redeemer. These characteristics all extend far beyond the human pale. But as the God of Justice, the "Judge of all the earth," he responds continuously to the behavior of his human creation.[1]

God established a working relationship with Israel that differed profoundly from that with the nations. As we have seen, they served principally as the "undifferentiated other," as amoral or immoral, stereotypical foils manipulated by the God of Israel for his holy purposes. But God grants to his people Israel the dignity of full human expression, i.e., they become free agents capable of moral choice. The core of the "domestic" relationship is chosenness: "I will walk among you," said the LORD, "and I will be your God, and you shall be my people."[2] From this intimacy, the notion of "covenant" (=testament) developed—an exclusive, "legal" contract binding the Deity and the people to one another in mutual love, loyalty, and obligation.[3]

Of the three major OT covenants with Israel, two are said to be "unconditional" and one "conditional." Those with Abraham (Gen. 12,15, etc.) and King David (2 Sam. 7) are unconditional in the sense that they represent free and gracious acts of God devoid of any specific demand upon the recipients. The Sinai, or Mosaic, covenant is conditional, carrying the unambiguous expectation that Israel must conform to divinely-prescribed behaviors with the threat of rupture if it fails to do so. Although a tension may be detected among some texts, the Sinai pact became the controlling paradigm and, in modified form, it remains so even unto the present day. Of course, the historical evidence cannot distinguish between punishment within the system and expulsion from it. In any event, as the prophets Jeremiah, Ezekiel, and Second Isaiah affirm, covenantal ruptures were rapidly repaired, and hence, short-lived.[4]

The covenant at Sinai included the Ten Commandments ("Ten Words"), but those precepts were only the beginning. Rabbinic tradition holds that, at Sinai, Moses received 613 commandments *(mitzvot),* 248 mandates and 365 prohibitions.[5] These commandments are scattered widely throughout the written Torah (Pentateuch), but the most concentrated statements on the essence of the Sinai agreement are found in Deuteronomy. Delivered as a sermon on the plains of Moab as the people prepare to invade Canaan, it provides both historical reflection and theological teaching. Through Moses, God instructs his people not only on the "rules of engagement" with the Canaanites but, much more importantly, on the rules of engagement with himself.

At the heart of this engagement is the principle of retribution, the response of the Judge to the behavior of the judged within a divinely prescribed system of justice or righteousness. Here, and only here, can human beings "control" the deity through the consequences of their own actions. As prosecutor, judge, and jury, God observes, records, and "retributes," i.e., "pays back," according to the dictates of his divinely ordained plan of justice. Contrary to much that has been written about it, a retributional system is not simply an arrangement for punishment of the wrongdoer. Rather, it is a symmetrical plan of morality and justice whereby God in heaven responds as appropriate to the attitudes and behaviors of the earthly actors—blessing the humble and devout, punishing the prideful and wayward. In this moral universe, a blessing is what you may expect when you are righteous; mercy is what you hope for when you are not. Grace is a free response of God outside a judicial context (Fig. 2).

A few passages from Deuteronomy convey the essence of the

message as it was delivered to the Israelites in the Transjordan. In the second of the Ten Commandments, the LORD makes clear the duality of the system:

> For I the LORD your God am a jealous God, punishing children for the iniquity of parents, to the third and fourth generation of those who reject me, but showing steadfast love to the thousandth generation of those who love me and keep my commandments.[6]

After receiving from the LORD "all the commandments, the statutes and the ordinances," Moses warned the people of the conditional nature of their tenure in Canaan:

> You must therefore be careful to do as the LORD your God has commanded you; you shall not turn to the right or to the left. You must follow exactly the path that the LORD your God has commanded you . . . that it may go well with you, and that you may live long in the land that you are to possess.
>
> —Deut. 5:32–33

In Deut. 11:26–28, Moses presents in black-and-white terms the moral choice before the nation:

> See, I am setting before you today a blessing and a curse: the blessing, if you obey the commandments of the LORD your God that I am commanding you today; and the curse, if you do not obey the commandments of the LORD your God, but turn . . . to follow other gods that you have not known.

Deuteronomy 28 offers the greatest elaboration of the blessing-and-curse theme found in the OT. In one of the longest and most undervalued chapters of the Bible, the LORD sets out in minute detail the consequences of the moral choice.[7] In fourteen verses of "blessings," God promises the nation, in obedience, an abundant material prosperity grounded in the fertility of womb, soil, and livestock. Its military enemies shall be routed as they "come out against you one way, and flee before you seven ways." All its endeavors shall receive divine blessing—for it will become "the head, and not the tail," live "only at the top, and not at the

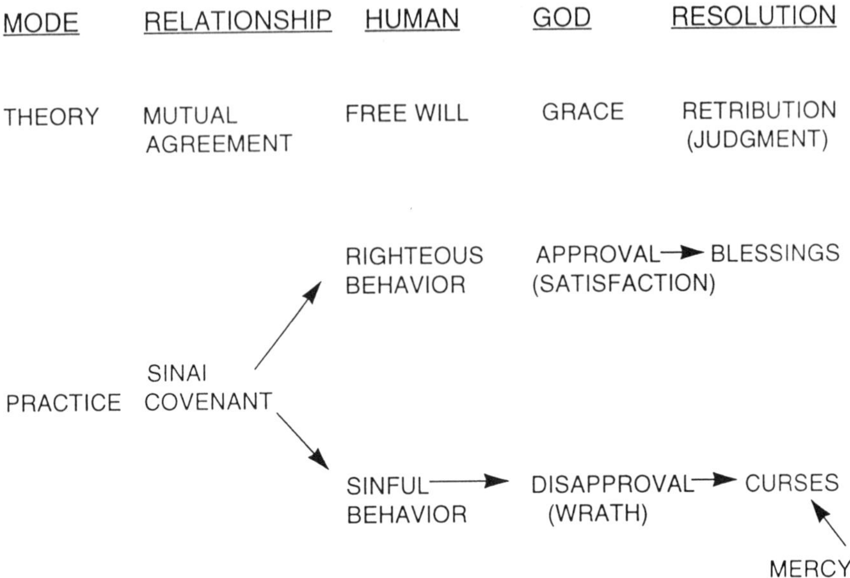

FIGURE 2. SCHEMATIC REPRESENTATION OF DIVINE JUSTICE. AT GOD'S DISCRETION, MERCY MAY TEMPER PUNISHMENT.

bottom." Exalting his covenanted people like the proverbial city on the hill, God vows to set the righteous Israelites "high above all the nations of the earth."

Of course, the moral coin bears a "curse" side, detailed in no less than fifty-four horrific verses calculated to frighten even the most impenitent sinner into obedience. Virtually every morbidity known to the Mediterranean world is threatened: itch, boils, fever, scurvy, hemorrhoids (JPS), pestilence, consumption, inflammation, blindness, madness, "confusion of mind," "severe and lasting" afflictions, and "grievous and lasting" maladies. Verse 61 provides a "pour-over" provision, a general warning of all those maladies "not recorded in the book of this law."

In the agricultural sector, infidelity to the covenantal law will bring in its wake worms, cicada, infertility, "blight and mildew," and a "fiery heat and drought," the latter the result of dust raining from a "bronze" sky in place of moisture. In disobedience, the Israelites shall be "continually abused and robbed"; their betrothed maidens shall lie with other men; their children shall be taken by "another people"; their unburied corpses shall attract every carrion-feeder of the air and earth. Indeed, in every possible undertaking, they shall experience only "disaster, panic and frustration."

Presumably influenced by the horrors of the Jerusalem siege of 586, the author of Deut. 28 warns that, as punishment for disobedience, the "most refined and gentle" of women will be reduced to eating their own afterbirth and their newborn infants, even begrudging this "food" to their families. The ultimate humiliation will find the Israelites returned to Egypt where they are offered for sale as slaves, "but there will be no buyer." The text asserts that if *all* the commandments are not fulfilled, *all* the ninety-eight enumerated curses "shall come upon you and overtake you."[8] As in the Conquest of Canaan, the LORD himself will not be a detached observer to the awesome events. As he took pleasure in making Israel prosperous and numerous, so, too, will the monistic God "take delight in bringing you to ruin and destruction."[9]

The Theory

Nearly all theological propositions make assertions that can neither be verified nor falsified within ordinary human experience. Since they defy testing, these statements have no standing as scientific hypotheses. Assertions that Yahweh created the heavens and the earth, that Moses wrote the Torah, or that Jesus arose on the third day can be confirmed only by faith, not reason. But in the retributional paradigm, in passages such as Deut. 28, elaborate cause-and-effect declarations are made about life on this earth. Righteous action will result in favorable socio-economic conditions, sinful behavior in misfortune or catastrophe. Two variables are involved and if, *in principle,* they can be measured, we have a testable, scientific hypothesis.

The two variables are socio-economic circumstance, or earthly lot, and virtue or morality as evaluated within a specific ethical system. Although a great deal of information would be needed to calculate a reliable measure for each, no *theoretical* reason precludes our doing so. In other words, in order to test our hypothesis, we need no supernatural aid, only mundane data available to ordinary human beings. The divinely ordained retributional schema asserts that the two variables are positively, if not perfectly, correlated. Theoretical scatter diagrams showing a high, positive correlation (approaching r=+1) and a negligible correlation (r=0) are presented in Fig. 3. Henceforth, we shall refer to the retributional plan as the "Deuteronomic Hypothesis" (DH).

Given a totality of information, including a set of moral priorities, assignment of individuals to a point on the grid would be relatively straightforward. In the absence of information and/or a confusion of moral priorities, assignment would prove more difficult. The ambivalent moral careers of, say, John Brown, Richard Nixon, and Oskar Schindler come to mind. Of course, we regularly make moral judgments of our fellows based on the information available and our prejudices, and will continue to do so. Though we leave the ultimate judgments to God, the notion that we have no powers of moral discrimination among our fellows is untenable. The Western world at least has come to an

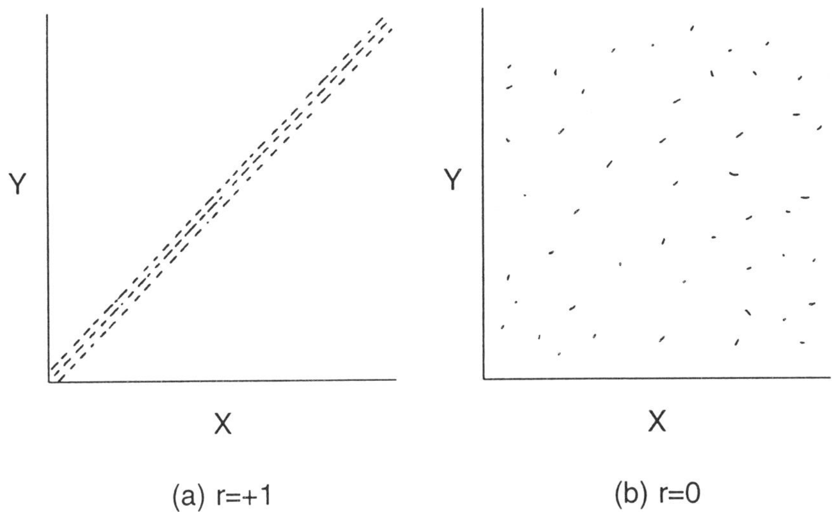

FIGURE 3. CORRELATION OF CIRCUMSTANCE AND VIRTUE. IN THESE SCATTER DIAGRAMS THE TWO VARIABLES, SOCIOECONOMIC CIRCUMSTANCE (X) AND MORALITY OR VIRTUE (Y), ARE POSITIVELY (r=+1) AND NEGLIGIBLY (r=0) CORRELATED. THE FORMER DEPICTS THE TRADITIONAL BELIEF; THE LATTER, THE REAL WORLD.

overwhelming consensus regarding the validity of the Deuteronomic Hypothesis.

We may theoretically construct such "moral" scatter diagrams, but the God of Justice may, at specific junctures, impose upon the moral continuum a discontinuous, or dichotomous, judgment. He may separate individuals into the absolutes of sheep and goats, obedient and disobedient, righteous and wicked. In explanation, the OT offers only broad and variable criteria for defining the two groups. With only these generalities at hand, bisection of a normal, ethically heterogeneous population becomes rationally impossible.

The difficulties become compounded when we focus on the entire group or nation, rather than on the single individual. Obviously, individuals within a society will carry different moral scores and, therefore, deserve different living conditions. But, especially in the pre-exilic era, God tended to judge all as one. Given the 613 *mitzvot,* which theoretically could be violated by everyone every day, a population of, say, 300,000 could generate a maximum of 67 billion sins over the course of a single year! Of course, the Bible makes no claim of equality for all sins or sinners. But with few exceptions, the text makes no systematic pairing of sin and consequence, most especially as regards the fate of the entire nation. Only God could work his way through that moral morass.

The problem of a single judgment on a differentially righteous population is confronted early in the biblical story. Abraham pressed God on the issue as the latter contemplated the total destruction of the pagan cities of Sodom and Gomorrah (Gen. 18). At Abraham's urging, the "Judge of all the earth" agreed that if so many as ten righteous could be found among the wicked inhabitants, he would spare the cities. Such an outcome would result in "justice" for the righteous and "mercy" for the wicked. But the pagans failed to muster a single worthy and the cities went up in a rain of sulfur and fire.[10] We may note, in passing, that God does not require Lot's family to meet a "righteous" test, only a "blood" test. They are saved, not through merit, but because of their familial ties to Abraham.

The problem of rendering justice within a morally diverse population presented itself again during the wilderness trek, but this time God—apparently once more needing a little help from his friends—reached a more satisfactory conclusion. Some 250 Levites rebelled against Moses and his brother, Aaron, and demanded to be elevated to the priesthood. An irate Yahweh resolved to destroy the entire congregation, but Moses and Aaron dissuaded him by questioning whether the entire group should be eradicated for the sins of the few. Endorsing the proffered solution, the LORD ordered the innocent to segregate themselves from the guilty. Thereupon, the earth conveniently "opened its mouth and swallowed them up" (Num. 16).

The Text

The Deuteronomic Hypothesis permeates every nook and cranny of the OT. Normative in the ANE long before Sinai, it is prominent in the Torah, the Writings, and the Prophets, both the major and the minor. It pervades the primary history and the secondary history and informs both pre-exilic and post-exilic theology. In an altered form, it continued as a dominant theme in the intertestamental texts, the rabbinic writings, and the NT. To the present day, it remains as a major theological principle, outlining and governing the divine–human interaction and expectation.

At the beginning of creation, humankind encountered the judgmental reaction of God to its misdeeds. The LORD God (Yahweh Elohim) had to expel Adam and Eve from the Garden of Eden for listening credulously to the too-persuasive snake. For this insubordination the Almighty decreed that, henceforth, humankind would experience the pain of childbirth, the misery of toil for its daily bread, and, most distressing of all, the permanent loss of the possibility of immortality (Gen. 3).

In the tenth generation from Adam and Eve, the LORD despaired that the inclination of the human heart had become "only evil continually." Regretting that he had ever created such a "corrupt" species, the immutable Deity opted for the elimination of "all flesh" in a universal flood. Only Noah—declared "righteous" for reasons unspecified—his family, and a breeding pair from every animal group would survive the inundation, to repopulate the earth. With the "pleasing odor" of Noah's burnt offerings regaling his nostrils, the LORD promised never again to destroy all earthly life, though he had to resign himself to the abiding fact that the human heart remained "evil from youth."[11]

Several hundred years later, at the celebrated theophany on Mount Sinai, the Israelites, led by Aaron, fashioned and worshiped a golden calf while Moses was receiving the two tablets of the covenant "written with the finger of God." The wrath of the LORD burned so hot against the stiff-necked, idolatrous people that he decided to liquidate them all and start over with the righteous Moses, just as he had done with Noah. But Moses implored the

LORD to stay his hand lest the Egyptians cast aspersions on the divine character, and the divine promises to the patriarchs go unfulfilled. Apparently impressed by Moses' logic, the unalterable LORD "changed his mind about the disaster that he planned to bring on his people."[12]

Once we pass the Sinai event, the DH comes into full view, though some scholars maintain that short, "primitive" cause-and-effect linkages may be found scattered here and there throughout the biblical text. In these sequences, a "fate-producing deed" triggers its own built-in consequence, thereby reducing significantly the judicial role of Yahweh and bringing us close to "magic." One may envision a judicial "reflex arc" in which a stimulus triggers a response without the benefit of the judgment of the higher moral center. In other words, your sins as well as your good deeds will automatically find you out. In this conception, Yahweh acts more as a catalyst or midwife than as an independent judge, merely bringing to a foregone conclusion that which the deed itself had initiated.[13]

A few "act-consequence" passages may be identified in the prophets: "For they sow the wind, and they shall reap the whirlwind" (Hos. 8:7); "You have plowed wickedness, you have reaped injustice, you have eaten the fruit of lies" (Hos. 10:13). They are most common in the Proverbs and Psalms, where the deeds of the wicked guarantee their fate:

Whoever digs a pit will fall into it,
and a stone will come back on
the one who starts it rolling.

—Prov. 26:27

They make a pit, digging it out,
and fall into the hole that they
have made.
Their mischief returns upon their
own heads,
and on their own heads their
violence descends.

—Ps. 7:15–16

God plays a more directing role in circumstances that produce a "poetic justice," or retributional measure-for-measure. In these texts, we find a correspondence of the crime and its punishment—in the "eye-for-eye" talionic spirit of Ex 21:23–25—but without the sense of a rigid predetermination of it.[14] For example, in the period of the judges, the Israelites captured a Canaanite king and cut off his thumbs and big toes. The king admitted that he had similarly mutilated seventy kings: "As I have done, so God has paid me back" (Judg. 1:6–7). The similarity of sin and judgment may be more general and rely on word play, as in Deut. 32:21, where God threatens an idolatrous Israel with retribution at the hands of a pagan nation:

> They made me jealous with what
> is no god,
> provoked me with their idols.
> So I will make them jealous with
> what is a no people,
> provoke them with a foolish nation.

King David had to face a payback, in kind, after he had arranged for the death of Uriah, the Hittite, and married his beautiful widow, Bathsheba (2 Sam. 12). Via the prophet Nathan, the LORD declared that since David had employed the sword to dispose of Uriah and had taken his wife, "therefore the sword shall never depart from your house. . . . I will take your wives before your eyes, and give them to your neighbor, and he shall lie with your wives in the sight of this very sun." David himself was to be spared, but as for the fruit of his union with Bathsheba, "the child that is born to you shall die." And so it did seven days later.

In the foreboding days before the fatal attack on Jerusalem by Nebuchadnezzar, some prophets had prophesied—in the name of the LORD and contrary to Jeremiah—that all was well, that "sword and famine" would not visit the capital city. The LORD proceeded to execute poetic justice on these false prophets and on the foolish people who had listened to them (Jer. 14). He announced that "By sword and famine those prophets shall be consumed. And the people to whom they prophesy shall be thrown out into the streets of Jerusalem, victims of famine and sword."

Measure-for-measure retribution did not necessarily entail matters of the greatest national importance. It could also find out those—like the "haughty" women of Jerusalem—who strutted about with "outstretched necks, glancing wantonly with their eyes . . . tinkling with their feet." "In that day," the LORD would strip away the finery of these women, would "wash away the filth" of the daughters of Zion (Isa. 3:16,18;4:4):

> Instead of perfume there will be a stench;
> and instead of a sash, a rope;
> and instead of well-set hair, baldness;
> and instead of a rich robe, a
> binding of sackcloth;
> instead of beauty, shame.
>
> —Isa. 3:24

A more complex case of retribution presenting a nexus of questionable justice, corporate responsibility, and the concept of the ban, or "holy war," is found at Josh. 7. After their initial success at Jericho, the invading Israelites were repulsed at the nearby city of Ai, losing thirty-six men in the failed effort. When the distraught Joshua inquired of the Lord GOD, he learned that the theft of "devoted things" at Jericho had caused the LORD to withdraw his support at Ai. He would be with Israel "no more" until the stolen goods had been identified and destroyed. The Israelites were instructed to destroy the culprit "together with all that he has, for having transgressed the covenant of the LORD and for having done an outrageous thing in Israel."

Under duress, Achan of the tribe of Judah confessed to the taking of silver and gold booty at Jericho and burying it inside his tent. In pronouncing sentence, Joshua declared that since Achan had brought "trouble" on Israel, the LORD would bring "trouble on you today." All that Achan had was destroyed along with him—the offending objects, his livestock, and his sons and daughters. We struggle to understand the concept of "justice" that required the destruction of the entire family of the single sinner, the death of the thirty-six men in the futile attack, and the vulnerability of the entire camp to the enemy during the period in which God's protection was withdrawn. All of these divinely sanctioned consequences flow from the theft of a few material items by one individual!

After a thorough analysis of the incident, Joel S. Kaminsky has concluded that when understood in its own terms, it manifests an "internal coherence." In ancient Israel, a man's family was often considered as his property. When Achan received the death penalty by stoning, his nearest relatives went with him, not because of guilt on their part, only the bald fact of kinship. The tabooed status of "devoted things" could be transmitted like an infection to other objects in their vicinity. After Achan had buried the silver and gold in his tent, the LORD declared that the entire community had become "a thing devoted for destruction."

The purloined objects had violated camp purity or holiness, creating a contaminated condition inhospitable to the Presence. Since the Israelite camp no longer maintained the proper ritual state, Kaminsky argues, God had no choice but to abandon his people whatever the consequence. The entire group had the responsibility of maintaining an environment sufficiently holy for God to manifest his power. Therefore, the whole community could be held responsible for the transgressions of its individual members.[15]

Another celebrated incident in which the many suffer for the sins of the few is described in 2 Sam. 24, casting yet another dark shadow on the character of the OT God. In "anger" at Israel for reasons unspecified, the LORD "incited" King David against it by directing him to take a census of the entire country. Census-taking was unpopular with the people since it was closely tied to taxation and military conscription. Some ten months later, the head count had been completed and God's anger had apparently been assuaged. But suddenly, the erratic David protested to the LORD that he had "sinned greatly" in the undertaking, though he had, in fact, only served as God's coerced agent. Though the LORD had initiated the project of his own free will, in his response to David, he chose not to dwell on that point; rather, he seemed anxious to relieve the king of his newly discovered guilt through harsh punitive measures.

In an unusual gesture, the LORD offered David three options for "his" punishment, two of which placed the people as a whole at great risk. David could choose between three years of famine in the land, three months of flight before his enemies, or three days of pestilence in the land. The second option would have placed his subjects at least risk, but David chose the third. He reasoned that he would rather fall into the hands of the Almighty than into human hands, "for his mercy is great."

The divinely commissioned plague arrived on schedule, ravaging the nation from Dan in the north to Beersheba in the south. The LORD demonstrated his "mercy" by eventually calling off the angel in charge of plagues, but only after seventy thousand innocent souls had perished. Originally David had shunned option number two, but after he viewed the extent of the carnage on his people, he cried to the LORD that since he alone had sinned, he alone should pay the price. Some interpreters have attempted to shine light into this moral miasma by suggesting that it represents an example of "ruler punishment," wherein the king is "punished" for his sins by the decimation of his flock.[16] Whether the LORD our God, who instigated the whole affair, so viewed it, remains unknown to this day.

One of the variables of interest in the retributional equation is timing, i.e., the interval elapsing between the human deed and its divinely directed consequence. In his universal principle of "moral balance," St. Augustine claimed that no interval at all elapses between "failure to do what ought to be done and suffering what ought to be suffered."[17] Unfortunately for that concept, the Bible knows no such consistent coupling of act and consequence. A statement of principle in Deut. 7:9–10 suggests that, typically, punishment may be somewhat more immediate and personal than reward: "Know therefore that the LORD . . . maintains covenant loyalty with those who love him and keep his commandments, to a thousand generations, and who . . . does not delay but repays in their own person those who reject him."

Examples of immediate punishment are not difficult to find. When escaping from the doomed city of Sodom, Lot's wife disobediently "looked back" and instantly became transformed into the famous pillar of salt (Gen. 19:17,26). As David's entourage was carrying the Ark of God toward Jerusalem, Uzzah reached out innocently to steady the tottering shrine. God immediately struck him down, presumably because he had violated the holiness of the sacred object (2 Sam. 6:6–8). Earlier, after the Philistines had returned the captured Ark, at least seventy Israelites had been struck down because they had peered into the chest (1 Sam. 6:19). In the wilderness, Moses's siblings, Aaron and Miriam, mount one of several challenges to his authority. This palace revolt caused the LORD's anger to be kindled against them both, though inexplicably only Miriam felt the heat. Her punishment came in the form of a leprous condition which made her skin "as white as snow" (Num. 12:1–10).

Although not as common, divine rewards may also be dispensed on the spot. At Mount Sinai, total disaster was averted in the golden calf episode, but the LORD did demand recompense for the gross idolatry. Sacrifice of the son at the behest of the father is present, though rare, in both testaments; but on a particularly bloody day on the sacred mountain, it became commonplace. Moses called for all those "on the LORD's side" to step forward; in response, all the members of the tribe of Levi gathered around the prophet. The LORD commanded each of them to strap on his sword and slaughter in cold blood his sons, brothers, friends, and neighbors. The reported carnage came to about three thousand. As an immediate reward for this fratricide, Moses ordained into the priesthood each of the Levites, thereby bringing the ultimate divine blessing on their zealous work for the LORD (Exod. 32:25–29).

Another incident of undelayed blessing resulting from righteous violence produced an everlasting priesthood for Aaron's lineage. While still encamped opposite Jericho, Israelite men in some numbers had begun to be attracted to the pagan women of the area and even worse, to their idolatrous religion. Aaron's grandson, Phinehas, enraged at the sight of an Israelite and a Midianite woman in copula, pierced them both "through the belly" with his spear. For this heroic act of atonement for Israelite sin, God granted Phinehas and his lineage a "covenant of perpetual priesthood." Phinehas's spear ended not only the couple in coitus but also a heaven-sent plague that had terminated the lives of no less than twenty-four thousand of the iniquitous Israelites (Num. 25:1–13). (For encouraging this apostasy, God also directed the ethnic cleansing of the Midianites, resulting in the slaughter of all the non-virginal females and every male, both the mature and the "little ones" [Num.31]).

Immediate retribution tends to be less common when it involves larger groups and more momentous events. The act-consequence interval lengthens to years and to generations, eventually stretching all the way to infinity. That consequences can be both immediate and delayed is demonstrated by the twelve scouts sent by Moses to reconnoiter the Promised Land. The majority report that a successful invasion appeared impossible so inflamed the LORD that he caused the faithless messengers to die from the seemingly omnipresent plague. But he spared the lives of the two spies (Joshua and Caleb) who had given a bullish report that was much more to his liking. When Israel settled in the subdued land forty-five years later, the LORD remembered and rewarded his servants with a handsome inheritance of land (Num. 13–14; Josh 14:6–15).

Inter-generational responsibility—corporate responsibility in its temporal form—moves to the foreground in 2 Sam. 21. David learned from the LORD that a three-year famine was the result of Saul's alleged mistreatment of the Gibeonites several years earlier. Since Saul had passed on, David turned over to the Gibeonites the seven sons and grandsons of the dead king as his living representatives. After the seven had been ritually "impaled," but subsequently given an honorable burial, God once again "heeded supplications for the land."

The reservoir of good-will generated by the memory of a former favorite could persuade God to delay justice for a generation or more. Although King Solomon possessed many admirable qualities, he had included a number of foreign women among his one thousand wives. In his dotage, these wives "turned away his heart after other gods." He even built altars in "high places" for the worship of the "abominations" of the Ammonites, the Moabites, and other pagan peoples. Naturally, this evil behavior evoked the extreme displeasure of the LORD, who resolved to sunder all the tribes except one from Solomon's united kingdom.

But, because the LORD held his father, David, in such high esteem, he promised Solomon that "I will not do it in your lifetime" (Kings 11:1–13).

The common man and woman of biblical Israel would hardly have been privy to intimate conversations between God and king. How was their faith in this-worldly retribution, as the overarching system of divine justice, sustained in the face of overwhelming evidence to the contrary? Societal authority figures—the court, priests, prophets, and wisemen—exerted a strong influence, no doubt, but there are common-sense limits to credulity about a world that is perceived daily by one's senses. The faithful didn't automatically read their neighbors' merit, or their own, in their fortune. They knew that the righteous didn't retire each night to a bed of roses, the wicked to a bed of nails. Timing, hope, and patience become critical elements to sustain belief. Although it is far better known for other themes, the little Book of Ruth may offer a realistic portrayal of how the DH was perceived to operate among ordinary folk.

Naomi and her very ordinary family experienced economic hardships so severe that they were forced to immigrate to a nearby country. First, her husband dies and then both of her adult sons. A God-fearing woman perplexed by the heartbreaking turn of events, Naomi informs her pagan daughters-in-law that "it has been far more bitter for me than for you, because the hand of the LORD has turned against me." Following her return to Bethlehem, the widow asked her friends to start calling her "Mara," which means "Bitter," rather than Naomi, which means "Pleasant." "I went away full," she lamented, "but the LORD has brought me back empty." The proud woman is filled with resentment, not repentance; she doesn't attribute her misfortune to sin, but rather to the inscrutable ways of the LORD.

Old, bitter, and stripped of male support, Naomi brightens a bit when she learns that Boaz has taken favorable notice of Ruth, a hopeful sign that the LORD has begun finally to bless them. By the end of the harvest season, Naomi was fully energized, giving Ruth detailed instructions on how to catch Boaz. After the marriage and birth of the child, the village women cry out to Naomi, "Blessed be the LORD." The DH has been abundantly confirmed, but only across the full span of a lifetime. Good things come to the good woman but only in God's good time. As Ps. 27:14 puts it: "Wait for the LORD; be strong, and let your heart take courage; wait for the LORD!"

Not surprisingly, patience is a necessary virtue in a tradition that begins with a five-hundred-year hiatus between the promise of land and its fulfillment. Indeed for millennia, waiting for divine justice to be perfected has been a forced requirement among Jews and Christians, as they anticipate the eschatological appearance of the Messiah and Jesus Christ, respectively. But, as the non-Israelite prophet, Balaam, assures the faithful:

> God is not a human being, that he
>   should lie,
>   or a mortal, that he should
>   change his mind.
> Has he promised, and will he not
>   do it?
>   Has he spoken, and will he not
>   fulfill it?
>
> —Num. 23:19

Waiting for God to act can be extremely frustrating, most especially if he has elected to go into hiding. It turns out that God does not invariably manifest his displeasure in the angry response or the commissioning of an instrument to effect justice. He may simply "hide his face" or withdraw from active engagement with humankind. The concept of the *Deus Absconditus,* the self-concealing God, is prominent both among biblical and post-Holocaust writers. God is said to be "elusive" or "silent," but the retreat is almost always envisioned by his human subjects as temporary. That is, the *possibility* of his return to active duty always remains open.[18]

In Isa. 8:17, the themes of human waiting and divine hiding are connected: "I will wait for the LORD, who is hiding his face from the house of Jacob, and I will hope in him." In Isa. 54:8, God confesses to Israel that "in overflowing wrath for a moment I hid my face from you." In Isa. 1:15, God declares that he will neither see nor hear the petitions of a sinful Israel: "When you stretch out your hands, I will hide my eyes from you; even though you make many prayers, I will not listen."

A tone of impatience and frustration with the *Deus Abscon-ditus* dominates a number of Psalms, particularly so in times of crisis:

How long, O LORD? Will you
    hide yourself forever?
  How long will your wrath burn
    like fire? . . .
Why, O LORD, do you stand far
    off?
  Why do you hide yourself in
    times of trouble?

—Ps. 89:46;10:1

The most famous cry of all to the absent God comes from Ps. 22, the first line of which was quoted by Jesus on the cross (Mark 15:34):

My God, my God, why have you
    forsaken me?
  Why are you so far from
    helping me, from the
    words of my groaning?

—Ps. 22:1–2

In addition to these more episodic withdrawals, over the centuries God also appears to have removed himself gradually from direct intervention in human affairs. Mircea Eliade has observed that this enduring trend is a "primary" fact among the religions of the world. Supreme beings, he states, "tend to disappear . . . they depart from among men, withdraw to the sky, and become remote, inactive gods (*dei otiosi*)."[19] In a brilliant, recent study, Richard E. Friedman has traced the gradual disappearance of Yahweh from the pages of the OT over the course of Israelite history. Correlated with divine disengagement, so his argument runs, is the increasing freedom, knowledge, and responsibility of humankind, painfully inching ever closer to its full potential.[20]

Catastrophic Judgment

In theory, the system of distributive justice appears symmetrical, a balance of blessings and curses, but in actual practice, the latter received much more biblical attention than the former. Rather than experiencing the sustained blessing of an ongoing felicitous relationship, the disobedient population came to rely increasingly on the LORD to salvage a remnant, to season his justice with mercy. Of his own gracious free will, God had elected Israel and granted it the rights and responsibilities that flow therefrom—love, intimacy, covenant, commandments to live by, a system of retributional justice, and promises of fame, land, and population expansion. The Israelites' lengthy and undeserved service as bondsmen in Egypt had only enhanced their stature in the eyes of the Almighty. In spite of the grumbling that he had heard on the forty-year trek in the wilderness, he did deliver fully on his long-delayed, real estate promise to the patriarchs.

At the conclusion of the hostilities in Canaan, Joshua had gathered the people at Shechem in a grand ceremony to reaffirm their covenantal loyalty. The assemblage enthusiastically and unanimously proclaimed: "We will serve the LORD!" Indeed, they did faithfully keep their promise "all the days of Joshua, and all the days of the elders who outlived Joshua and had known all the work that the LORD did for Israel" (Josh. 24:21,31). At this historical juncture, the LORD and Israel were "even," so to speak: both parties seemed well-pleased with the arrangement and the future appeared bright. But human nature being what it is—that is, what God made it to be—over the centuries the relationship grew progressively strained to reach finally the breaking point six hundred years later.

The Deuteronomic Hypothesis is inextricably interwoven into the fabric of the two greatest tragedies in the biblical history of Israel: the obliteration of the northern kingdom (Israel in the *sensu stricto*) in 721 B.C.E. and the destruction of the southern kingdom (Judah) in 586 B.C.E. As the unambiguous theological explanation of these historical occurrences, the DH permeates the primary and secondary histories, the prophets and the psalms. Some theological propositions may appear nebulous, equivocal, or beyond our comprehension, but the one, true, and judging LORD speaks clearly and loudly and repeatedly regarding the causation of the two mega-calamities of Israel.

The catastrophic judgments of the LORD did not occur suddenly or without warning but came to pass only after centuries of disobedience, beginning with the schism of the united kingdom. David (1005–965), it is true, had presented a slightly soiled character as an adulterer, murderer, military oppressor, and ethnic cleanser. But the LORD elevated him and his memory to the heights of unsurpassable human virtue, primarily because his cultic heart was pure. His son Solomon (965-928) fell from grace as a result of his flirtation with foreign gods and women, but Yahweh delayed retribution for a generation because of his high regard for David. In 928, the united nation split into a southern kingdom of Judah under Solomon's son, Rehoboam, and a northern kingdom consisting of ten tribes under the non-Davidic king, Jeroboam I.[21]

As an "industrious" worker on state-sponsored projects, Jeroboam had attracted the attention of Solomon, who placed him in charge of the "forced labor" contingent in the northern region of the realm. Later, when the ambitious Jeroboam rebelled against Solomon's authority, the king attempted to have him killed, but the would-be usurper escaped to Egypt where he remained until after Solomon's death. Jeroboam had caught the eye not only of the king but of the LORD as well. Because of Solomon's idolatry, Jeroboam received the northern tribes, but in a very conditional grant. The LORD promised Jeroboam that he would build him an "enduring house" provided that he did what was right "by keeping my statutes and my commandments, as David my servant did" (1 Kings 11:26–40).

Through the prophets, God sometimes scolded the Israelites for their treatment of the poor, orphans, widows, and resident aliens. But the transgressions that counted the most and resulted in the loss of the two kingdoms involved the proper worship of the LORD. Following his anointment, Jeroboam proceeded to commit cultic sins so reprehensible that God used them throughout the remainder of the history of the northern kingdom as world-class standards of unforgivable behavior.

The king appointed non-levitical priests who served at "high places" where "other gods" were worshiped with paraphernalia such as "sacred poles." But the most disturbing transgression by far was the placement of two "calves of gold," one each at sanctuaries near the northern border (Dan) and the southern border (Bethel). This royal initiative was calculated to provide convenient sites for worship within the newly-established kingdom and counter any tendencies that the citizenry might harbor to look fondly toward Jerusalem and its magnificent temple.[22]

Because of these apostatic acts, the God of Israel was beside himself with rage, vowing to bring "evil" on the house of Jeroboam. The king and his family would be incinerated "as one burns up dung until it is gone." In tension with this disposition, the LORD asserted that everyone connected with the king who died would lie unburied in the street or field, his body an open invitation to the indignities of carrion-feeders. The entire nation could anticipate being rooted up and scattered "beyond the Euphrates." Hence, at its very inception, the LORD doomed to total extinction the northern kingdom because of the sins of its first king (1 Kings 14:9–16). But the consequence did not follow the deed for some ten generations, or two hundred years.

The "sins of Jeroboam, which he sinned and which he caused Israel to commit" became a cliché in the evaluation of the eighteen kings of nine different "houses" who succeeded Jeroboam on the throne. All nineteen kings are found wanting and in sixteen instances some version of the "sins of Jeroboam" formula is invoked.[23] Of the entire royal roster, King Jehu received the most favorable notice from God for his valiant efforts in reducing the size of the sinful royal houses and in making Baal-worship in Israel such a hazardous undertaking (chapter 2). His failure to remove the golden calves constituted his sole demerit.

Modern theologians often claim that the DH was implemented in a routine or "mechanical" manner, implying that such an arrangement could not derive from a loving and merciful God. In this regard, the evaluations of a number of northern kings catch the eye, all of which testify to the erratic fashion in which

God did, in fact, put the DH into practice. It becomes virtually impossible to predict how a given king will fare in longevity or other measures based upon his moral stature.

Although Jeroboam is the paradigmatic sinner of the entire sequence, his reign (928–907) lasted twice as long as the northern average of eleven years and is permitted to continue through an heir, a privilege denied to four other rulers. Zimri (882) received the standard censure for "walking in the way of Jeroboam," though his tenure lasted only seven days! Omri (882–871) is said to have done more evil "than all who were before him," yet the sole charge against him is his perpetuation of the sins of Jeroboam. One would expect that the king who presided over the demise of the nation would have been in particular divine disfavor. Yet we find that, though Hoshea (732–724) did do evil in the LORD's eyes, he was "not like the kings of Israel who were before him."[24]

In 721, following the deportation of King Hoshea and a three-year siege of the capital city of Samaria, the nation fell to the Assyrians. The conquerors deported twenty-seven thousand inhabitants to sundry locales within their far-flung empire and brought in other thousands from conquered nations. The anthropological result was a hybrid people who developed a syncretic form of Yahwism, which the traditionalists of Judah found blasphemous. A mutual hostility arose, which continued through the era of the Hasmoneans into NT times, when a "good Samaritan" was understood as an oxymoron. The ten tribes of Israel had become permanently "lost."

The theological causes of the historical event are catalogued in a spirit of righteous indignation in 2 Kings 17. In addition to the continuing affront of the golden calves, the Israelites had embraced the religious customs of the Canaanites, worshiping Baal and other gods with pillars and sacred poles (Asherim) "on every high hill and under every green tree." They had served idols, worshiped the stars, employed divination and augury. Eventually, they had come to "despise" the LORD's commandments and even his covenant.

The Israelites had persisted in these "wicked things" in spite of repeated warnings by the LORD's spokesmen—the prophets

Amos and Hosea—that without repentance, disaster was imminent. For all these transgressions over the period of two centuries, the divine patience ran thin and eventually ran out. The LORD had become so angry with the Israelites that he finally had to remove them "out of his sight." Only the small kingdom of Judah remained to carry on the tradition of God's elect.

Twenty kings occupied the throne of Judah from Rehoboam (928–911), son of Solomon, to Zedekiah (596–586), who was blinded by his conquerors and led off to Babylon. As a group, these representatives of the house of David fared considerably better than their northern counterparts in the eyes of the LORD and the Deuteronomistic historian, as detailed in 1–2 Kings. The average length of tenure was seventeen years, fifty percent greater than that in the north, reflecting the greater stability of the Davidic lineage. Still, their cultic sins were more than sufficient in both quantity and quality to bring down the kingdom after nearly three hundred fifty years of existence.

Eight of the twenty kings may be categorized as "good," the remaining twelve as "bad," all the evaluations being based on the degree of adherence to the cultic norms of Yahwism. There is a positive correlation between royal virtue and length of rule, the good kings averaging twenty-seven years, the bad only eleven years. But beyond this superficial correspondence, the association breaks down at numerous points, revealing a pattern of sin-consequence as erratic as we found in the northern kingdom.

Among the eight good kings, only Hezekiah (727–698) and Josiah (639–609) aggressively destroyed the "high places" and their sacred paraphernalia. The other six permitted them to remain. But the tenures of Hezekiah and Josiah were exceeded in length by three kings not rated as highly. Among the wicked kings, the worst, by far, was Manasseh (698–642) whose heinous cultic sins recall those of Jeroboam. But Manasseh's reign lasted fifty-six years, the longest of any king, good or bad, north or south!

Good kings could become seriously ill, be assassinated, or die in battle, while bad kings might die a natural death in bed after a long life. Both types paid tribute to overlords, entered into foreign alliances, and suffered through long, debilitating wars.

Asa (908–867) "did what was right in the sight of the LORD" by removing idols and temple prostitutes from the land. He also removed his own mother as the queen mother because she had fashioned "an abominable image for Asherah," the female consort of Baal. But the conscientious Asa tolerated the high places for which Solomon had been chastised and the united kingdom split asunder.[25]

The modern concept of "justice delayed, justice denied" did not impinge significantly on the act-consequence loop in ancient Israel. The "ancestral merit" of King David influenced the timing of divine retribution long after his death. During the reign of the "bad" King Jehoram (851–843), the LORD forestalled destruction of Judah in order to perpetuate the royal "lamp," which he had promised to David "forever." In the late eighth century, the LORD answered the prayer of a desperately-ill King Hezekiah who was struggling to keep the Assyrians out of Jerusalem. Though Hezekiah had richly earned divine approval in his own right, the LORD chose to draw on his fond memory of David in response. He promised to heal the king, add fifteen years to his life, and save the city "for my own sake and for my servant David's sake."[26]

On occasion, the virtue of the reigning monarch so impressed the Deity that the forthcoming favors were in the king's own name. In the late seventh century, King Josiah heard the disturbing words of the newly discovered "book of the law"—probably an early edition of Deuteronomy, which included the alarming curses of chapter 28. This reading so energized the young ruler that he soon became the most ruthless foe of the Baalists since Jehu.

Josiah burned images of Asherah and defiantly scattered the ashes over the graves of the "common people." He defiled tombs in Samaria, littered the high places with human bones, and slaughtered on their altars the priests of the despised rival religion. For this and much more, of Josiah it was proudly written that "before him there was no king like him . . . nor did any like him arise after him." As a reward for this pious industry, the LORD promised his servant that the destruction of Judah would be postponed to such a time that he would not have to witness "all the disaster that I will bring on this place."[27]

God spared King Josiah (actually, he fell in battle with Egypt in 609), but he did not spare the nation. Since Judah had witnessed the downfall of its sister kingdom, it had had the opportunity to know first hand the horrifying consequences of unrepentant sin. But the stubborn Judahites proved no more educable than their erstwhile neighbors to the north. God, himself, grieved that the Judahites would "not listen or incline their ear; they stiffened their necks and would not hear or receive instruction" (Jer. 17:23).

King Manasseh represented the paragon of cultic evil in Judah in much the manner as Jeroboam I in the north, and for much the same reasons. In all, he encouraged the Judeans to do "things more wicked" than even the Godforsaken Canaanites had done. During Manasseh's tenure, the LORD announced that, because of his abominations, he would bring upon the nation "such evil that the ears of everyone who hears of it will tingle." In Jeremiah's time, the LORD reiterated the theme of the unpardonable transgressions, declaring that even the intercessions of such paragons of virtue as Moses and Samuel would not expiate the sins of Manasseh. Even so, as we observed with the sins of Jeroboam, the consequence trailed the deed by generations.[28]

As the hour of reckoning drew nigh, the LORD began to reject the cultic offerings of the Jerusalemites and cautioned Jeremiah not to pray for them. Through Jeremiah, he promised to bring against the city his three traditional weapons of sword, famine, and pestilence. A little later, through Ezekiel, he added a fourth: wild animals. Among the iniquitous Judahites, foreign gods had become as plentiful as the towns of Judah; Baalist altars as numerous as the streets of Jerusalem. In a desperate bid for a divine pardon, Jeremiah searched those streets for a single person who "acts justly and seeks truth." But he turned up as emptyhanded as did Abraham at Sodom. "Shall I not bring retribution on a nation such as this?" cried the LORD.[29]

In one context or another, God blamed everyone in sight and out for the impending disaster—kings, priests, prophets, the ancestors, and the "stubborn evil will" of the common people. And the iniquity had been of long standing. Jerusalem had aroused the LORD's anger "from the day it was built"; the people of Judah had "done nothing but evil . . . from their youth." This unrelieved record of disobedience so provoked the LORD that finally—with the aid of the strong arm of his servant Nebuchadnezzar—he "expelled them from his presence."[30]

In both Judah and Israel, we have repeatedly observed examples of "punishment displacement" wherein those who appear to be innocent have suffered for the acts of others in the same or an earlier generation. In the pre-exilic era, the text embraces unhesitatingly the notion of corporate or group responsibility in both its spatial (intra-generational) and temporal (inter-generational) dimensions. The crisis of 586 prompted its anguished victims to question the theological theory that explained in large part their suffering as the consequence of the accumulated sins of generations past. The prophet Ezekiel responded to this outcry by changing the retributional rules, or at least altering their emphasis. In so doing, he attempted to instill a renewed sense of hope and responsibility in the despairing community.

Ezekiel addressed the problem by reconsidering the old adage that the children's teeth are set on edge whenever the parents eat sour grapes. Henceforth, parents and children would not suffer for one another's sins; the individual deed would receive an individual response. If the wicked person repented of his evil ways, he would "live," just as the righteous person who later stumbled would "die." "Therefore I will judge you, O house of Israel," said the Lord GOD, "all of you according to your ways."[31]

Scholars have cautioned that Ezekiel's revisionism did not signal a sea change whereby the individual replaced the group as the sole focus of retribution. Both ethnic and individual modes remained important in the OT and into the Common Era.[32] Though it developed as a more "individualistic," non-ethnic offshoot of Judaism, Christianity also inherited the notion of corporate personality. The idea of "original sin" could only be seriously entertained in a tradition that felt comfortable with the concept of collective responsibility. As we shall explore in chapter 7, Christian views of the afterlife have been profoundly influenced by the Jewish belief in group responsibility or ethnic fate.

In the wake of the brutal siege, the stunned survivors paused to contemplate the meaning from every theological prospect. The Book of Lamentations furnishes a virtual eye-witness account of the desolation and suffering from both the community and the individual perspectives.[33] The once-proud city is reduced to shambles; the pain, suffering, and disillusionment are palpable. Crying babies starve; starving mothers devour their newborn; priests and prophets lie slaughtered in the LORD's house. Amid the bitterness and the sorrow, the pleas for mercy, and the cursing of the despised Edom, one discovers an abiding hope in the God of Israel and the complete acceptance of his retributive system. The contrite victims affirm their suffering as deserved and repent of their former transgressions:

> The LORD is in the right,
> for I have rebelled against
> his word. . . .
> The LORD is good to those who
> wait for him,
> to the soul that seeks him. . . .
> Why should any who draw breath
> complain
> about the punishment of
> their sins?
> Let us test and examine our ways,
> and return to the LORD.
>
> —Lam. 1:18a;3:25,39–40

Jeremiah and Ezekiel spoke of a "new heart" and a "new covenant" for a new Israel, but the old DH survived the catastrophe intact and remained as the ruling paradigm into the far distant future.[34] Meanwhile, in a small refugee colony down in Egypt, a group of Israelite women did raise serious questions about the efficacy of the LORD's sin-consequence program. In one of the few instances in the OT in which a group of dissidents are permitted to make a reasonable case, the skeptical women openly defied the aging Jeremiah. Contrary to his teachings, they insisted that when they had worshiped the "queen of heaven," the goddess Ishtar, they had prospered, and when they stopped, disaster struck. On this evidence, they declared boldly that they would return to making cakes and pouring out libations in honor of the Mesopotamian goddess.[35] In due course, other dissenters arose who would challenge even more substantially the Deuteronomic Hypothesis.

6

Dissent and Its Aftermath

In the pre-exilic and exilic eras, the Deuteronomic Hypothesis received overwhelming support from all quarters of the OT. Questions arose here and there concerning God's justice, though typically the doubts were either weakly developed or quickly extinguished. Given the problematic nature of the evidence, the only surprise is that more frequent and substantial dissent did not appear. Of course, the extant text represents the residuum that survived a rigorous and lengthy process of "unnatural selection" at the hands of innumerable and intolerant editors. It appears likely that the most trenchant dissent ended up on the cutting-room floor.

Basically, two types of empirically grounded complaints could be lodged against the DH: Why do the wicked prosper? Why do the righteous suffer? Since a pervasive sinfulness was widely acknowledged, at least among the religious elite, worldly success of the wicked produced a more nagging dissonance for the defenders of the tradition. Jeremiah, himself, had expressed a concern, derived from his own observations, years before his confrontation in Egypt with the apostatic women. In the first of a series of "personal laments," the prophet plaintively asked the LORD to explain why the guilty seemed to prosper, why the "treacherous" thrived. As for the falsehearted—those pseudo-pious who held the LORD "near in their mouths yet far from their hearts"—the no-nonsense seer called on the LORD to "set them apart for the day of slaughter" (Jer. 12:1–3).

The late seventh-century prophet Habukkuk opened his dialogue with the LORD in a questioning mood. The prophet complained that his cries for help had gone unanswered, that the LORD's justice never seemed to prevail. Since the eyes of the Almighty were "too pure to behold evil," Habukkuk was puzzled that the Deity could remain so inactive when he saw the wicked "swallow" the righteous. In his stock reply, the LORD assured his anxious servant that divine justice was on its way: "If it seems to tarry, wait for it; it will surely come, it will not delay" (Hab. 1:1–4,13;2:3).

That the wicked may frequently acquire more wealth and prestige than the righteous seemed to be widely acknowledged and, therefore, in need of reconciliation with the requirements of the DH. In Psalm 37, the Psalmist counsels his brethren not to "fret" over the wicked or be "envious" of their success. In fact, one could expect that material rewards would flow from piety, since taking "delight" in the LORD would produce "the desires of your heart." The poet then contradicted this traditional thought by admitting that wrongdoers often luxuriate in "abundance" while the faithful struggle to get by on "a little." But in that great future day planned by the LORD, the children of the wicked would be "cut off" and the progeny of the righteous would "abide forever." In an all-encompassing confirmation of the DH, the Psalmist soberly asserted (v. 25) that never in his long life had he ever seen the righteous "forsaken" or their children "begging bread."[1]

The author of Psalm 49 takes a somewhat less traditional approach, while still struggling to explain the conjunction of wealth and wickedness. He recognizes that this association is not a temporary aberration and seeks to temper its significance by focusing his audience's attention on the ephemerality and indiscrimination of life. Everyone—the rich, the poor, the wise, the foolish—arrives at the same ultimate destination on his earthly journey. God cannot be bribed by wealth to postpone death indefinitely nor do the goods of the wealthy "go down after them." In a tone of barely-concealed gratification, the Psalmist declares that the successful may seem to live a "happy" life, blessed with respect, praise and worldly goods, but they, too, are destined to join "the company of their ancestors, who will never again see the light."[2]

Before Job, approaches to the problem of the suffering righteous typically stopped short of calling God's justice seriously into question. The frequent pleas for divine intervention in the psalms of personal and national lament do not accuse God of infidelity. Nearly everyone accepted the anthropological proposition, affirmed in both theory and experience, that humankind, if not inherently wicked, exhibited a prodigious capacity for sinfulness.

In Psalm 73, extolled as "a masterpiece, one of the great spiritual works of all time," the righteous protagonist, beset by a sea of troubles, is attracted to the life of the wicked, but virtue triumphs in the end.[3] The Psalmist confesses that he had grown "envious" of the success of the sinful whose lives seemed almost problem-free. He had even begun to question whether his obedience to God's admonitions to keep a "clean heart" had not been "all in vain." But a numinous experience in the temple quickly restored his orthodox belief that God sets the wicked in "slippery places" and is "good" to the "pure in heart."

The author of Psalm 44 assumes a more aggressive stance in contemplation of God's justice. Described as a poem of "rage," the post-exilic psalm demands that the Deity rouse himself and forthwith right the wrongs that beleaguer the community—all the while protesting the innocence of the victims.[4] The nation was being persecuted unmercifully by its enemies who made of it a "laughingstock" among its neighbors. "Because of you," the poet rails at his Creator, the Israelites were "being killed all day long, and accounted as sheep for the slaughter." Flying directly in the face of the conventional theodicy, the Psalmist claims that the people suffer undeservedly since they had neither "forgotten" their God nor been "false" to their covenant with him. In exasperation, the Psalmist attempts to provoke the *Deus Absconditus* into taking action:

> Rouse yourself! Why do you
> sleep, O Lord?
> Awake, do not cast us off
> forever!
> Why do you hide your face?
> Why do you forget our
> affliction and oppression? . . .
> Rise up, come to our help.

Redeem us for the sake of your
steadfast love.

—Ps. 44:23–24,26

Job

We have now arrived at the famous Book of Job, the classical locus for addressing the problem of the suffering righteous or unexplained evil. The "Mt. Everest" of the OT, this product of a poetic genius stands unchallenged as the principal voice of dissent from the system of divine retribution so richly documented in the pages of Scripture. Line for line, pound for pound, Job has evoked a more passionate response from its readers than any other OT book. The dramatic story has captured the considered attention of an array of giants that includes John Calvin, Thomas Carlyle, Daniel Webster, Alfred Lord Tennyson, Carl Jung, D.H. Lawrence, Thomas Wolfe, Archibald MacLeish, and Robert Frost, among numerous others.[5]

At least two major, and closely related, reasons for this enduring fascination may be identified. No matter how pious or disciplined, every human being is inclined, now and again, to shake her fist defiantly at God and cry out in pain for immediate relief. We instinctively identify with the long-suffering Job who struggles heroically to understand the meaning hidden behind his personal, apparently heaven-sent, catastrophe. In addition, though the book is not formally "philosophical," it probes the profound issue of theodicy ("God's justice") in a more engaging fashion than any other book in the Bible or, arguably, in the literature of the world.

Job consists of an ancient tale—now divided into a prose prologue (chapters 1 and 2) and epilogue (chapter 42:7–17)—which frames a central poetic section (3–41). The work belongs to the genre of "wisdom" literature, produced by sages or "wisemen," who tended to address cosmopolitan themes rather than more narrow, parochial questions. Job and his compatriots hail from the "land of Uz," provisionally identified as Edom, but they obediently worship Yahweh, assumed to be a universal God. Following the direction pointed in Ezek. 18, the retributional problem focuses on the individual rather than the nation. Since, at times, the questioning of God's ways borders on the blasphemous, the unorthodox utterances may have been placed in the mouth of a "foreigner" in order to dampen their heretical impact among the more intolerant of the Israelite faithful.

Though unsurpassed in literary merit, the book can scarcely claim priority in the field of the righteous sufferer. At least fifteen hundred years before Job, the theme had been thoroughly explored in Egypt and in Mesopotamia.[6] Estimates of the date of the final recension of Job range over several centuries, since the text itself offers almost no solid chronological clues. A scholarly consensus clusters around the sixth to fifth centuries B.C.E., i.e., in the disillusioning aftermath of the tragedy of 586. Stimulated by that historic event and the evidence derived from his everyday observations, the author dares to look unblinkingly at the alleged correspondence between reality and the retributional hypothesis.

In the opening scene, God is in his heavens and all is right with the world. The "blameless and upright" Job possesses all that a man could desire—ten fine adult children, "very many" servants, and vast herds of livestock. In fact, he had become "the greatest of all the people of the east." The righteous man is richly blessed; the DH functions as biblically advertised.

Meanwhile in the celestial court, one of the "heavenly beings," the Satan ("the Adversary"), suggests to God that the saintly Job doesn't fear him "for nought" (KJV). That is, Job's piety may owe more to the anticipation of reward than to the pure love of God. For the author, true piety is found only in those attitudes and actions that go beyond, or rise above, the retributional schema. In effect, God and the Satan wager on the possibility of *disinterested* obedience among humans. To test the proposition, God suspends the DH, leading to an abrupt change in the fortunes of his servant Job.

Approved by the Deity and effected by the Satan, Job's catastrophe includes the loss of children, servants, and livestock and affliction with "loathsome sores" from head to foot. Physical adversity leads to social ostracism and the insufferable status of "laughingstock" among his neighbors. When his wife encourages him to "curse God, and die," the ever-righteous Job responds from his ashheap with the resigned query: "Shall we receive the good at the hand of God, and not receive the bad?"

In the poetic core of the book, Job's mood changes radically. No longer the proverbial man of "patience" known to NT readers, he turns progressively distraught, embittered, and, finally, openly confrontational with the Power of the universe.[7] Three old friends steeped in the wisdom tradition arrive to commiserate with their colleague who has suffered such a radical deterioration of fortune. Their dialogue with Job starts in a polite and sympathetic key but escalates to such an emotional intensity that, by the third round of exchanges, far more heat than light is being shed on the central issue.

A firm believer in the DH throughout his life and for good reason, Job now flatly repudiates the hypothesis in his own God-forsaken case. Eventually, he shifts his focus to ponder the general condition of humankind and its implications for the character and providence of the LORD. He observes that the rich regularly abuse the poor who, "like wild asses in the desert," scavenge in harvested fields for food for their children. The wealthy "snatch the orphan child from the breast, and take as a pledge the infant of the poor." From the city arise the terminal groans of the "dying" and the pitiful petitions of the "wounded," but God "pays no attention to their prayers" (24:5–6,9,12).

The outraged sufferer mounts an all-out attack on the dogma that the LORD will re-tribute the wicked:

> Why do the wicked live on,
> reach old age, and grow mighty in power?
> Their children are established in their presence,
> and their offspring before their eyes.
> Their houses are safe from fear,
> and no rod of God is upon them. . . .
> They spend their days in prosperity,

and in peace they go down to
Sheol.
They say to God, "Leave us alone!
We do not desire to know your
ways . . . "

21:7–9,13–14

Job rejects outright the "justice" inherent in the doctrine of inter-generational responsibility. The orthodox recognized that not all the wicked would personally feel the hand of the LORD though their descendants certainly would. Job proposed that justice would be served only if the evildoers saw with "their own eyes" the retributive destruction, only if they themselves should "drink of the wrath of the Almighty." After all, when their days on earth had ended, why should the iniquitous "care for their household after them"? (21:19-21).

Job recognized that divine retribution in a post-mortem life would neatly solve his problem. He took up the possibility in some detail but in the end rejected it totally. Heretical with respect to the DH, he affirmed the OT dogma that life ends for all in a shadowy netherworld called Sheol. A judgmental afterlife was an idea whose time had not yet arrived in Israel.

A mortal, born of woman,
few of days and full of
trouble,
comes up like a flower and
withers,
flees like a shadow and does not
last. . . .
For there is hope for a tree,
if it is cut down, that it will
sprout again,
and that its shoots will not
cease. . . .
But mortals die, and are laid low;
humans expire, and where are
they?
As waters fail from a lake,
and a river wastes away and

dries up,
so mortals lie down and do not
rise again;
until the heavens are no more,
they will not awake
or be roused out of their sleep.

14:1–2,7,10–12.

Like the author of Ps. 49, the poet connected the failure of retribution to impact the lives of either the righteous or the wicked to their common fates at death:

One dies in full prosperity,
being wholly at ease and secure,
his loins full of milk
and the marrow of his bones
moist.
Another dies in bitterness of soul,
never having tasted of good.
They lie down alike in the dust,
and the worms cover them.

21:23–26.

The three friends defended the conventional wisdom in a very conventional manner. They offered no rigid formulas, idiosyncratic theories, or eccentric views of the divine economy—only the studied observations and convictions of the sage. Before their exchanges with Job turned into shouting matches, the wisemen adduced experience, ancestral wisdom, and the mercy and trustworthiness of God in support of their case. Their theodicy would have been comfortably at home in most every book of the OT.

The senior friend, Eliphaz, asked Job to recall all those past experiences that confirmed the DH:

Think now, who that was
innocent ever perished?
Or where were the upright cut
off?
As I have seen, those who plow

iniquity
and sow trouble reap the same.
By the breath of God they perish,
and by the blast of his anger
they are consumed.

4:7–9.

When a human being persists in his claims of sinlessness, even his most empathetic friends may be inclined to raise a skeptical eyebrow. To Job's protestations of innocence, Eliphaz gently responds that "human beings are born to trouble just as sparks fly upward." As an alternative to sin as the explanation of suffering, Eliphaz introduces the possibility of "discipline" at the hands of a monistic God: "How happy is the one whom God reproves; therefore do not despise the discipline of the Almighty. For he wounds, but he binds up; he strikes, but his hands heal." Another friend, Zophar, reminds Job of God's abiding inclination to temper his justice with mercy, which in reality meant that he "exacts of you less than your guilt deserves."[8]

The friends' defense of the God-given concept of retribution has triggered a barrage of scorn and derision among modern critics. The friends are altogether vilified as "miserable comforters" and the biblical system of retribution distorted into shapes that defy recognition.[9] The wisemen are accused of "superficiality" and "formulaic and sloganeering dogmatism."[10] They are found guilty of "pious lies" and "hypocritical sycophancy"—of offering Job, in place of understanding, only "sanctimonious platitudes" and "conventional clichés and empty phrases."[11] Above all, they had fallen victim to the theologians' "occupational hazard," which is to forget that he probes into God's eternal mystery. The friends had had the temerity to consider the Divine and his laws as subjects to be "analysed, predicted and understood."[12]

In criticizing the friends, theologians have caricatured divine retribution so severely that neither Moses nor God would recognize it. As we saw in Chapter 5, the DH is, in fact, a grand, sprawling concept in application, pregnant with generational slippage, and totally devoid of predictability in the individual case. The targeted unit ranges from the individual, through groups of varying sizes, to the nation as a whole. The act-consequence timing is so indeterminate that it often requires the "patience of Job" to witness its complete manifestation. The initial agent may be requited immediately, or ten generations later his descendants may suffer the consequences. God may impose a judgmental dichotomy upon part or all of the population in a wholly unfathomable manner. He may delay, forgive, or temper his judgments with covenantal mercy—or he may not. The only constant is his assurance, as a moral accountant, that in the fullness of time, human behavior will be re-tributed.

In direct contradiction of this biblically-derived picture, many Job interpreters fabricate an inflexible, mechanical DH that is said to be constrained by a "strict calculus."[13] The friends' God is the "Lord of retribution," an "ice-cold engineer who enforces the steely mechanisms" of reprisal. In this scenario, God becomes a "marionette" in a predictable system of act-consequence. Eventually, the Almighty is "imprisoned" by his own merciless and immoral system, a victim who forfeits his freedom and sovereignty.[14] This disparaging image of a mechanical Deity is difficult to reconcile with his widely touted virtue as the unerodable Rock, the immutable Presence, the only Constant in an ever-changing world. The critics' problem apparently rests more with God as the moral accountant than with his specific mode of operation.

A provocative variation on the theme of the "prisoner God" has been proposed recently by James L. Crenshaw, a leading student of the problem of unexplained evil. He labels the DH as a "magical assumption," insisting that magical "manipulation" of Deity is an inherent component of the retributional program. The friends' God is demoted to the "god of magic"; the DH regresses to the unenviable status of "faith's worst enemy."[15]

The difficulty with regarding the DH as a type of magic is that the concept is ethical in its essence, as magic is not, and derives from the holy God who, by definition, cannot be co-opted. When man acts and Deity reacts within the divinely-prescribed, ethical system, neither is "manipulated" in any meaningful sense. In freedom, God set out the ground rules of covenantal obligation; with free-will, man strives to obey the divine commandments.[16]

Following repeated imprecations from Job, God finally roused himself to speak "out of the whirlwind." The Almighty upbraided Job for his reproving attitude and puny perspective on the cosmos, but addressed not at all the burning question of retribution. For many readers, the divine speeches represent a curious and disappointing response—a "magnificent irrelevance"—since Job had questioned God's justice, not his omnipotence.[17]

In the final chapter, an humbled and awed Job confesses before the LORD: "I despise myself, and repent in dust and ashes." The LORD inexplicably informs the friends that they have not spoken of him "what is right" as his servant Job had! That startling judgment—which hardly follows from the preceding forty-one chapters of dialogue—would seem to cast a divine shadow on the DH as well as its defenders. But God promptly restores to the aggrieved Job "twice as much as he had before." The Satan goes unmentioned and the "test" results go unannounced. Most readers would agree that Job "passed" or came as close as it is humanly possible to do.

Given the ambiguity in God's speeches and his errant behavior in the epilogue, all interpretive points of view can claim at least partial victory. One enthusiast even found profundity in the equivocalness of the conclusion, declaring that "the genius of this climax . . . lives in the way it requires each reader to construe the resolution for him- or herself. . . . "[18] But those who have seen in Job a significant turning point for Israelite religion and its latter-day heirs have carried the day.

According to many of its modern admirers, Job had single-handedly and permanently disposed of the biblical doctrine of retribution. They have claimed that the "discredited" idea belonged to a bygone era, to the "adolescence of religion."[19] Its "bankruptcy" and "intellectual and ethical inadequacy" had become apparent; the poet-Job had refuted it "once and for all."[20] The theological implications for the future were momentous. In Job, God had been taken "entirely out of moral law enforcement." Theology was "never the same" after the DH "got what it deserved."[21] Indeed, the author of Job had dealt a veritable "death blow" to God's system of retribution. [22] This modern attitude is reflected in the absence of a "retribution" entry in the authoritative, six-volume, *Anchor Bible Dictionary* published in 1992.

Although the poet-Job obviously wanted to explore in depth the problem of the suffering innocent, his story, on its face, does not really challenge the DH at all. In this view, God does not bother to defend his retributional principle because he knows that it has only been suspended temporarily. From the DH perspective, Job is "connected" at the outset, disconnected during the prolonged test of his character, and re-connected in the epilogue. He resembles a man who loses his electric power at dusk and frets all night that the entire universe is suffering a calamitous power outage, only to discover at dawn a tree limb on the line leading to his house.

To expect a seismic shift in the theodicean ground of Israel as a result of Job is unrealistic. The centripetal force generated continuously by theological dogma is routinely undervalued. A culture doesn't alter its fundamental theological understandings with the seasons or the latest poetry, no matter how excellent. Although it could bring pain—as post-586 Israel knew only too well—retributional theology also brought a credible answer to the perennial longing of the human soul for overarching order, meaning, and purpose. It supplied an effective antidote to fear and uncertainty in a frightening and chaotic world.[23]

The omnipotent moral Policeman might bring harsh judgment, but at least you knew that he was watching and that he *cared.* As mother nature abhors a vacuum, so human nature abhors purposelessness. In this respect, our needs have changed scarcely at all through the millennia. Tortured by pointless suffering and cosmic uncertainty, individually and collectively we frequently cry out the universal "why?" (see Appendix B). The retributional idea has functioned so satisfactorily in response that, even when significant modification did occur, the core idea remained untouched, and so it continues to the present day.

Although the long-term impact of Job on retributional thinking was limited, some scholars have seen the book as a theological turning point of a different order. The God of the prologue and epilogue was absorbed fully in human affairs, the classical "Lord of History." But the Voice from the whirlwind came from a transcendent creator who is remote and eventually falls silent, the classical *Deus Absconditus.* This transformation accords with the apparent progressive withdrawal of the Deity from direct involvement in history, and from the pages of the Bible.[24]

The most enduring contribution of Job to the retributional matrix was the firm establishment of the possibility that divine testing or discipline could explain misfortune, in addition to the old standby, sin. As for the correspondence of the DH to reality—confirmed by leading Israelite theologians for centuries—an old adage, inverted, helps explain the remarkable longevity of the hypothesis in the face of its manifest disconfirmation: "If they hadn't believed it, they wouldn't have seen it."

A curious feature of Job interpretation is the rarity with which the Originator of the orthodox view is openly acknowledged. Tracing the concept to its scriptural source does not require high-tech equipment. Critics heap abuse on intermediate targets—the beleaguered friends, the religious elite, the impersonal tradition, the too-human biblical authorship—that could be directed more appropriately to the responsible Party. Throughout the OT, the retributional doctrine issues directly from the lips of the one, true and judging God. Facing squarely the implications for the integrity of the Bible is difficult since the retributional principle informs—indeed, saturates—its pages. If the DH is labelled flatly as "false" doctrine—rather than merely too "mechanical" in execution—a mainstay of biblical theology crumbles into dust. But did the God of Justice decide to jettison the judgmental paradigm as we are encouraged to believe? Were subsequent biblical authors as impressed with the theology of Job as modern writers have been?

The Post-Joban Biblical Response

The tension created by Job did produce "a crack in the door" of retribution by encouraging a broader community response to those experiencing pain and suffering. But a more flexible dogma meant confusion and ambiguity rather than clarity and comprehensibility. So the ranks of orthodoxy closed quickly to forestall an instability that could have resulted from the dissonance introduced by Job.[25] The traditional view remained alive and well in the post-Joban era, as if the classical portrayal of the innocent sufferer had never been written.

The most extensive OT expression of post-Joban theology is found in the sixty-five chapters of the Books of Chronicles, probably written toward the end of the fourth century B.C.E. Basically a re-write of the Books of Kings, 1–2 Chronicles presents a second version of the pre-586 history of Israel. In it the Deuteronomic Hypothesis emerges as an even more salient principle than in the primary account. In the nineteenth century, the eminent biblical scholar, Julius Wellhausen, noted that for the Chronicler, "Never does sin miss its punishment, and never where misfortune occurs is guilt wanting."[26]

In his zeal for the DH, the Chronicler determined that "each and every deed" must be requited—a refinement that has been called the "imperative of reward and punishment." As we have observed, the timing of sin and retribution in the Books of Kings is untidy in the extreme. In reworking these materials, the Chronicler clears a shorter and more certain path between act and consequence. Developing Ezekiel's emphasis on the individual as the primary unit of justice, he mutes or eliminates entirely the retributional dimensions of ancestral merit and corporate responsibility. In Chronicles, God acts within a very restricted time frame to reward or punish his people.[27] Ironically, his picture of cause-and-effect is closer to that painted by the modern critics of Job's friends than by the friends themselves.

As a revealing example, the Chronicler revises radically the attribution of the downfall of Judah to the abominations of King Manasseh one hundred years earlier, as described in 2 Kings 21. In the latter-day version, the LORD brings the Assyrian army against an unrepentant Manasseh who is captured and led away in chains. Suddenly contrite, the king "humbled himself greatly" before God who just as promptly restored him to his throne in Judah. Now a dedicated Baal-basher in the tradition of Jehu, Hezekiah, and Josiah, the king destroyed the numerous altars to the foreign gods that years earlier he, himself, had erected (2 Chron. 33:10–16). These virtuous acts were calculated to go a long way toward explaining his unequaled tenure of fifty-six years. Additionally, the Chronicler shifts the proximate cause of the collapse of Judah to the last king, Zedekiah, and his generation, whose sins are appropriately expanded over the 2 Kings account (2 Chr. 36:12–16).

In the Books of Ezra and Nehemiah, traditionally ascribed to the Chronicler, the orthodox system of justice continues to hold full sway. In prayer, the priest Ezra begs God's forgiveness for the manifold sins of his countrymen, most especially their predilection to mix their "holy seed" with the polluted germ plasm of the Canaanites. Ezra acknowledged that the Israelites had indeed suffered greatly for their past "evil deeds" but, even so, the merciful God had punished them less than their sins deserved (Ezra 9).

In his so-called "great confession" to God, Ezra reviews the lengthy covenantal relationship between the Deity and his people (Neh. 9). Again and again, the Israelites had rebelled against God whose great forbearance eventually evaporated, delivering the wicked nation into the hands of its enemies. But thanks to his "great mercies," God never forsook them or made "an end of them." In summation, the pious priest says it all: "You have been just in all that has come upon us, for you have dealt faithfully and we have acted wickedly. . . . " (9:33).

Some late prophetic books apply the DH to very concrete problems that the post-exilic community had to face. By 520 B.C.E., nearly two decades after the first exiles had returned from Babylon, no serious effort had been made to rebuild the Jerusalem temple. Through the prophet Haggai, the LORD announced to the returnees that the difficult economic conditions that they had been experiencing were because "my house lies in ruins, while all of you hurry off to your own houses." Furthermore, he continued, "I have called for a drought on the land." Later on, he brought "blight and mildew and hail" against the sinful people. But after the foundation of the temple had been laid, the economic picture changed abruptly. "From this day on," declared the LORD, "I will bless you" (Hag. 1:9,11;2:17,19).

Through the prophet Malachi, the LORD engaged in a series of acrimonious exchanges with the restless Israelites who had "wearied" him by asking "Where is the God of Justice?" For his part, God accused them of "robbing" him. "How are we robbing you?" they asked. "In your tithes and offerings!" he responded. In recompense for this lapse, God brought a "curse" on the nation in the form of voracious insects and a devastating drought. But in a gesture of conciliation, he made them a dramatic offer: if they would begin to bring in the full tithe, he would "rebuke" the locusts and "open the windows" of heaven. In this bold challenge, the LORD invited the people to "put me to the test"—and, of course, his system of retribution as well (Mal. 2:17;3:8–11).

In the Book of Ecclesiastes, the third-century B.C.E. Teacher, Qoheleth or the "Preacher," brought his dark pessimism to bear on all forms of theology, including the retributional theory. "Fear of God" remained a virtue, but mere mortals could not begin to fathom God's mysterious ways.[28] The DH is not rejected outright, but it, too, remains incomprehensible.[29] Since "all is vanity," the Teacher recommends that everyone eat, drink, and "be merry."[30] But orthodoxy gains the last word in an epilogue (12:9–14) in which an editor endorses the Teacher's wisdom but moderates his extreme skepticism. Thus, ironically, the book closes with a ringing endorsement of the DH: "For God will bring every deed into judgment, including every secret thing, whether good or evil."

The celebrated sage, Ben Sirach, disputed with those of his time, circa 180 B.C.E., who would doubt the efficacy of God's retributive justice. In a line of argument that reprises that of Eliphaz, Sirach asks his audience to recall the experience of generations past: Had anyone ever "trusted in the LORD and been disappointed?" The sage held that God had established such a perfect harmony in his creation that everything in the universe had its purpose and its "appointed" time. This position even induced him to tackle the difficult problem of natural evil. Natural disasters, such as wind, fire, hail, and famine, he insisted, are but retributive agents of the LORD. They "take delight in doing his bidding . . . and when their time comes they never disobey his command."[31]

By Sirach's time, winds that would significantly transform the DH had begun to blow. Nevertheless, he held steadfastly to the tradition of the ambivalent God that had been passed down through the ages:

> For mercy and wrath are with the
> Lord;
> he is mighty to forgive—but he
> also pours out wrath.
> Great as his mercy, so also is his
> chastisement;
> he judges a person according to
> one's deeds.
> The sinner will not escape with
> plunder,
> and the patience of the godly
> will not be frustrated.
>
> —Sir. 16:11b–13.

In the second and first centuries B.C.E., the sectarians (Essenes?) at Qumran wrote and collected the massive library that has become known as the Dead Sea Scrolls. Arguably the most important archaeological find of the twentieth century, these writings have significantly advanced our understanding of Judaic thought in the two centuries before the Christian era. Not surprisingly, divine retribution emerges as one of the most salient theological principles. The sectarians endorsed with enthusiasm the full operation of the DH in the biblical past, their Hasmonean-Age present and the End of Days future. Incidentally, although Job is represented in the collection, it was not among the community's favorites.[32]

Conclusions Regarding the Divine Character

A sufficient number of texts in which God engages the nations or Israel have now been examined to draw some general conclusions about his character, especially as it relates to "justice." The NRSV states that the character of God, as derived from the Bible, is "known and reliable."[33] However, modern readers may be dismayed or repulsed by the "known and reliable" words and deeds of the OT God. Approximately one thousand passages link Yahweh to violence, either directly or through his human instruments.[34] For Christians, the temptation has been great to contrast the OT God of wrath, law, and justice with the NT God of love, gospel, and mercy. In its introduction to the Book of Joshua, the RSV asserts that "many have felt—no doubt rightly—that the God of Joshua is infinitely remote from the God of Jesus."[35]

Before the Second World War, Christian theologians did not hesitate to contrast the two testaments, the two religions, even the two peoples. Early in this century, the prominent German scholar, Hermann Gunkel, wrote that the "simplicity" of the "Hebrew mind" rendered it "hardly capable of philosophic thought." The OT was the product of a fanatical people and their "volcanic" Deity. "Unlike Christianity," Gunkel said, "his [the Hebrew's] religion does not exhort him to gentleness, and his hot blood impels him to deeds of passionate energy, sometimes even of violence and fanaticism. And as was the people, so was its history."[36]

In the post-Holocaust era, some interpreters have rushed to the opposite extreme by denying that any significant differences in the mood and behavior of God exist at all between the testaments. In these assessments of the attributes of the OT God, "justice" tends to be slighted in favor of "creator," "rescuer," "restorer," and the like. Only a "widespread confusion," it is said, could contrast the "strict" God of the OT with the "friendly" God of the NT. To contrast the two testaments is to make a "fallacious" comparison or perpetuate the "stereotype" of wrath versus love since both qualities may be found in both testaments.[37]

To try to understand the differences that do exist between the portrayals of God in the two testaments seems more useful than to vaporize them into thin air through apology. By any objective measure, the OT God is far more bellicose, wrathful, and retributive than his NT counterpart. It should be noted in passing that, in the NT, God nearly disappears as a first-person actor. As the Father, he is almost totally eclipsed in deference to the Son. Spoken of a good deal, he speaks hardly at all.[38]

As we saw in chapters 1 through 4, the key to understanding Israel's relation with its neighbors was the "us-them" perspective, in which the "not-us" is viewed as belonging to a radically different, and inferior, group or "species." Irrationally, God chooses and loves only Israel; irrationally, the unchosen are despised because they are "Godless" and practice exotic religious "abominations." If the circumstances required "moral surgery" to remove the pagan pollution, a genocidal "Doctor God" stood by with a willing scalpel. In other words, the God of Israel behaved like—well, the God of Israel. But these hostile engagements of Yahweh with the "other" are typical of nationalistic gods the world over fiercely defending their ethnic turf. Modern believers—callous to the plight of the unchosen, yet uncomfortable with the "God of Joshua"—manage to forgive Yahweh for his manifold assaults on the heathenish pagans. They regard it as an unfortunate, but necessary, price for the establishment and maintenance of God's own in his Promised Land. Or they may resort to the double-speak of the Presbyterian Confession that declares: "God's love never changes. Against all who oppose him, God expresses his love in wrath."[39]

The covenantal relationship with Israel also evoked a plethora of "wrathful" violence that is often contrasted with the more irenic landscape of the NT. This more intimate affinity requires a more detailed analysis to appreciate its OT milieu and to identify the critical changes that occurred in the NT. As in a human family, the character of God may be revealed most profoundly in his relationships with his own.

We can identify five basic parameters that for a millennium operated to shape the character of the OT God of Justice:

1 God is one, i.e., no other divine providence is recognized.
2 God is immanent, participating actively in history.
3 God is just, interacting retributively with his people.
4 A systematic conception of a judgmental afterlife is absent.

5 An independent source of evil, a Satan, is absent.

We could append to this list the enduring propensity of human beings to sin and the absolute necessity, in a "God-intoxicated" society, of offering theological explanations for historical events. Given these divinely-ordained bounds, Yahweh is, in effect, constrained or "boxed-in," though hardly "manipulated." Punishments for the wayward—either the individual or the nation—must be meted out on this earth and within a time-frame that bears some relation to the causal event—what has been called "terrestrial eschatology."[40] The result is a monistic God who appears "angry" much of the time because human behavior and the divine system of justice require it.

Throughout the OT, a bipolar, ambivalent Deity dispenses both blessings and antithetical curses with a self-confident equanimity. Hundreds upon hundreds of passages witness to the concrete activities of this scriptural God. In addition, a number of terse passages insist on divine ambivalence as an abstract theological principle. Among these, we select a few representative examples:

> I kill and I make alive;
> I wound and I heal;
> and no one can deliver from my hand.
>
> —Deut. 32:39

> If you forsake the LORD and serve foreign gods, then he will turn and do you harm, and consume you, after having done you good.
>
> —Josh. 24:20

> The LORD kills and brings to life;
> he brings down to Sheol and
> raises up.
> The LORD makes poor and makes rich;
> he brings low, he also exalts.
>
> —1 Sam. 2:6–7

> I form light and create darkness,
> I make weal and create woe;

I the LORD do all these things.

—Isa. 45:7

Is it not from the mouth of the Most High
that good and bad come?

—Lam. 3:38[41]

In a deuterocanonical work written around the turn of the era, the Prayer of Manasseh, the petitioner—the pseudonymous and infamous King Manasseh—accepts fully the duality inherent in the Godhead. This classical sinner of Judah prays earnestly to "you who made heaven and earth"

who confined the deep
and sealed it with your terrible
and glorious name;
at whom all things shudder,
and tremble before your power,
for your glorious splendor cannot
be borne,
and the wrath of your threat to
sinners is unendurable;
yet immeasurable and unsearchable
is your promised mercy,
for you are the Lord Most High,
of great compassion,
long-suffering, and very
merciful,
and you relent at human suffering.

In the NT, God remains monotheistic (barely!), immanent and retributional. But the statuses of Satan and the afterlife change radically—though both mutations predate the Christ-event. An independent Satan, or Devil, and a matured conception of the hereafter make it possible for the more odious aspects of judgment to be attributed immediately to the one, or postponed indefinitely to the other. In addition, no pagans had to be ousted from their homeland and no historical crises threatened the nascent Christian community—as 721 and 586 did the Israelites—which demanded a retributional explanation in the here and now. During the first Christian decades, the major calamity in Israel—the destruction of the Jerusalem temple in 70 C.E.—actually fortified the Christian position. Following the inexorable logic of the Hebrew Bible, that event obviously manifested God's wrath against the unbelieving Jews, as Jesus then and Christians thereafter never tired of proclaiming.[42]

As a consequence of the convergence of these several vectors, the God of the NT—at least prior to the Book of Revelation—is measurably more benign than his OT counterpart. Reconciliation becomes even more difficult if the dogma of divine immutability is invoked. But, in spite of some misgivings, Christians insist, as a primary article of faith, that the "God of Jesus" is the very same Deity as the "God of Joshua." However, they have difficulty embracing the bipolar God, a God who will both "make weal and create woe." This reluctance continues despite the fact that, from the Deuteronomist to Ben Sirach, we encounter a Deity who—though as merciful as he deems appropriate—still "delights" in visiting the full measure of his justice on a sinful people. Christians have been conditioned by a NT "God of love," a theology that has relegated the "bad stuff" to the Devil and to the hereafter. To follow the development of these radical modifications to the DH is our primary goal in chapter 7.

7
The Afterlife Solution

The unvarnished Deuteronomic Hypothesis remained a pillar of the theological edifice of Israel throughout its OT history. The nuclear idea of a caring, watching, and judging God survived intact even after significant change did finally arrive in the form of a judgmental afterlife. This veritable revolution in Israelite thinking occurred during the so-called intertestamental, or Greco-Roman period, three centuries that began somewhat before 200 B.C.E. In turning a single page of the Christian Bible—from Malachi to Matthew—one leaps, perhaps unknowingly, across a vast chronological chasm onto a radically-altered theological landscape.[1]

The Old Testament and the Afterlife

Most OT readers simply assume, or are taught, that its pages include a systematic exposition of the afterlife, one with which they are familiar from the Talmud or the NT. But modern biblical scholarship is nearly unanimous in its insistence that valid OT references to an afterlife are "rare, obscure . . . and late."[2] The Scottish scholar Robert Davidson has described the consequences for many: "For those for whom religion is primarily concerned with death and life hereafter the OT must be a very disappointing book."[3] In the first seventy-seven percent of the Christian Bible and one hundred percent of the Hebrew Bible, silence on the hereafter is deafening. Discourse on an afterlife does not issue from the lips of priests, prophets, sages—or God.

In the normative view of the OT, God's justice, though perhaps delayed for generations, was always carried out on this earth. The detailed retributional catalogs of Deut. 28 and Lev. 26 give no hint that either the "blessings" or the "curses" will be realized in part or in toto in an afterlife. Some modern theologians have reasoned that "If there is a God, and if he is just, there must be an afterlife."[4] The Israelites certainly believed in God, and in a God that was just, but for fifteen hundred years—from Abraham to Ben Sirach—they would have taken sharp exception to such thinking.

For the Israelites and their God, death marked the normal end of the life and expectations of the individual, as natural as birth or breathing. In the pre-exilic era—dominated as it was by the idea of corporate responsibility—perpetuation of the nation loomed much larger in the political and religious mind than persistence of the individual. Of course, death could induce anxiety and fear, especially if its mode and timing were inappropriate. A "good" death followed a life "full of days" that was blessed with numerous children and ended in peace. Contrariwise, a "bad" death resulted from a premature or violent ending, without offspring or a proper burial.[5]

Of course, curiosity and imagination regarding some sort of afterlife existence probably marks the human species from its inception over one hundred thousand years ago. Therefore, to understand that ancient Israel entertained no thoughts at all regarding a post-mortem life would be inaccurate. The religious elite did admonish the populace—though often futilely—to desist from those family-centered, "cult of the dead" activities whose practice threatened the centralized norm of Yahwism. The prophets railed against necromancers, mediums, wizards, demons and the like—all popular avenues throughout the ANE of interactions with the deceased.[6] But as the major official concession to afterlife "pressure" from the ANE, the Yahwistic tradition recognized only the concept of Sheol, the gloomy netherworld that comprised the eternal home of the dead.

Closely associated with graves, Sheol was conceived as the polar opposite of heaven ("deep as Sheol or high as heaven," Isa. 7:11). A completely democratic country, the "Pit" welcomed entrants on an equal basis from all points on the moral compass. Its inhabitants, the "shades," led a kind of nonlife devoid of purpose, meaning or the possibility of return.[7] God seems largely to have ignored the place, though in his omnipotence, he could appear there if he willed (Prov. 15:11). For the pious, the most painful aspect of the prospect of Sheol was the cessation of all communication with the Almighty. For example, in Ps. 6:5, a gravely ill petitioner reminds the LORD that "in death there is no remembrance of you; in Sheol who can give you praise?"

In theory, Sheol was the most egalitarian of kingdoms. Nevertheless, some prophets couldn't resist the temptation to assign especially dishonorable sections to some of Israel's most despised enemies. Ezekiel consigned the armies of Egypt to an area reserved for the warriors of oppressor nations. There it joined the hordes of Assyria whose graves were to be found "in the uttermost parts of the Pit." And, of course, that is where one would expect to find Edom, whose rulers were laid among those who "are killed by the sword; they lie with the uncircumcised, with those who go down to the Pit." (Ezek. 32:20–22,29).

To a significant degree, Israel's lack of interest in an organized afterlife reflected the ANE environment in which it was immersed and to which it was a relatively late comer. In Mesopotamia, the dead all journeyed to "the land of no return," a Sheol-like abode "bereft of light where their sustenance is dust and their food is clay."[8] As in Israel, a "bad" death included a dishonorable disposition of the body or dying in an unknown locale. The shades of these restless souls roamed the land endlessly, bringing disease and other misfortune on the living. But in the entire ANE outside of Egypt, no compelling evidence has been adduced that points to a post-mortem judgment of the deceased.[9]

In sharp contrast to this picture of the ancient world, Egypt developed the first and most elaborate system of an organized afterlife, including bodily resurrection. By the thirteenth century B.C.E., when Moses led the children of Israel out of Egyptian bondage, the idea of judging the moral attributes of the resurrected individual had been in place for at least a millennium. In one version of this tradition, a person's good and bad deeds are arranged in "heaps" before a tribunal of severe judges. In another, the decedent's heart is weighed on a balance against a feather, the symbol of "truth" or justice.[10] Whether the Israelites consciously rejected such theodicy because it derived from their hated oppressors, must remain conjectural.

Though a full-fledged post-mortem existence is not portrayed in the OT, as it happened, several established principles of Yahwism were "pre-adapted" to this idea. By pre-adaptation, we refer to those concepts that arise and function in one context, but subsequently facilitate the maturation of other, very different, ideas. The tradition of judgment that bipolarized the populace into "righteous" and "wicked," the post-exilic, Job-type frustration with the DH, and the increasing recognition that sin might not be the sole cause of suffering—all these served as congenial antecedents to the reformulation of the retributional principle.

The notion of a precipitous action by God in judgment against Israel and/or the nations—variously known as "that day," the "Day of the LORD" and similar formulations—preconditioned the faithful to the expectation of a certain date of reckoning. In the seventh century B.C.E. Book of Zephaniah, the LORD, in retribution for cultic sins, threatens to "sweep away everything from the face of the earth" (1:2). The day of judgment approached rapidly:

> The great day of the LORD is near,
> near and hastening fast;
> the sound of the day of the LORD is bitter,
> the warrior cries aloud there.
> That day will be a day of wrath,
> a day of distress and anguish,
> a day of ruin and devastation,
> a day of darkness and gloom. . . .
>
> —Zeph. 1:14–15

The most significant single factor promoting the shift in retributional venue was the mind-set that produced writing known as apocalyptic (="revelation"). In this colorful, "not yet" literature, God reveals—through visions, dreams, and angelic mediators—a transcendent time and place in which the righteous and wicked are to be judged and requited for their earthly deeds. Most apocalypses are thought to have been produced in sects or communities that suffered at the hands of the political and/or religious power structure. As a result, these alienated segments of society had lost their faith in the inclination or ability of God to maintain his traditional retributional program. In this radically new (for Israel) world view, the focus shifts from the "here and now" to the "there and then."

Many scholars find an embryonic form of the full-blown apocalypse in the work of post-exilic prophets, which stressed an eschatological (End-time) judgment. Drawing a sharply definitive line between the prophetic and apocalyptic world views is impossible. The prophetic retains the traditional hope that retributional solutions to the community's problems can be realized on this earth within an historical context. In the more pessimistic apocalyptic perspective, such hope is abandoned. The utopian apocalyptist looks beyond the irredeemable evil on earth to a supernatural time and place where God's sovereignty will be restored and the righteous vindicated.[11]

A transition from prophetic eschatology toward the apocalyptic is found in the late sixth-century prophet, the so-called "Third Isaiah" (Isa. 56–66). In the following "early apocalyptic" passage, the LORD projects a radical transformation, but one that will remain within the bounds of history:

> For I am about to create new heavens
> and a new earth;
> the former things shall not be remembered
> or come to mind. . . .
> I will rejoice in Jerusalem,
> and delight in my people;
> no more shall the sound of
> weeping be heard in it,
> or the cry of distress.
> No more shall there be in it
> an infant that lives but a few days,
> or an old person who does not
> live out a lifetime. . . .
>
> —Isa. 65:17,19–20a

The Radical Shift in Retributional Venue

The eschatological vision alters drastically in 1 Enoch, a collection of writings that includes the earliest true apocalypses, which date to the late third century B.C.E. 1 Enoch is one of the Pseudepigrapha, intertestamental books that influenced both the Jewish and Christian canons but, for one reason or another, were not included in them. The apocalyptists chose Enoch as their pseudonym in recognition of the ancient worthy in the seventh generation from Adam whom God translated directly into heaven (Gen. 5:24).

In 1 Enoch 1–36, holy angels conduct Enoch on a tour of the heavens and the far corners of the earth that "none among human beings" had ever seen before. In these exotic environs, he observes "the cornerstone of the earth," the "pillars of heaven," and souls "carried by the clouds." Sheol was located inside a great mountain and had taken on an entirely new function. It now served as a receptacle for the souls of the dead until the spiritual resurrection at the time of the "great judgment." In Sheol, Enoch could hear the troubled voice of Abel, the first human to die unjustly, calling eerily and unendingly to his assailant, Cain.[12]

The souls-in-waiting in Sheol had been segregated into the righteous, the sinners who had not been sufficiently punished during their lifetimes, and those who had. Those in the second category experience "great pain" as they await the great judgment; those in the third, who died violently on earth, are considered by that fact to have received adequate recompense (1 Enoch 22). Thus in the first detailed description of post-mortem retribution, we discover both an immediate and a final judgment. And, of course, judgment is wedded inseparately to the hereafter; we never find the latter without the former.

A second-century B.C.E. conclusion to 1 Enoch (Chapters 92–105) takes up anew the cognitive dissonance generated by the health and happiness of the wicked and the poverty and oppression of the righteous. But 1 Enoch offers a very different solution than that proffered by the prophets, the Psalms, or Job. Enoch counsels the suffering righteous not to be "sad" because, in proportion to their goodness, they had "fared not well" on earth (102:5). As one consolation, and unlike the sinners, they would have no need to "hide" on the day of the great judgment (104:5). Enoch swears that "the tablets of heaven," which had been revealed to him, disclosed that God had prepared for the righteous "all good things, and joy and honor." And in a declaration that the prophets could not make—and Job's God did not deign to make—Enoch asserts that "the spirits of those who died in righteousness shall live and rejoice; their spirits shall not perish, nor their memorial from before the face of the Great One unto all the generations of the world" (103:1–4).

Enoch identifies the wicked as the wealthy who oppress the poor and show no sign of misgiving for their behavior. Given their favorable socio-economic status, they are much more reluctant to give up the traditional view—that success derives from virtue— than are the poor. The normative DH places the prosperous in a positive light and suggests that their accusers may be less virtuous than they purport to be.[13]

Putting their faith in death as the great democratizer, the unrepentant wicked gloat that "As we die, so do the righteous die. What then have they gained by their deeds? . . . From now on we have become equal" (102:6–7). The ungodly also claim that their misdeeds go unnoticed by the Great One. Not so, counters Enoch—he has it on good Authority that their iniquities are recorded "every day" (104:7). At death, the souls of the wicked will descend to Sheol where they will experience "evil and great tribulation—in darkness, nets, and burning flame" (103:7). And all of this misery occurs prior to the great judgment! The doomed wicked must still face the prospect of unrelieved punishment: "Woe unto you, for there is no peace for you!" (103:8).

From the rich eschatological feast of 1 Enoch, we move to the more paltry fare of Daniel 12:1–3. Though it tantalizes with its brevity, this passage is significant because it represents the only unambiguous statement on post-mortem existence in the Hebrew Bible. An apocalypse, Daniel was written about 165 B.C.E. in the tense days of Antiochus IV Epiphanes (God made "manifest"), the Syrian Greek ruler of Israel and military heir of Alexander the Great. His persecution of the pious— principally the *hasidim* ("Faithful Ones"), the progenitors of the Pharisees—included prohibitions on circumcision and Torah study. It culminated in the "abomination that makes desolate," the placement of a statue of the Greek god Zeus within the precincts of Yahweh's holy temple.[14]

An angel conveys to Daniel the knowledge inscribed in "the book of truth," a vision of the turbulent last days of the present age (10:21). Following the death of the wicked Antiochus, in a time of great anguish, the archangel Michael shall arise to deliver Daniel's people, i.e., those whose names are "written in the book" (12:1). The focus then shifts to those who have gone down to Sheol:

> Many of those who sleep in the dust of the earth shall awake, some to everlasting life, and some to shame and everlasting contempt. Those who are wise shall shine like the brightness of the sky, and those who lead many to righteousness, like the stars forever and ever.
>
> —Dan. 12:2–3

This less-than-universal resurrection leaves many questions unresolved, but it did provide an answer to the most critical problem of the day—the apparent failure of God's system of justice in troubled times. The evidence of the senses could no longer be denied: contrary to the conventional teaching, those obedient to the Torah were the most likely candidates for a violent death at the hands of the wicked. Fortune and virtue had become uncoupled, or more accurately, had become inversely correlated. Since the righteous had manifestly not received justice in this world, God must have arranged for it in the next.[15]

The resurrectional fog of Dan. 12:1–3 lifts appreciably in 2 Maccabees, one of the Apocrypha ("hidden books") for Protestants, the last book in the OT canon for Roman Catholics. Written toward the end of the second century B.C.E. concerning events in the first half of the century, 2 Maccabees purports to be an historical narrative portraying the dramatic struggles within the Jewish community and between it and its Syrian Greek oppressors. In response to the depredations of Antiochus IV, the Maccabean family, led by Judas, spearheaded a successful revolt against their persecutors. That uprising eventually established the family (as the Hasmonean dynasty) as the dominant power in Israel in both the religious and political realms.

In 2 Maccabees, we witness a literal life-and-death struggle for the souls of men and women between two deities: King Antiochus, who considered himself an earthly manifestation of Greek divinity, and Yahweh, the demanding, unyielding and retributing God of Israel. In 2 Macc. 7, an "admirable" mother and her seven sons prepare to die rather than transgress the laws of the holy Torah—specifically the injunction against eating pork. Most significantly, their faith in divine justice now requires recompense in an afterlife.

In his dying breath, one son defiantly declared to Antiochus ("You accursed wretch") that though the king dispatched them from this life, God would raise them up "to an everlasting renewal of life, because we have died for his laws." Another brother, holding out his hands, announced his full faith in bodily resurrection: "I got these from Heaven . . . and from him I hope to get them back again." The youngest brother combined the traditional theology with the new. He admitted that God, in anger, had inflicted suffering on them "for a little while" because of their sins. But after this brief period of affliction, he and his family would drink "of ever-flowing life, under God's covenant."

A remarkable passage in 12:39–45 affirms the resurrection faith and introduces the idea of intercession by the living for the dead. These verses became the canonical basis of the Catholic doctrine that prayers for those in purgatory could be efficacious. Judas Maccabeus had discovered that a number of his fallen soldiers wore "sacred tokens" of idols under their tunics, a practice strictly forbidden by the Mosaic law. Attributing the soldiers' deaths to this sin, Judas took up a "sin offering" of silver in atonement and led prayers that the transgression might be wholly erased. In so doing, he affirmed his belief in the resurrection in the face of skeptics:

> For if he were not expecting that those who had fallen would rise again, it would have been superfluous and foolish to pray for the dead. But if he was looking to the splendid reward that is laid up for those who fall asleep in godliness, it was a holy and pious

thought. Therefore he made atonement for the dead, so that they might be delivered from their sin.

—2 Macc. 12:44–45

In the period following upon the Maccabean revolt, then, divine retribution of some type in an afterlife of some sort had become well-established, though it hardly progressed in a rectilinear fashion and was far from being endorsed unanimously. In the face of the very public fate of the martyrs, confidence in the efficacy of this-worldly judgment was badly shaken. The discordance was simply too great and too patent between what "was" and what "should be." As the theologian E. Renan has observed: "the blood of the martyrs was the veritable creator of belief in a second life."[16] Eventually, resurrection theology would lose its close association with persecution and become the standard mode of retribution for earthly deeds. But the oppression-persecution *Sitz im Leben* served as the trigger on the weapon that fatally wounded the long-standing orthodoxy.[17]

Viewed in terms of the statistical model presented in chapter 5, during the period from the third to the first century B.C.E., the actual correlation between virtue and circumstance shifted from nil (r=0) toward the negative (r=-1) (Fig. 4). Given the slippage built into the DH that we observed in chapter 5, the faithful could maintain confidence in the correlation of merit and fortune (r=+1), even though in reality there was little or none (r=0). But as piety came to be increasingly yoked to calamity (r=-1), the tension between the observed and the theoretical could no longer support belief. The radical modification of the DH that resulted removed it from the realm of verification and, therefore, from its status as a scientific hypothesis. The new solution would be no more subject to confirmation than the number of angels that can cavort on the head of a pin.

Released from the restraint of verification, the human imagination received a carte blanche to explore the possibilities of post-mortem judgment unembarrassed by facts—and explore them it did! During the intertestamental era, pluralism became the hallmark to such an extent that identifying a normative position is virtually impossible. Not until the first centuries of the Common Era—when the rabbinical and Christian positions

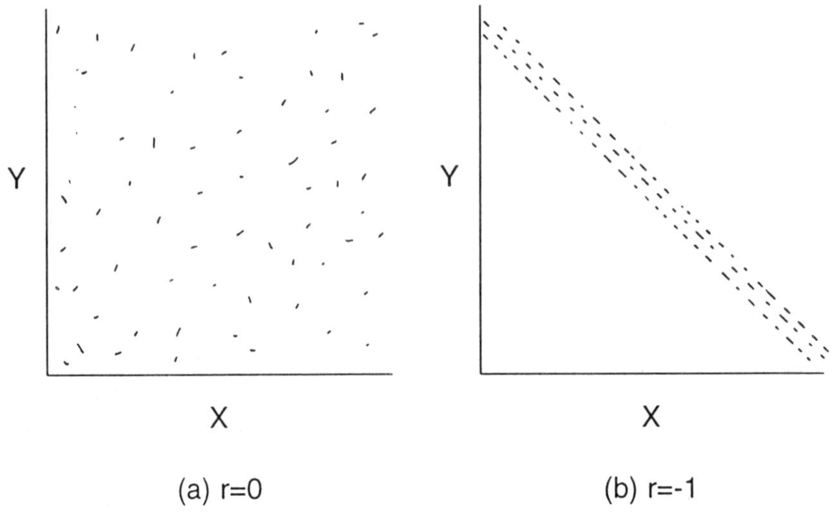

FIGURE 4. CORRELATION OF CIRCUMSTANCE AND VIRTUE. IN THESE THEORETICAL SCATTER DIAGRAMS, THE TWO VARIABLES, SOCIOECONOMIC CIRCUMSTANCE (X) AND MORALITY OR VIRTUE (Y), ARE NEGLIGIBLY (r=0) AND NEGATIVELY (r=-1) CORRELATED. IN THE LATTER CASE, THE PIOUS SUFFER MARTYRDOM FOR THEIR BELIEFS IN A PUBLIC MANNER.

emerged as dominant—would retributional orthodoxy be reestablished, and then only within quite broad limits.

Several major texts of the period make no mention at all of a judgmental hereafter—e.g., Esther, Ben Sirach, Tobit, Judith, 1 Baruch, 1 Maccabees, and 3 Maccabees among several others. On the other hand, the Testament of Abraham envisions three modes of judgment (fire, records, scales) and three separate judgments: by Abel immediately post-mortem; by all Israel of the Gentiles; by God in final determination for all.

While 2 Maccabees emphasizes resurrection of the body, 4 Maccabees—which covers much the same ground—eschews bodily resurrection in favor of the Greek-influenced idea of immortality of the soul. The canonical Wisdom of Solomon also features non-corporeal immortality and is entirely silent on resurrection—a difficult fact for some Christian interpreters since resurrection plays such a prominent role in Christian dogmatics.[18]

The Qumran community that preserved the Dead Sea Scrolls held decidedly apocalyptic world views, but ironically its texts rarely speak unambiguously of resurrection or a judgmental afterlife. This xenophobic sect perceived the outside world as Sheol and full acceptance into its community as the equivalent of obtaining eternal life. For them, biological death was inconsequential, since they lived within a frame of "realized eschatology" whereby the here and now is in continuity with the salvation promised at the End of Days.[19] This proleptic philosophy is also developed in the biblical Gospels and the Pauline Epistles.

Two Jewish apocalypses written in the wake of the destruction of Jerusalem in 70 C.E., 2 Baruch and 2 Esdras (= 4 Ezra), confront the difficult questions raised by that catastrophe and offer very different answers than the prophets who interpreted the events of 586 B.C.E. In the intertestamental literature generally, descriptions of the hereafter are abbreviated, opaque, and/or contradictory. But these two authors deal forthrightly and expansively with God's purposes for the world, and in so doing, describe in unique detail, the life of the world-to-come.

2 Baruch furnishes the most explicit description of the appearance of the resurrected body found in the intertestamental literature.[20] The precise nature of the resurrected body had become a concern in the contemporary Jewish and Christian literature, as exemplified in Paul's treatment of the problem in 1 Cor. 15. Concerned about perpetuation of the corrupt earthly bodies "by which evils are accomplished," Baruch questions God about the shape of the arisen forms (49:3). God responds that initially all bodies will retain their familiar shape in order to refute those who scoff at the possibility of resurrection. After this recognition has satisfied the doubters, the fate of the corporeal righteous and wicked will differ drastically:

> For the shape of those who now act wickedly will be made more evil than it is (now) so that they shall suffer torment. Also, as for the glory of those who proved to be righteous on account of my law . . . their splendor will then be glorified by transformations, and

> the shape of their face will be changed into the light of their beauty. . . . [T]hen both these and those will be changed, these into the splendor of angels and those into startling visions and horrible shapes. . . .
>
> —2 Bar. 51:2–3,5

The intertestamental literature frequently refers to a Final Judgment, which involves the collective resurrection of Israel or humanity at large. The same or other texts also depict an immediate post-mortem judgment, but make little effort to integrate the two judgments into a coherent pattern.[21] In fact, a completely satisfactory reconciliation of the two has eluded Judaism and Christianity down to the present day. 2 Esdras attempts to harmonize the two with an intermediate stage that receives a more detailed consideration than in any other writing.[22]

Through an angelic interpreter, God informs Ezra that at death the soul separates from the body and returns "to him who gave it" (7:78). The souls of the wicked do not enter into storehouses called "habitations," but immediately begin to "wander about in torments, always grieving and sad, in seven ways" (7:80). These seven modes of torment are largely contemplative and anticipatory, the most wretched being, ironically, the sight of "the glory of the Most High," against whom they had sinned grievously (7:87). Likewise, in this intermediate state, the righteous experience seven kinds of joy, the ultimate being the opportunity to gaze on "the face of him whom they served in life" (7:98). But the blessed enjoy their "freedom" for only seven days, after which they are "gathered in their habitations" to await, quite impatiently, the Final Judgment (7:101).

How long must the saved wait for their Grand Day? Here the LORD is much less forthcoming. The End-time will not arrive until a predetermined quota of the righteous has been realized, not until "that measure is fulfilled" (4:37). When the Final Day is at last reached, souls shall be reunited with their bodies and God shall assume his place on the "seat of judgment." At this late hour, intercessionary prayers for the wicked shall be futile: "compassion shall pass away, and patience shall be withdrawn. Only judgment shall remain. . . . " (7:33–34). Recompense follows swiftly: "The pit of torment shall appear, and opposite it shall be the place of rest; and the furnace of hell shall be disclosed, and opposite it the paradise of delight" (7:36).

The author of 2 Esdras attempts to extract cosmic meaning from the destruction of Jerusalem by the Romans. The seer Ezra adopts an aggressive, Joban stance in his queries to God, an attitude that yields valuable insights into the LORD's character and his Grand Design for the universe. God confirms that Jerusalem's demise stemmed from Israel's sins, an evil inclination that originated with Adam's transgression (3:21). But since God had blessed the Israelites with an infallible guide for godly behavior—the Torah—they were held fully accountable for their misdeeds (9:32–33).

But the disquieted Ezra was not easily turned aside. He was troubled by the ancient problem of the potency of a deity whose people have been subjugated by "them." The equally ancient answer of "divine wrath" no longer seemed to suffice. Granted that Israel had committed enormities, were they really any greater than those of the wicked "nations"? Why had the Most High permitted his chosen people to be dominated by heathens who, he had said, were no more than "spittle" in his creation? "If the world has indeed been created for us," Ezra asks, "why do we not possess our world as an inheritance? How long will this be so?" (6:55–59).

The numbers of those who suffered in the 70 C.E. calamity were so massive that Ezra was persuaded to move beyond strictly ethnic concerns to contemplate the plight of all humankind under God's grand plan. In addition to the present world of suffering, Ezra now knew that the hereafter promised to bring "delight to few, but torments to many" (7:47). Since all of God's children are inevitably "full of sins," they would be much better off in a world devoid of post-mortem retribution (7:68–69). Indeed, even the cattle and beasts of the field were better off, for they "do not look for a judgment" (7:66).

In response, God showed little sympathy for Ezra's sensitivities. To explain the huge disparity in the lost-to-saved ratio, he offered analogies drawn from both the physical and biological worlds. In the deposits of the earth, that which is more plentiful, such as lead and clay, is necessarily less valuable than the more rare elements, such as silver and gold (7:52–58). Just as the farmer sows many seeds that do not produce, so too those who "have been sown in the world will not all be saved" (8:41).

In several replies, the LORD appears totally callous to the predicament of the wayward. In a tone of indifference, he declares that "Many have been created, but only a few shall be saved" (8:3). In answer to Ezra's passionate solicitude for the multitude of lost souls, the God of Mercy states coldly that "I will not grieve over the great number of those who perish," for "they are set on fire and burn hotly, and are extinguished" (7:61).

Basically, God gives Ezra two answers to his deeply troubled questions, neither of which is satisfying. Like Job, he is reproached as a mere mortal for attempting to comprehend the inscrutable ways of God with man (4:2; 5:35). The more prominent response derives from the assertion that God made "not one world but two" (7:50). This solution requires the "patience" of the righteous—both in this world and the next—a virtue much celebrated in the tradition. An exasperated angel asks Ezra why he doesn't redirect his attention from "what is now present" to "what is to come" (7:16). It is painfully obvious that the Most High would rather promise the future than explain the present.[23]

The Appearance of Satan

In addition to the judgmental afterlife, another basic concept with an anemic OT career manifests itself full-blown in the Talmud and NT. In these later texts, a source of universal power, entirely evil, i.e., Satan or the Devil, comes to operate independently of the one omnipotent God. In the entire Hebrew Bible, a celestial Satan ("Adversary" or "Accuser") makes but three named appearances, and in each instance, he acts only under narrowly-circumscribed, divine direction. Of these, the most startling is 1 Chron. 21:1 where the Chronicler jolts the reader with the substitution of "Satan" for "God" as the initiator of the infamous census of Israel (2 Sam. 24). In this passage, theological progress may also be reflected in the name as a proper noun,

"Satan," as distinguished from the other two instances where it is a common noun indicating an office or function ("the Satan").[24]

In several intertestamental creation mythologies, Satan appears as an angel (Satanael) who is in good standing in the heavenly court. Blessed with a surfeit of angelic hubris, he refuses to bow down to the "mud and dirt" represented by the subsequently-created Adam. Responding to this rebellion, God stripped the "- el" (="God") from his name and expelled him and his angelic cohorts from heaven. Subsequently, the antigod becomes associated with all manner of natural and human evil, the implacable enemy of the true God. The tardiness with which this dualistic concept captured ancient Israel must be attributed to the impressive hold of the monotheistic ideal. The Israelites preferred to attribute evil to sin rather than entertain the possibility of a universal power not totally subservient to the monistic Deity. [25]

During the intertestamental period—rich in angelology and demonology—the most powerful of these celestial figures comes fully into his own. The expansive literature of the era fills the gap between the weak Satanic images of the OT and the robust ones of the Common Era writers. The variety of names and activities of the "evil one" is so great that identification of a tradition norm is not possible. Functional synonyms—often more popular that "Satan"—include Belial, Mastema, Sammael, Asmodeus, Apollyon, Beelzebub, and Prince of Darkness. The Hebrew "Satan" translates into Greek as *diabolos,* which becomes "devil" in English.

Many writers of the Greco-Roman period took advantage of the emergence of this new, autonomous center of power to absolve God from any "evil" intent or conduct. Like the Chronicler at 1 Chron. 21:1, they revisit some of the more celebrated OT incidents and assign to Satan the role originally played by God. In so doing, they restrict the character of the Deity to his more positive attributes. This sea change in the providence of God lends support to the contention that Satan may be perceived profitably as the dark side of God when he was fully monistic. The metamorphosis has had a profound impact on the perceptions of the Deity to the present day.[26]

Recasting the role of God is prominent in Jubilees, a mid–second century B.C.E. writing popular with the sect that produced the Dead Sea Scrolls. Chock full of angels and demons, it purports to be a revelation divulged to Moses at Mount Sinai. Jubilees takes a harsh "us-them" position, declaring flatly that all the uncircumscribed are destined for total annihilation (15:26). All nations belonged to the LORD, but he had "sanctified" only Israel, and had commissioned duplicitous angels to lead the Gentiles "astray" from following him (15:31).

In Jubilees, evil derives from a supernatural source, but one that specifically excludes God. At several morally questionable junctures in Scripture, the author replaces God with the perfectly evil Satan. It is now Satan (called "Mastema," which means "hatred") who suggests that Abraham's merit be tested by directing him to sacrifice his son Isaac (17:15–16; cf Gen. 22:1). It is "Prince Mastema" who makes the enigmatic attack on Moses on his return to Egypt (48:2-3; cf Exod. 4:24). And it is Mastema who hardens the hearts of the Egyptians (48:17; cf Exod. 4:21) and slaughters the first-born of Egypt (49:2; cf Ex. 12:29). In these roles, Mastema performs as a semi-autonomous agent, still responding to God's will but growing increasingly independent of it.

In other writings, Satan—now unchained from his ties to the Godhead—freely engages in activities that God at his most truculent would have pursued only reluctantly. In the dualistic Martyrdom and Ascension of Isaiah—the core of which dates to the second century B.C.E.—the biblical contrast between the "good" King Hezekiah and his idolatrous son, Manasseh, is heightened by the introduction of a very independent Satan. Evidently unimpressed with the Chronicler's attempted rehabilitation of Manasseh, the author portrays the wicked king in the thrall of Satan, "the angel of iniquity who rules this world" (2:4). The prophet Isaiah—appalled by Manasseh's cultic enormities in Jerusalem—distanced himself from the abominations by withdrawing to a remote location in the desert (2:7–8). But with the help of a "bad" Samaritan, the Satan-possessed Manasseh seized the prophet and "sawed him in half with a wood saw" (5:11).

Thus Satan and his angelic accomplices came to patrol the earth and the heavens as they willed, promoting misfortune and misery wherever they roamed. In Jewish tradition, the person of Satan became identified with the *yezer ha-ra,* an "inclination to evil," which makes its appearance at birth in every individual. This view of the psychological constitution of humankind was encouraged by biblical passages such as Gen. 8:21 in which the human heart is said to be "evil from youth." Unfortunately, the evil inclination gets an enormous head start in ontogeny since the *yezer ha-tov,* the inclination to good, does not appear on the scene until puberty.[27]

The potent adversary of Jesus whom the reader encounters early in the NT text would have been familiar enough to the contemporary audience but a puzzle to OT authors from Moses to Malachi. But a major article of Christian faith has been the insistence that in the end—that is, at the Final Judgment—the Prince of Darkness will be utterly destroyed. In the canon, that "ancient serpent" is cast into the "lake of fire" to be tormented "day and night forever and ever" (Rev. 20:10). By just that margin is Christianity saved from its own "lake of fire," for it avoids thereby that most unwelcome of theological epithets—a "dualistic" religion.

Salvation Prospects for Jews and Gentiles

With the establishment of the afterlife solution early in the Common Era, religious authorities scrambled to anchor the new doctrine firmly in traditional soil. Theirs was not an easy task since, as we have noted, the OT hardly knows the concept. Nevertheless, the leaders of Pharisaic-rabbinic Judaism sought to prove by the written Torah (Scripture) that afterlife propositions in the oral Torah (Mishnah) were valid. Specifically, they wanted to demonstrate that the Mishnaic declaration—"All Israelites have a share in the world to come"— could be derived from the Bible. Such a "proof" was especially critical since denial that the statement carried biblical authority excluded one from its benefits.

The ingenious rabbis adduced "evidence" from all three divisions of Scripture, employing the allegorical method, which probes for "deeper meanings" of the text. Their approach may be demonstrated by their interpretation of Exod. 6:4, a passage wherein God states that he established his covenant with the Patriarchs "to give them" the land of Canaan. Since the Patriarchs died long before Israel subdued the land, this statement could only mean that the Patriarchs would possess the land in a future resurrected state.[28]

Around the turn of the era, in both Palestinian and Hellenistic Judaism, the primary focus of salvation remained on the corporate, i.e., the nation of Israel, rather than on the individual, though the two modes were combined with some frequency. As E.P. Sanders has described the predominant salvific mode: "salvation comes by *membership* in the covenant, while obedience to the commandments *preserves* one's place in the covenant."[29] Losing that largely hereditary place was not easy; it could only be achieved, if at all, through the most gross transgressions, such as rank apostasy or an "incurable" predisposition to sin.[30]

On the prospects of a promising hereafter for non-Israelites, opinions varied, though they tended to be pessimistic. A few texts, such as 2 Esdras, value only individual merit independent of ethnicity. Many, such as 2 Baruch, underscore the salvific value of God's covenant with Israel, though admitting of the possibility that the most righteous Gentiles might be saved. Still others, such as Jubilees and the Dead Sea Scrolls, foreclose that possibility altogether.[31]

Early in the Common Era, the rabbis approved a legal code defining divine expectations of Gentiles that has framed the relationship between Judaism and all other peoples to the present day. This "judicial" exercise served principally as a vehicle to define both "us" and "them"—an "as if" fantasy of the marginalized. It could not have represented practical legislation since, after 70 C.E., a Jewish state did not wield political power over non-Jews.[32]

The rabbis taught that, following the universal flood, God had given to the sons of Noah, i.e., all humankind, a set of moral precepts that he expected them to observe (Gen. 9:1–17). The seven "Noahide Laws" include the mandate to establish a system of just laws and prohibitions against idolatry, blasphemy, homicide, theft, sexual immorality, and—the easiest to observe—eating flesh torn from a living animal. It was held that if the Canaanites had obeyed the seven laws, God would not have driven them out of the land. A Gentile who did accept the laws was considered a *ger toshab* ("resident alien") or even a "semi-convert" to Judaism. Violation of any of the seven, the rabbis ruled, would bring a sentence from a Jewish court of death by decapitation.[33]

Although seven pales in comparison with the 613 *mitzvot* that Jews are expected to keep, the Noahide "laws" may more accurately be viewed as legislative areas, since each implies a number of commandments. Aaron Lichtenstein has calculated that at least 66 of the 613 *mitzvot* are implicated. For example, "sexual immorality" follows closely the several proscriptions of Lev. 18, including that which prohibits homosexuality. Since only 271 *mitzvot* are operative in the absence of the Jerusalem temple, the overall ratio reduces to 271 to 66, or approximately 4:1.[34] But for those committed to a different faith tradition—e.g., the one billion Hindus and Buddhists—keeping the Noahide Seven becomes an impossibility since the practices of these religions were, and are, considered "truly idolatrous.[35]

During the first centuries of the Common Era, the rabbis also decreed that "All the righteous men of the nations of the world have a share in the world to come." This doctrine of salvation for the non-Jew appears generous since it does not require conversion to Judaism—most especially when contrasted with the traditional position of Christianity that "outside the Church there is no salvation."[36] The issue then narrows to the controlling definition of a "righteous" Gentile (*hasidei ummot ha-olam*).

A more precise answer to the question had to await the twelfth-century advent of Moses Maimonides ("Rambam"), said to be "the most illustrious figure in Judaism in the post-talmudic era, and one of the greatest of all time."[37] Maimonides linked the Noahide Laws to the definition of a "righteous Gentile," asserting that complete fulfillment of the former enlisted one forever in the ranks of the latter. But he joined them in a manner that has remained controversial to the present day.

Maimonides confirmed that while no coercion should be exerted on Gentiles to convert to Judaism, they could be compelled, upon penalty of death, to accept the Noahide Seven. The "righteous heathen" would have a portion in the world to come provided that he fulfilled the letter of the seven laws—and provided that he believed that the God of Israel, Yahweh, had revealed them to Moses, and not because of his own "reasoned conclusion."[38] He based this theological thunderbolt on his conviction that our sense of morality must derive ultimately, not from reason or natural law alone, but from divine revelation. The great philosopher's proposition has remained controversial especially since it tends to subvert the traditional position of Judaism that it is a religion of "doing" while Christianity is a religion of "believing."[39]

The fact that the Noahide laws may be found in the codes of the ANE two or more millennia before their rabbinic formulation testifies to their universality. The resourceful Christian theologian Wilhelm Vischer interpreted the laws as universal "emergency orders" that God had issued to sustain the heathen until the coming of Jesus Christ.[40] The laws have been widely praised by both Christians and Jews because they set only "the bare minimum standards" for Gentile morality and impose no conversion requirement.[41] As a significant step toward universal tolerance and understanding, they have been lauded as "one of the most remarkable initiatives in the history of the monotheistic religions."[42]

But a concept that excludes from the hereafter major segments of humankind, prescribes capital punishment for its violation, and, in its major formulation, insists that all humanity recognize the power of its God—such a doctrine is in need of additional work as an instrument of universalism. In their eisegetical enthusiasm, its advocates have read more universality into it than its particularism will sustain. The idea that the universal God tolerates, even champions, any sort of selective standard among his children is insulting on its face. As the distinguished Jewish scholar Jacob Neusner laments with respect to the differential expectations: "Of you God wants civility; of us, holiness."[43]

Christianity

Christianity brought to the world its own unique requirements for salvation, but the NT writers enfolded the afterlife version of the retributional principle smoothly and firmly into the heart of their theology. Given the Judaic milieu of first-century Palestine and the Diaspora, Christianity proffered few retributional innovations outside the specifics related to the Christ-event. That event altered only the mode, not the essence, of the traditional judgmental principle. God watched, recorded in a "book of life," and on a Day of Judgment imposed upon all his subjects a sharply-dichotomous verdict. For the righteous, that meant eternal life, for the wicked, eternal damnation.

The nuclear ideas would have been commonplace to first-century Jews. It was "a fearful thing" to fall into the hands of the Almighty (Heb. 10:31); nevertheless, everyone must stand before the "judgment seat of God" (Rom. 14:10). The peoples of all nations assembled before him would be segregated from one another "as a shepherd separates the sheep from the goats" (Matt. 25:32). One could expect to receive firm and just recompense without "partiality" (Acts 10:34): "The one who believes and is baptized will be saved; but the one who does not believe will be condemned" (Mark 16:16). Jesus taught that in the everlasting kingdom the righteous would "shine like the sun" while the evildoers would be thrown into the "furnace of fire, where there will be weeping and gnashing of teeth" (Matt. 13:42–43).

But with a potent Devil and post-mortem recompense in play, the Son does not approach the OT God of Justice in this-worldly "harshness" or "wrath." Under the New Covenant, the loving and redeeming Son almost totally eclipses the Father who had brought both weal and woe in the here and now to a Satanless, OT world. In the Gospel of John, Jesus declares that "just as the Father raises the dead and gives them life, so also the Son gives life to whomever he wishes. The Father judges no one but has given all judgment to the Son. . . . " (5:21–22). On the Last Day, Jesus will resurrect those who have died (John 6:40) and then, as the one "ordained by God," will judge the living and the dead (Acts 10:42; 2 Tim. 4:1). This function is confirmed in the

Apostle's Creed where, after his ascension, Jesus sits at the right hand of God and "From thence he shall come to judge the quick and the dead." The Son will judge—and judge severely—but only in the world to come.

The criteria for judgment in the NT vary from author to author— and even within the writings of a single author. But, basically, they collect around one of two poles: faith and works. The tension between the two has resulted in disputes among Christians from the first century to the present time. Stripped to its core, the faith-works issue is identical to the one Maimonides addressed in the twelfth century with respect to the righteous Gentiles and the Noahide laws.

Many passages suggest that faith in the risen Christ appears to obviate the necessity of those deeds that had been a mainstay of salvation in Judaism. In John 6:40, Jesus states baldly that it is God's will that "all who see the Son and believe in him may have eternal life." In his heroic attempts to define the nascent movement ("us") vis-à-vis the parent religion ("them"), Paul repeatedly extols the primacy of faith: "God decided . . . to save those who believe" (1 Cor. 1:21); "For Christ is the end of the law so that there may be righteousness for everyone who believes" (Rom. 10:4); "a person is justified not by the works of the law but through faith in Jesus Christ" (Gal. 2:16). And, of course, there is the famous John 3:16: "For God so loved the world. . . . "

Other passages support the traditional position of Judaism that deeds are the sine qua non of salvation. The Judge was expected to "repay everyone for what has been done" (Matt. 16:27); he would re-tribute "according to each one's deeds" (Rom. 2:6). At the End-time, the dead would arise from their graves—"those who have done good, to the resurrection of life, and those who have done evil, to the resurrection of condemnation" (John 5:29). In his famous answer to the lawyer's question about the criteria for eternal life, Jesus declares that acts of love toward God and man represent fulfillment of the greatest commandments (Luke 10:25–28; Mark 12:28–34).

For most modern believers, the most satisfying resolution is that which rejects the "either-or" approach to "faith" and "works." In theory, if the former is sufficiently potent, the latter will necessarily follow. In the early Christian community, "James" disdained the inclination of some to rest their laurels on faith alone, devoid of deeds. He countered that "just as the body without the spirit is dead, so faith without works is dead" (Jas. 2:26).

The authors of the NT lived in times marked by strong eschatological expectations, a keen anticipation that the "last days" were at hand, perhaps to arrive even before Jesus' generation had passed away (Matt. 16:28). This line of thought culminates appropriately in the NT's closing book, Revelation, an apocalypse written late in the first century during a period of Roman persecution. If the Father and Son had become "domesticated" in the Gospels and Epistles, their inherently bipolar nature reappears with a vengeance in the Last Days. Christians who prate about the biblical "God of love" haven't read the last chapter of the Book.[44]

The function of Revelation is similar to that of Deuteronomy 28 though their retributional venues differ radically: to impress indelibly upon the audience the horrific fate that awaits the habitual sinner. In Revelation, "John" describes visions of the End-time that Jesus the Christ had revealed to him. Surrealistic imagery and mysterious symbols dominate the writing and invite a wide range of interpretations. But a focus on the retributional theme reveals, in bold outline, the primary message of God and the author.

Revelation draws extensively on the OT tradition; 278 of its 404 verses carry allusions to OT passages, though direct quotation is uncommon.[45] It describes in vivid and repetitive detail the judgment of God and Christ and the multiple and prolonged suffering of all humanity in the End-time. The lost-to-saved ratio is congruent with that envisioned in 2 Esdras, but no Ezra appears to shed tears for the multitudes that fail to meet the criteria. In fact, sadistic pleasure in the hopeless plight of the damned dominates the book, a sentiment that the Church enshrined as the "abominable fancy." The terroristic keynote is sounded at 8:13: "Woe, woe, woe to the inhabitants of the earth. . . . "

For five excruciating months, locusts torture those who lack the "seal of God" on their foreheads, inflicting on them such unbearable pain that they "long to die." But environmentalists may take comfort in the fact that God's angels instruct the voracious insects to avoid damaging the grass or "any green growth" (9:3–6). On signal from an angelic trumpeter, the people are peppered with hail and fire that is "mixed with blood" (8:7). Hailstones weighing some one hundred pounds brought such "fearful" destruction that the victims could only "curse God" (16:21). With a sharp sickle in hand, an angelic vintner collected "the vintage of the earth," threw it into "the great wine press of the wrath of God," from whence blood flowed "as high as a horse's bridle," for a distance of two hundred miles (14:17–20).

Still in the "pre-Judgment" phase—though still in fulfillment of God's eternal purposes—the wicked are tormented with "fire and sulphur" in the continuing presence of the angelic host and the Lamb (14:10). Eventually—and to the blessed relief of all but the most demoniacal—the final curtain begins its descent. Christ announces that he will "repay according to everyone's work" (22:12). The people are judged "according to their works" before the "great white throne" of God. The righteous take up residence in the New Jerusalem, a holy city in no need of illumination from the sun or the moon, for "the glory of God is its light, and its lamp is the Lamb" (21:23). Those whose names cannot be found in the "book of life" are pitched summarily into the "lake of fire," there to join the world's most evil entities—Rome, Satan, Death, and Hades (20:11–15).

Revelation is a fitting denouement of the Bible since it radiates the intolerance that so characterizes both testaments. To a world desperately in need of forbearance, then as well as now, it offers only a mean-spirited parochialism. Certainly the authors of Deuteronomy, Ezra, Matthew, and John, inter alia, would have appreciated its uncompromising exclusivity and its religious imperialism. Like Third Isaiah, the author is at pains to denominate God as "King of the nations!"; to picture all the nations walking by the light of God's glory (21:24); and to fantasize that all peoples will bring to the New Jerusalem "the glory and honor of the nations" (21:26).

In the Eschaton the heathen, by definition, would be found outside the gates of the heavenly city, in the company of "dogs . . .

and idolaters, and everyone who loves and practices falsehood" (22:15). But in a triumphalist image that quickens the pulse of every evangelist, a "great multitude" from every ethnic, political, and linguistic entity on earth assembles before the great throne and cries out in unison: "Salvation belongs to our God who is seated on the throne, and to the Lamb!" (7:9–10).

While Revelation provides colorful minutia of End-time events, it doesn't confront at all the problem of double judgment, one of Christianity's most questionable legacies from Judaism. So long as the faithful anticipated the Last Day in the foreseeable future, the interval between the individual's death and the Last Judgment could not become an issue. But as the world stubbornly persisted—and the interval lengthened to years, generations and centuries—the question of an immediate judgment came to the fore. Exactly what took place at death, at the Last Judgment, and during the lengthy, and lengthening, intervening period? Were two judgments—an immediate or particular and a final or general— really just or even necessary?[46]

From the apocalyptic tradition of Judaism, Christianity inherited the notion of bodily resurrection at the End-time, a complex that is linked closely to the judgment of ethnic groups, Jews and non-Jews. But Christianity broke through the bounds of ethnicity to focus on the individual and, in addition, it had to adjust to the afterlife implications of the disconfirmation produced by the delayed Parousia. Some NT passages (e.g., Luke 16:19–31; 23:43)suggest that immediate judgment is possible, though the norm remains elusive. The NT produces nothing like the vivid description of the intermediate state found in 2 Esdras.

A partial solution came in the form of purgatory, an intermediate state perceived by the Church as an opportunity for expiatory purification for those who die in God's grace but stand in need of additional atonement. But this concept left unanswered a host of questions, some of which have received Papal attention over the centuries. For example, did the blessed experience the full glory of God at death, or did that come only after the long wait for the Final Judgment?[47] Protestants rejected purgatory altogether since in their minds it was too closely associated with the administrative abuses of the Church. That rejection re-created the problem that purgatory was designed to fix.

In whatever manner the intermediate state is conceived, the bald fact remains that Christianity inherited "one judgment too many."[48] But in both the Catholic and Protestant traditions—utilizing mental gymnastics that the British call "jiggery-pokery"—the historic trend has been to empower the immediate judgment, leaving the Final Judgment in an otiose state. This trajectory undoubtedly devolves from the human inclination to impatience at having to wait "forever" for final results, whether the issue be an election, a horse race, or the fate of the immortal soul. In consequence, the Final Judgment has become a vestigial structure, a theological wisdom tooth or vermiform appendix.

Continued This-Worldly Retribution

Though the principal venue of divine justice shifted permanently to the hereafter, humankind has refused to let go entirely of the idea of retribution in the here and now. A God disengaged from this-worldly affairs—even if still available for comfort and guidance through prayer—is far too distant and Deistic for most mortals, though the price may be to understand pain as punishment. The upshot is an unpatterned, catch-as-catch-can doctrine, but, nonetheless, one that remains as a significant, supplementary component of theodicy. Over the centuries, the faithful have often employed it in explanation of the misfortune of their enemies, though it may be turned back on "us" as well.

Among the early Jewish thinkers, the notion of at least occasional this-worldly recompense rested comfortably and unsystematically alongside the more carefully-developed post-mortem paradigm. In the Wisdom of Solomon, which includes an unambiguous portrayal of a judgmental afterlife, the author still takes comfort in the fact that, though Israel had been judged with "strictness," God, in his "goodness," had punished its enemies "ten thousand times more" (12:21-22). In 2 Maccabees, the seven sons persecuted unto death by Antiochus IV acknowledge that their present suffering derives from their sins (7:18,32). As we have seen, when Judas Maccabeus discovered idolatrous amulets on the bodies of Jewish soldiers, "it became clear to all that this was the reason these men had fallen" (12:40).

But this-worldly and other-worldly punishment may be correlated, and in an inverse fashion. In 1 Enoch, one of the receptacles in Sheol is reserved for those souls whose violent deaths exempted them from post-mortem judgment (22:12–13). In the Testament of Abraham, God states flatly that "those whom I destroy while they are living on the earth, I do not requite in death" (14:15). The seer in 2 Baruch comforts the Israelites with the thought that their current suffering will immunize them from eschatological judgment, so that they may not "be condemned at the end and be tormented" (78:6). In the NT story of the rich man and the poor man (Lazarus), their afterlife fates are exact reciprocals of their earthly circumstances (Luke 16:19–31).

Early in the Common Era, the rabbis honed to a fine point the concept of retributional reciprocity. They reasoned that since our earthly existence was so fleeting, ultimate justice could be achieved only in the hereafter, where each person would receive just one type of recompense. In a decided advance over the absolutism of most biblical writers, they recognized that each individual represented a moral mosaic of good and evil. This ambivalence had to be accounted for somehow in this-worldly retribution, "For God is not suspected to execute judgement without justice."[49] The delicate balancing of earthly reward and punishment established "a sort of divine economy, lest the harmony of the next world should be disturbed."[50]

In this more nuanced theodicy, prosperity and suffering could signal moral standings in diametrical opposition to their traditional meanings. The basically wicked person who performed some good deeds would be rewarded for those in this life, so that the way would be paved for her unrelieved punishment in the next. The righteous who had sinned—as indeed all had—suffered in this world so that she might receive an uninterrupted blessing in the next. In this understanding—unfortunately not available to Job— misfortune no longer marked the incorrigibly wicked and became instead a desideratum—well, almost. One rabbi taught that if a person passed so much as forty days without adversity, he had already received his share of the world-to-come. Another held that if one suffered no major problems in this life, he should no longer even be considered a Jew.[51]

The dominant explanation of the mega-event of the era—the destruction of Jerusalem in 70 C.E.—fell back on the traditional DH that is trumpeted so loudly in the OT. As Jacob Neusner has observed, "all Judaic thinkers took for granted that the tragic events conveyed God's will and judgement."[52] The sin-solution has even found its way into modern Jewish liturgy where God's destruction of the second temple is attributed to "our sins."[53] Since the historic options narrowed to the admission of massive guilt or a declaration that impugned God's justice, the choice is not surprising.[54]

Though post-mortem judgment suffuses the NT, it also tantalizes with the possibility that the traditional DH may appear now and again. On occasion, Jesus appears to link sin and morbidity (e.g., Mark 2:1–12). In a type of vignette rare in the NT but relatively common in the OT, Ananias and his wife, Sapphira, lie about financial resources that they had promised to the Christian community. After they have been found out, each of the sinners drops dead on the spot (Acts 5:1–11). King Herod Agrippa is struck down by an "angel of the Lord" immediately after being hailed as a god by the people (Acts 12:23). Paul suggests to members of the church at Corinth that their abuse of the Lord's Supper has caused many to become ill and some to die (1 Cor. 11:30). On a much broader scale, Jesus predicts the destruction of the temple as a consequence of Jewish sin, thereby confirming Jewish theodicy.[55] Beyond this meager collection, more-or-less normal events that rely on the traditional DH for explication are rare.

In tension with the possibility of this-worldly retribution are passages that suggest that it is either of minor importance or nonexistent. Jesus recommends to a rich young man that he sell his possessions, give the proceeds to the indigent and thus build up his "treasure in heaven" (Matt. 19:21; see also Matt. 6:19–20). In response to queries concerning the relative moral standing of those who die violently, Jesus confirms that they are no worse sinners than those who survive (Luke 13:1–5). He rebukes those Disciples who want to call down heaven's fire on unfriendly Samaritans (Luke 9:54–55) and those who attribute blindness to either the sins of the victim or his parents (John 9:1–3). In a celebrated verse (Matt. 5:45), Jesus asserts that the Father causes the sun to rise on both the righteous and the wicked, brings rain on both the just and the unjust. Paul goes so far as to claim that God has delegated to the civil authorities his judicial role in mundane affairs. In this reading, it is the state judicial apparatus, as "the servant of God," that brings down divine "wrath" on the miscreant (Rom. 13:1–7).

Despite problematical NT "proof," Christians have often seen the hand of the God of Justice in earthly affairs, in either the normal course of events or as a result of their prayers. A God who takes note of the sparrows' fate and counts the hairs of the head (Matt. 10:29–30) can be expected to engage now and again in some this-worldly retributory activity. Earthquakes, floods, eclipses, comets, meteorites, and malformed animals are taken as "signs" that God contemplates momentous action. Prosperity may be interpreted readily as the smile of God, a view that Americans, Calvinists most especially, have cherished from the very beginning of their national history. In his farewell address, George Washington asked rhetorically whether "Providence has not connected the permanent felicity of a Nation with its virtue?"[56] Adversity may be perceived as the frown of God, particularly in the area of sexual behavior. For centuries, the devout have held that God invented venereal diseases to punish the promiscuous. The incidence of AIDS in the homosexual community has occasioned the most recent manifestation of this moralistic interpretation of naturalistic events.

For two millennia, Christians have taken a particular interest in the circumstance of their Jewish brethren, since in their wretched state, one could read directly the operation of God's justice and God's plan. From this linkage came the concept of the "reprobate" Jew, despised of God for his ancient role as Christ-killer and his continued rejection of the Son. The miserable condition of the "wandering Jew" in the Diaspora became living proof that God requited his "enemies" daily for their rejection of

Christian truth. In the Middle Ages and later, European states promulgated numerous laws severely restricting Jewish movement and economic opportunity—thus giving a significant human boost to the divinely-decreed, inverse correlation of Jewish sin and Jewish circumstance.[57]

This brings us to the controversial and emotional issue of the theology of the Holocaust. In 1948—just three years after the death camps had ceased their murderous work—a group of German Evangelical theologians declared that God had instituted the Holocaust as retribution for Jewish sin.[58] The Germans had evidently been doing the LORD's work. But in the decades that followed, that early straw proved to be a false indicator of Christian reaction. Protestant and Catholic officialdom responded overwhelmingly with a massive *mea culpa,* either expressed or implied. Their agreement that God's covenant with the Jewish people remains intact represents a major theological shift. Both peoples could now be considered as God's "elect" and as "partners in waiting" for the Eschaton. Of course, the man and woman in the pew may retain a somewhat less liberal view of the matter.[59]

Ironically, the most vocal exponents of the Holocaust-as-punishment theology have come from the ranks of Jewish Orthodoxy. Some ultra-Orthodox rabbis have interpreted Auschwitz variously as divine response to the eating of pork, the alleged enormities of Polish Jewry, the Zionist movement devoted to the establishment of a Jewish state, and in direct contradiction, the neglect of the self-same Zionist movement.[60]

Reaction among the more mainstream commentators to this radical theodicy has frequently shed more heat than light. The Jewish theologian Jonathan Sacks states, understandably, that "At some point the religious imagination rebels against adding to the evil of [the victims'] death the indignity of saying that it was justified."[61] The president of Yeshiva University, Norman Lamm, declares that the recourse to sin-as-explanation is "massively irrelevant, impudent, and insensitive." For him, "The enormity of this callousness, the outrageousness of such insensitive arrogance . . . is mindboggling. It is . . . unforgiveable."[62] The Christian theologian A. Roy Eckardt, who has proposed the ultimate Christian *mea culpa*—that Christ's resurrection somehow led to Auschwitz— recommends unceasing torture for those who perceive in the "Final Solution" the judgment of God.[63]

For our purposes, the question is restricted to the nature of divine justice and the character of God as revealed in Scripture. In super-heated discussions of Holocaust causation, appeal to the canon for guidance is nearly always finessed. We ask whether the idea of Holocaust-as-judgment is a reasonable deduction from the biblical principles of divine justice that we have been examining. We ask further if the implication of divine participation in the Holocaust is a justifiable inference from the biblically-derived character of God as we have drawn it.

Would the sanguinary God of Deut. 32:42, 2 Kings 10:30, Jer. 25:33, and Rev. 14:20 have grown faint at the sight of the blood of a sea of victims? Would the ethnic Cleanser of Num. 31:17, Deut. 20:16, 1 Sam. 15:3, 2 Kings 17:18, and Mal. 1:4 have hesitated to perform "moral surgery" on a population of "sinful" human beings? Would the Author of the "deserved" catastrophes of 721 B.C.E., 586 B.C.E., 167 B.C.E., and 70 C.E. have blanched before that of 1945 C.E.? Only our reluctance to accept the bipolar scriptural God clouds the answer. If one cannot live with reasonable deductions from the principles of the scriptural judicial system and its God, perhaps one needs to take a second look at that canon and its usefulness for the twenty-first century.[64]

8
The Ghost of Marcion

Nearly two thousand years ago, a charismatic spiritual leader left obscurity to energetically traverse the rugged countryside of the Near East. Attracting thousands of enthusiastic followers to his banner, he preached a message of love and asceticism, founded a popular Christian church and produced the first NT canon. Despised by the religious establishment for his innovative ideas, it vilified him in life and for centuries after his death. He lived in second-century C.E. Asia Minor (modern Turkey) and his name was Marcion.[1]

A century after Jesus' death, Christianity's growth potential clearly lay beyond Palestine in the Gentile world, primarily as a result of the apostle Paul's missionary activity. The time, the place, and the people had all shifted significantly from the first-century Palestine of the first Jewish Christians. The new recruits flocked in droves to the unadorned Christian message of love, redemption, and the promise of eternal life. They had no ethnic predisposition toward the people, the places, or the canon of Judaism. At this juncture, the nascent religion, itself, had no formal canon, creed, or authority structure. In this indeterminate theological milieu, Marcionism made its appearance and nearly carried the day.

Marcion's concerns centered on what today we recognize reluctantly as the discordance between the OT and the NT, the theological gulf that separates Malachi from Matthew. A plethora of basic questions assaulted his literalistic mind: the contradiction between Christianity's fervent claim to "newness" and its equally-passionate insistence that its roots reached deep into antiquity; the apprehensiveness inherent in embracing a God who, after thirteen hundred years, discards his people and covenant for an entirely different people and covenant; and the casuistry in adopting the Hebrew Bible as sacred Scripture, yet disdaining to keep its divine law or rituals, and despising those who do. If Christians could reject the Mosaic law, then why not the God who gave it?[2]

For Marcion, the utter contrast between the character of Yahweh and the Father of Jesus represented the ultimate issue. Marcion construed this materialistic world as a sorry and nonsensical place, replete with contradiction, violence, and suffering. Such an absurd and evil world could not possibly have been created and maintained by the loving Father who had sent his Son to redeem it. Informed by this understanding, Marcion took the logical, but very radical, step into ditheism—he recognized not one God, but two!

The God of the Hebrew Bible, Yahweh, had created the cosmos and ruled it as the God of Justice. He did not represent evil personified, i.e., he did not supplant the Devil. But he was characteristically harsh, arbitrary, and capricious. Above all— as the Hebrew Bible repeatedly confirms—he was concerned to render justice for humankind. The antithesis of the God of Justice was the Father of Jesus, a superior God of pure love and grace who had acted only recently through his Son to save the world from Yahweh. Strongly influenced by Paul's writings, which assigned primacy to faith over works (or the spirit over the flesh), Marcion gave the dichotomy its ultimate expression. He distanced the Christian Gods from the harshness of "justice" with a single, but significant, exception. Though the loving Christ was divested of retributional powers in this world, he assuredly would preside as the resolute Judge in the next.[3]

Since the Hebrew Bible served as the canon of the God of Justice, it necessarily followed that it could not play that role for Marcionite Christians. They were forced to look elsewhere for their sacred texts. They found them in a modified version of Luke as the sole gospel, the ten Pauline letters as the apostolic component, and Marcion's own "Antitheses," an appendage that reviewed the disparities between the Hebrew Bible and Jesus' teachings. These three documents represented the earliest known canon of a Christian community. Many scholars believe that its appearance provoked the development of the orthodox canon later in the second century.

Marcion was no scholarly recluse thinking deep thoughts in his ivory tower, but rather a practical, personable evangelical who took his simple message directly to the Gentile masses. They responded in such numbers that a dynamic church was soon established. It spread rapidly throughout the Roman empire and beyond, reaching its zenith in the latter decades of the second century when it may have rivalled in membership the orthodox institutions. By the third century, it had begun to decline, though it continued a presence into the fifth century especially in the eastern reaches of the empire.

Marcionite identification went beyond its distinctive theology. The church adopted several "Protestant" innovations, including the substitution of water for wine in the liturgy, the assignment of women to a prominent cultic role including that of baptizers, and the development of a weak administrative structure that encouraged the interaction of clergy and laity. Ironically, its ultimate demise can probably be attributed more to its biological than its theological demands. Evidently the church could live, even thrive, with the radical doctrine of ditheism and the ahistorical God of Love. But it couldn't survive its own Draconian criterion for membership: the insistence on the promise of celibacy as a prerequisite for baptism!

All that we know today of Marcion and his church comes from the writings of his enemies. The chief defenders of the orthodox faith, the Church Fathers, reacted to the threat with "horror and vehemence."[4] Their well-stocked verbal arsenal included the savage ad hominem attack. Irenaeus claimed that Marcion was "the proper mouthpiece of the Devil" who "countermands the truth in every detail."[5] For Polycarp, Marcion had become "the first-born of Satan," the Antichrist himself.[6] The most vociferous of Marcion's critics, Tertullian, said that—though Marcion's home region on the Black Sea had a dark reputation for "savagery"—the "most barbarous and melancholy thing" that had ever occurred there was the birth of the heretic. Marcion, Tertullian wrote, had attempted to abolish marriage, "nibbled away" the gospels, and "torn God Almight to bits with [his] blasphemies."[7]

The patristic response to the Marcionite theology drew extensively on the *Adversus Judaeos* (anti-Judaic) tradition that had its literary origins in the NT, especially in the Books of Matthew and John. (Even Jesus is said to have participated in this tradition; see, e.g., Mark 10:2–5.) In their energetic defense of the Jewish God, the Christian Fathers did not hesitate to denigrate the Jewish people. The dark side of Yahweh's persona that had been of such concern to Marcion was held to have been wholly necessary to control the intransigent Hebrews who had repeatedly rejected Christ's truth. If the particularities of the Mosaic law were to be discarded—as all Christians agreed—that repudiation did not reflect discredit on their divine author, but rather on the sinful dregs of humanity with which God had had to deal in the old, superseded dispensation.

Nevertheless, the Church Fathers argued that the Hebrew Bible contained such indispensable divine truths that it had to be stitched into the fabric of the Christian faith. The destruction of Jerusalem, the reprobate condition of the dispersed Jews, the replacement of the Jews by the Christians as God's elect—all this and more had been foreseen in the very texts that the heretic Marcion wanted to exclude. The "holy voices" in Scripture, Tertullian said, had warned the stiff-necked Jews that the fateful day would arrive when God would "transfer his favor" to worshipers who were "much more faithful."[8] Origen asserted that the heinous sins of the Jews, which included deicide, had caused God to destroy their nation. As a consequence, the Almighty had extended an "invitation to blessedness" to the Gentiles who welcomed in the new teaching "the simple and pure worship of God."[9]

The Fathers also attacked Marcion's "good" God, the "God of Love," because he had appeared so late on the scene. In the history of religion, the establishment of any ahistorical deity has been notoriously difficult and, indeed, this feature did represent a major embarrassment for the Marcionites. This was especially true in a cultural milieu that found no discordance between the age of the earth as popularly understood and that declared in the

Hebrew Bible. But modern scientists estimate the age of *Homo sapiens* at 100,000 years at least and the earth at 6 billion years. Within this chronological frame, the biblically based ages of Christ (2,000 years), Yahweh (3,300 years) and Elohim (6,000 years) all appear to be those of "late-comers."

Many interpreters have seen Marcion's Christianity as anti-Judaic, and so it may seem at superficial glance. But his theology left Judaism intact for the Jews—their God, Scripture, election, and Messiah. It eliminated heated claims of the rivals to a common text—precluding, for example, puerile contention over which tradition Jacob represented in the Jacob-Esau saga.[10] It also furnished critical "breathing room" for the antagonists, affording each the opportunity to develop a more dispassionate view of the "other." Certainly Marcion proclaimed the superiority of Christianity, but no more vigorously than did the rabbis Judaism. The full acceptance of any one tradition always carries with it the implicit rejection of all others, in the sense, say, that a serious Baptist implicitly rejects the Book of Mormon and the Catholic catechism.

But the orthodox theologians won the day, perfecting a dogma in which the inferiority of the Jewish people replaced the scandalousness of Marcion's Jewish God. The Fathers redeemed the reputation of God at the expense of God's elect. In this hermeneutic, Christians capture the Jewish God, Scriptures, election, and Messiah. Stripped of their ancient moorings, the despised and disinherited Jews are left to wander aimlessly over the earth, an horrific object lesson in God's judgment on the ungodly.[11] From this foul and dark soil grew the supersessionistic mushroom that has only begun to be reevaluated by Christians in the late twentieth century.

Since the Christian-specific message of the OT isn't apparent to the unaided eye, interpreters from NT times to the present day have struggled heroically to extract hidden or "spiritual" meanings from the ancient and obdurate text. Utilizing exegetical techniques that include chiefly prophecy, typology, and allegory, they attempt to uncover exotic designs totally foreign to the original authors, their redactors, and their audiences. In this hermeneutical world, Moses prefigures the cross in his upraised arms at the battle with Amalek (Exod. 17); the "virgin" in Isa. 7:14 predicts the appearance of Mary, the mother of Jesus, some seven hundred years later[12]; and everyone from Adam and Joshua to the Suffering Servant (Isa. 53) and the Red Heifer (Num. 19) become types of Christ. When the OT is properly interpreted, Gaetano Cardinal Stefanescki declares, it is nothing less than "pregnant with Christ."[13] This huge hermeneutical effort has been expended primarily to answer the implicit question that every novel religious movement must face: "Where has your God been?" Toward that end the first church historian, Eusebius, writing circa 300 C.E., declared that Christianity was the most ancient of all religions, though its central figure had appeared on the scene just three centuries earlier.

In the modern era, the "Christianization" of the OT has continued apace, but characteristically in a more subtle and sophisticated mode. In the field of "Biblical Theology," dedicated Christian scholars earnestly seek themes that will "unify" the Old Covenant and point it beyond itself toward its denouement in the New. Numerous candidates have been put forward—e.g., covenant, salvation history, promise-and-fulfillment, the Kingdom of God—but none has met with general acceptance or is likely to. The task is impossible simply because the OT represents the lengthy history of an ethnic unit, a *people,* embodying all the diversity of outlook and fluctuation of circumstance that the record of such an anthropological entity will necessarily entail. As Dale Patrick has wryly remarked, "The witness of the OT is radically pluralistic."[14] The OT refuses to give up its "unifying" theme because, as the diverse record of a people, it has none to give.

Marcionism per se disappeared well over a millennium ago, but the "ghost of Marcion" has continued to haunt the church.[15] It is said to have sponsored "creeping Marcionism"[16]; over the centuries a strong "tendency" to Marcionism [17] has remained "latent" in Christianity.[18] Many Christians—clerics and laypersons alike—have become "virtual Marcionites,"[19] drinking only reluctantly at the OT fount.The OT is said to "pose problems" for the minister "at every level," the most critical of which is "relevance."[20] Every preacher and Sunday school teacher knows that a great deal in the OT is "not easy" to relate to the Christian message, including lists of forbidding names that are "not even interesting."[21] The OT is said to represent the "biggest problem" in Bible-reading; it has become a matter of "grave concern," indeed it must be considered "a liability."[22] To see a Christian minister "torture and torment" an OT text into a "procrustean bed of . . . rigid hermeneutic" is indeed a "pitiful" sight.[23]

A leading champion of the OT cause, Elizabeth Achtemeier, deplores the infrequency with which the "old, old story" is preached from the modern pulpit. Since so many are "not very comfortable" with the OT or its God, it has become "largely a lost book" in many precincts of the church. For Achtemeier, the consequences of this neglect are "dreadful to behold." Without the foundation of the OT, she maintains, it becomes "almost impossible" to understand the character of our God, the nature of our world or ourselves as human beings.[24]

Faithful to two thousand years of Christian interpretation, Achtemeier affirms that Jesus the Christ was "the completion and fulfillment and final reinterpretation" of the nearly two thousand years of prior Jewish history. "Unless we preach from the Old Testament," she urges, "our people really cannot know who their Lord is."[25] Achtemeier would have saluted the Punic Church Father who found reading the OT prophets without reference to Christ a "tasteless and insipid" affair. But "find therein Christ," he enthused, "and what thou readest will not only prove agreeable, but will intoxicate thee."[26]

In contrast to this derivative paradigm, Judaism has understood those self-same Scriptures in a very different light. In the anthropological sense, Judaism is a "natural" religion. That is, it is the religious expression of a particular people—over a specific span of time and at a specific place—who share a particular government, economy, culture, history, language, cult, and God. At least up to the time of their dispersion after the destruction of the second temple, the Jewish people readily met every reasonable criterion of a distinctive ethnic community.

That natural community practiced a high degree of endogamy, which served to maintain its integrity as a biological unit semi-isolated from all other peoples. Like many similar anthropological units, it produced a written record of its history and its interaction with its God that we know as the Hebrew Bible (a.k.a. the Tanakh[27] and the OT). As the record of a specific human community over a lengthy period of time, the Hebrew Bible resists concepts such as "completion," "fulfillment," "solution," and "validation"[28] in the same manner as, say, the history of the Japanese or the Pawnee Indians. Most especially does it deny those concepts when they derive from another religion and people, from a "them."

Understandably, the people who produced the Book are much more emotionally attached to it than any other people are or can be. Christians know the first five books of the OT by the unlovely name of "Pentateuch" and treat them as just that—the first five books of the OT. But as the "Torah," Judaism received them as a special blessing from God that have come to play a central role in Jewish festivals, liturgy, study, and self-understanding. As the "constitution" of the Jewish community for twenty-five hundred years, the Torah has commanded a respect and reverence, even love, that no Christian community can begin to emulate.[29] In their vision of the ultimate in blessedness, the rabbis imagine God teaching Torah to the faithful in heaven. Each spring, while Christians are celebrating Pentecost, Jews observe Shavuot, a celebration of God's gift of Torah to Moses and the Jewish people.

Jewish intimacy with the Bible is recorded in the Book itself, especially in the Psalms. In the middle of Ps. 119—156 acrostic verses devoted exclusively to extolling the virtues of Torah—the Psalmist blurts out to the LORD, "Oh, how I love your law!" (v.97). In Ps. 19, the author rhapsodizes about Torah:

> The law of the LORD is perfect,
>   reviving the soul;
> the decrees of the LORD are sure,
>   making wise the simple;
> the precepts of the LORD are right,
>   rejoicing the heart . . .
> the ordinances of the LORD are true
>   and righteous altogether.
> More to be desired are they than gold,

even much fine gold;
sweeter also than honey,
and drippings of the honey comb.

—Ps. 19:7,8a,9b,10

In the critical matter of identity, the modern Jew reads in the biblical narrative that speaks of kings and priests and prophets, not an exotic "them," but an intimate "us." At the Seder meal that celebrates Passover, the prescribed reading actually incorporates the participants into the stirring events of yesteryear—the ancient time when "we" were slaves in Egypt and God rescued "us" with his mighty hand and outstretched arm (Exod. 6:6).[30] Such biblically based traditional ceremonies touch the Jewish soul in a manner that is not possible for any other people, even those who have "adopted" the Book and its stories. Rabbi W. Gunther Plaut states that the Torah is "a book which had its origin in the hearts and minds of the Jewish people."[31] The Hebrew Bible will inevitably mean more to the Jewish reader than to even the devout Christian, Rabbi Harold Kushner affirms, "because it is the book his relatives wrote."[32]

Whereas Judaism discovers both historical-genealogical and theological rationales for attachment to the Hebrew Bible, Gentile Christianity can identify only with the latter. The first Christian writers were almost all Jews, anxious to anchor the Christ-event in the only text and God that they knew. This entailed the monumental task of radically reorienting the nearly two-millennial "natural history" of a definitive ethnic population. Henceforth, every event from creation forward had to be refracted through the lens of a novel theological proposition, the "new covenant." When Christianity abrogated the Mosaic law, in Jewish eyes it passed from the status of "us" to "them," and supersessionism metamorphosed from internal reform to hostile takeover.

In this "unnatural" perspective, the "real" meaning of the ethnic experience had been concealed not only from the world at large, but more incredibly, from the very ones who had participated in it! The benighted people are now held to be "dull" (Acts 28:27), "not enlightened" (Rom. 10:2), "ignorant" (Rom. 10:3) and "blind" (Matt. 15:14; 23:16–19) to the basic truths of their own historic existence. As Paul states, "Whenever Moses is read, a veil lies over their minds; but when one turns to the Lord, the veil is removed" (2 Cor. 3:15–16). It is impossible to imagine that such thinking could have gained a broad and sympathetic audience save among Gentile peoples with no cultural or biological ties to the ancient community.

One of the twentieth century's most respected theologians, Gerhard von Rad, disdained the coarse Christological interpretations his predecessors had imposed routinely on an abused and protesting OT. To his intricate and sophisticated constructions, he brought the more enlightened attitude toward Judaism that typifies the Christian theologian in the post-Holocaust era. Yet, in essence, his is an understanding that remains firmly entrenched in the traditional position.

Somewhat plaintively, von Rad asks what relationship he, as a Christian communicant, can have with the OT since he cannot identify as his people the congregation of ancient Israel. He is neither a member of one of the twelve tribes, nor a worshiper at Jerusalem, nor even a proselyte. In effect, he has no place at the Seder table except as a guest.[33] God's "gracious provisions" for his people, he says, "seem to pass me by, because I do not belong to the historical people Israel."[34]

In his solution to this Christian dilemma, von Rad takes pride in the fact that it entails "no peddling of secret lore, no digging up of miracles." His typological conception shuns the crudities that have resulted from fixation on detailed correspondences between OT and NT. Rather, he focuses more broadly on the essential Christian creed that he claims to discern in the historic events. But he discovers in the facts of Israelite history only "something in preparation . . . of which the Old Testament witness is not itself aware." Across the full history of Israel, one may perceive "everywhere . . . the prefiguration of the Christ event." Above all, he states, modern typological interpretation recognizes the "incompleteness of the Old Covenant, in which God had not yet implanted his precepts in the hearts and will of men (Jer. 31:31ff)."[35]

Christianity, then, is an "unnatural" religion in the sense that it attempts to impose retroactively an exotic theological abstraction on an ethnic history. It does not represent the voice of a distinctive people and tradition but instead robs another of its heritage. In this strained interpretation, the divine promises made to Abraham and his offspring lay fallow for nearly two thousand years. They refer not to the people Israel, "as of many," but rather to the "one person, who is Christ" (Gal. 3:16). As Paul declared in his famous metaphor, Gentile Christianity had been grafted, "contrary to nature," onto an olive tree whose "natural branches" had been pruned because of incredulity (Rom. 11:24). Essentially, the people of the New Covenant must capture a canon, a cult, and a God, transferring them from the "other" to "us." In this supersessionistic maneuver, inappropriate concepts such as "preparation," "promise," and "completion" are forced upon an unwilling ethnic populace, its history, and its texts. The only pillar that can possibly support the "imposing" edifice is ceaseless appeal to a supernatural Providence.

As rationalistic enterprises, all attempts to find Christian blood in the OT turnip are doomed to failure. Christianity per se is no more evident in the OT than in the Talmud or the Dead Sea Scrolls. The cause-and-effect arrows simply point in the wrong direction. It is one thing to understand—with Second Isaiah—that a later event, the Exile, can be illuminated by the light of a prior event, the Exodus. It is another matter altogether to insist that the "real" meaning of the prior event is revealed thereby—centuries later and to another people. For our belief system, it makes all the difference whether the Suffering Servant prefigured Christ or served as a literary model for Christ. The latter possibility can be entertained rationally, the former—exempted from all intervening, natural contingencies—can be maintained only by "faith."

Faith is not to be despised, but it should be used thoughtfully and sparingly. It can give only that "assurance" generated by "hope," only that "conviction" produced by things "not seen" (Heb 11:1). For the Christian, the critical question is whether the traditional interpretation is absolutely essential to support his belief system. Why multiply the improbability (not impossibility) of Jesus-as-Son by the multiple improbabilities of finding him lurking behind every semicolon of the OT? The demands of the traditional hermeneutics tend to overwhelm the modern capacity to believe. Perhaps a version of Occam's Razor is in order: do not multiply theological improbabilities unnecessarily!

In recent decades, several interrelated trends among Christian interpreters fly directly in the face of the traditional replacement theology. These include abandonment of the term "Old Testament" in favor of "Hebrew Bible"; recognition of the integrity and *Sitz im Leben* of the OT authors; acceptance of the "natural history" of Israel unburdened by Christian dogmatics; and respect for Judaism as a viable religion in its own right. The most significant change has been the widespread acknowledgment among the churches that the Old Covenant has retained its validity.[36]

If the original covenant is so perceived, Jews should be released from the necessity of undergoing Christian-sponsored salvation. But the ancient habit of looking at Jews as potential converts and asking "Why not?" is difficult to break.[37] A declaration of Vatican II (*Nostra Aetate*) accepted the election of Jews, grounding its revised doctrine in Paul's assertion that "the calling of God [is] irrevocable" (Rom. 11:29).[38] But in a recent best-selling book, Pope John Paul II—like the apostle Paul before him—looks forward to the grand day when Jews will at last accept the Christian truth. "The time when the people of the Old Covenant will be able to see themselves as part of the New," he states, "is, naturally, a question to be left to the Holy Spirit. We, as human beings, try only not to put obstacles in the way."[39]

In this post-Auschwitz era, Christians continue to press their claim to the OT, but increasingly they must face a contrary and self-confident Jewish position. Elizabeth Achtemeier urges ministers to mine "this priceless lode" that has been "handed down to us as our own possession."[40] But Jon Levenson—in a review of a major commentary on Ezekiel by Walther Zimmerli—bristles at the thought of "a Christian interpretation of a non-Christian book."[41]

Specifically, Levenson objects to Zimmerli's application of 2 Cor. 5:17 ("So if anyone is in Christ, there is a new creation. . . . ") to Ezekiel's famous vision of Israel's restoration in the valley of the dry bones (Ezek. 37:1–14). The imposition of the Christian exegesis, Levenson maintains, "denationalizes" Ezekiel's prophecy, replacing the vision of the post-exilic, historic restoration of the Israelite *people* with the theological idea of the *individual* coming to Christ. The transformation is so severe, he states, that it could only derive from an "intellectual schizophrenia."[42] Obviously, the possibilities for Jewish-Christian disagreement on their "common text" are profound and endless.

In another arena that has only begun to be explored in the modern period, some Jewish scholars have challenged unreservedly the Christian dogma that the God of the NT is continuous with the God of the OT, that the voice at Calvary is necessarily the voice at Sinai. "[W]hat justification do Christians have," Michael Goldberg asks, "for identifying the deity whose salvific activity is depicted in the gospel story with the One whose saving acts are portrayed in Israel's prior story?"[43] More specifically, he questions whether the type of salvation offered to the people Israel at Sinai and that proffered to the Gentiles in the Gospels is fundamentally the same and a function of the same God.

Goldberg bases his argument on the rational expectation of narrative consistency across the two testaments and its implications for constancy in the divine character. Salvation, or blessing, under the Sinai pact is contingent upon the actions of both God and Israel, the traditional Deuteronomic retributional schema. But, he maintains, salvation in the Gospels appears to depend upon God's initiative alone. Would one and the same God have changed his salvific mode so abruptly? For these and other reasons, Goldberg concludes that the character of Christ appears to be discordant with that of the God at Sinai. Eventually, Christians may be forced to acknowledge that their canon includes "the chronicles of an alien religion"—thus confirming the Marcionian heresy.[44]

The Christian theologian Rudolph Bultmann—said by many to be the greatest NT scholar of the twentieth century—would affirm much of the OT-NT discordance that Goldberg identifies, and more.[45] Christian faith that relies on "impossible" OT proof texts is "no faith at all," Bultmann asserts; all forms of allegory are but "idle play or nonsense."[46] Eschewing the full Marcionite solution, he recommends that the church retain the OT for historical and pedagogical reasons, though for Christians it no longer represented revelation and is not "in the true sense" God's Word. The OT speaks of and to "a particular people" with "a particular ethnic history" and that history, Bultmann declares, is "not ours." Jesus—who put an end to all ethnic history—manifested a divine grace that differs "fundamentally" from that found in the OT. Insofar as the Old Covenant manifests God's grace at all, "such grace is not meant for us."[47]

The "ghost of Marcion" may also be detected in attempts to describe the character of the Christian Gods. It is particularly manifest in the popular, but simplistic, assertion that "God is love" and in the perception of many of discontinuous attributes in the OT Yahweh and the NT Jesus. The church has focused so intensely on *whether* one believes, Terence E. Fretheim states, that the *nature* of the Deity has often been neglected or given only stereotypical treatment.[48] The portrayal of Jesus as the loving, healing, merciful savior, Fretheim asserts, continues to stand in unresolved tension with the OT God of "wrath, power and justice." Believers may even go so far as to adopt the view that "Jesus is friend and God is enemy." The perception of atonement becomes so distorted that Jesus is seen as "the one who came to save us from God."[49] Marcion would certainly have concurred with that.

Many unanswered questions and unresolved issues remain for the twenty-first century agenda. Is it humanly possible to respect the integrity of Judaism and its central text and simultaneously impose the Christological "solution" thereon? Does not this retroactive imposition necessarily castrate the Hebrew Bible as a viable historical/theological record of the Jewish people? Does the Christian message *require* a typological-allegorical-prophetic reading of the OT? The kerygmatic nucleus celebrated in the popular song "He's Alive!" would seem to say it all: "He's alive—and I'm forgiven—heaven's gates are open wide."

The twenty-first century seems a propitious time to liberate ourselves from textual tyranny, to acknowledge the biblical truths that will set us free at last (John 8:32). In at least a dozen problem areas, the OT as wise and humane counselor would appear to be problematic at best and dysfunctional at worst: religious and ethnic tolerance; ethnic intermarriage; ethnic cleansing, genocide; capital punishment; the status of women, homosexuals, and the handicapped; and the problems created by those who would endorse the apocalyptic world view, the "us-them" mentality, or the actuality of divine retribution on planet earth. Above all, we need to muster the intellectual courage to face the fact that our Holy Bible includes much that is "pre-ethical" in addition to that which is "pre-scientific."

In the time-honored formulation of the problem of theodicy, God's omnipotence and omni-benevolence must be reconciled with the ugly fact of widespread evil (Appendix B). The questions raised in this biblical study pose yet another predicament for Christian theodicy. Traditional assertions regarding the loving nature and judicial character of the unipolar God of the OT are challenged flatly by the ethnocentric and retributory divine words and deeds in those self-same Scriptures. That is, claims that it is the loving, immutable Yahweh who acts in history and governs as the God of Justice for all humankind, collide head-on with manifold scriptural enormities, including multiple genocides, inflicted upon the human race, both the unchosen many and the chosen few. How does one explain to her children that Yahweh is the father of the loving Jesus?

Lastly, we must recognize the logical consequences of the most momentous theological development of the twentieth century, i.e., the acceptance of the continuing validity of the "old" covenant by mainstream Christianity. In the supersessionistic view of tradition, the OT is to be read as an incomplete, inferior and spiritually flawed writing—a mere preface to the salvific, a truncated promise that looks beyond itself to Christian fulfillment. With the recent mutation in understanding—a result of the *mea culpa* milieu of the post-Holocaust era—it must necessarily be acknowledged as an integral, self-validating, non-Christian history of the Jewish people. However, this concession poses a second major problem for Christianity. If presented with the rival claims on the text—the naturalistic proclamation of Judaism and its artificial Christian alternative—which perforce must the rational person choose?

But within these two predicaments, one may locate the germ

of their resolution. Reclassification of the OT from inspired moral authority to "foundational document" would reduce significantly the contemporary confusion and tension.[50] *Mirabile dictu*, adoption of a non-replacement theology centered on the Christ-event, would enable each of the two peoples to claim its own God, Messiah, covenant, and canon! Although this solution is not without difficulties, it deserves a much more thorough consideration than it has heretofore received. Is it possible that Marcionism may yet carry the day?

Appendix A
Chronological Table of the Salient Events in the Biblical History of Israel

1750	B.C.E.______	Age of Abraham, Isaac, and Jacob.
1300	B.C.E.______	
		Exodus from Egypt.
		Mt. Sinai theophany.
1200	B.C.E.______	Conquest of Canaan.
1100	B.C.E.______	Age of the Judges.
1000	B.C.E.______	Saul.
		David.
		Solomon. United Kingdom divided.
900	B.C.E.______	
		Ahab, Jezebel, Elijah.
		Moabite Stone.
800	B.C.E.______	Jehu.
		Fall of Northern Kingdom (Israel) to Assyria.
700	B.C.E.______	Hezekiah.
		Manasseh.
		Josiah.
600	B.C.E.______	Fall of Southern Kingdom (Judah) to Babylonia.
		Exile. Persia conquers Babylonia and Palestine.
500	B.C.E.______	Second temple constructed.
400	B.C.E.______	
		Alexander the Great controls Palestine.
300	B.C.E.______	
200	B.C.E.______	Seleucid Greeks control Palestine.
		Maccabean revolt against Antiochus IV.
100	B.C.E.______	Hasmonean Dynasty.
		Romans control Palestine.
0	______	Birth of Jesus.
		Paul's missionary journeys.
		Second temple destroyed by Romans.
100	C.E.______	

Appendix B
Theodicy

On Palm Sunday, 1994, a tornado demolished a United Methodist church in northern Alabama, killing 20 worshipers and injuring 90 in the congregation of 140. Among the six children killed was Hannah, the four-year-old daughter of the minister and her husband, also a Methodist minister. At the moment the twister struck, Hannah and her little friends, resplendent in their Easter finery, were waiting to perform in a crucifixion drama while the choir sang in joyous voices that "the LORD will provide." The anguished survivors pleaded with their minister to explain this "act of God." "There are no answers," she said later, "and there will be no answers, not in this life."[1]

In the Holocaust, the lights of a million Hannahs were extinguished; a million cries of "why?" rend the air. Perhaps the only rational response is the "no answer" of the minister-mother. Nevertheless, since time immemorial, humankind has proffered solutions of one type or another to the eternal problem. In its most elemental formulation, the monotheistic dilemma may be phrased by a question: How can an omnipotent and omnibenevolent God permit unmitigated evil, most especially when its victims are innocent children? If evil exists, God appears to be either powerless or unjust.[2] All three corners of the theodicean triangle—power, goodness, and evil—have been subject to extensive probing by a host of interpreters.

In recent decades, a popular solution has been to acknowledge God's impotence in historical events while insisting on his benevolence and the actuality of evil. In this paradigm, the ancient union of Deity and total power is dissolved. In a best-selling book, Rabbi Harold S. Kushner absolved God of responsibility for his young son's debilitating disease and early death. For Kushner, the hand of God could not be discerned in human tragedies: "I have seen the wrong people get sick, the wrong people be hurt, the wrong people die young." In his attempts to control mundane events, God is necessarily limited by natural law and human freedom. Although he can't contain evil, he shares the human frustration and anger generated by injustice.[3]

A number of variations on this basic theme have been advanced. Terence E. Fretheim has underscored God's empathetic role as a "mourner" and fellow "sufferer," even when divine justice has to be executed.[4] James L. Crenshaw abandons "power" as the "essential nature" of Deity in favor of "suffering," which is to be found "at the heart" of a benevolent God. In this understanding, God suffered in the ovens with the Jews; indeed, whenever misfortune afflicts the innocent, "God is there, shedding the first hot tear."[5] One is moved to ask whether the Auschwitz victims stood in greater need of more tears from the impotent or the "outstretched arm" of a rescuer, human or divine.

The notion of the *Deus Absconditus,* or self-concealing God, represents another nuance of the "Kushner solution." In theory Deity retains his omnipotence, but in the event he cannot be distinguished from the more impotent version. Jon Levenson has suggested that God was all-powerful at the creation and will be again at the Eschaton, but is largely absent in the intervening historical period.[6] David Birnbaum postulates that over the lengthy interval from Sinai to Auschwitz, the God of Israel progressively contracted his "consciousness" while granting to humankind ascending levels of freedom and knowledge.[7] Rabbi Norman Lamm imagines that a state of *Hester Panim* ("hiding of the face") was in effect from the destruction of the second temple to the Holocaust. During this "total eclipse" of Deity, the fortunes of the people depended solely upon chance and effort, not divine guidance.[8]

If both divine omnipotence and goodness are nonnegotiable—as in the more traditional solutions—evil must be finessed in some fashion. The Dutch theologian A. van de Beek recognized that while Marcion's ditheistic solution was too radical, the heretic did identify profound differences in God's character between the two testaments. Reconciliation of the two is contingent on the fact that God does change; the dogma of immutability is in error. For van de Beek, God's goodness is defined by his action at any particular moment. When God commanded Saul to hack to pieces the infants of Amalek (1 Sam. 15:3), "at that moment that is good." But God reserves the right to change his mind; the ethical norms changed radically when the Father introduced his Son to the world. Therefore, the goodness of God is "manifest in his action"; it is "the goodness of his history."[9] Since, by definition, God does only good, evil vanishes as a divine possibility.

Traditional theologians have tended to arrive at or near van de Beek's position—exculpating an omnipotent Deity from evil actions or intent through a wide variety of theological mechanisms. The Church Father Origen insisted that Deity could do no evil, that "nothing is to be said of God that is unworthy of him."[10] St. Augustine held that "all evil is either sin or the punishment for sin."[11] Fundamentalists such as the televangelist Oral Roberts attribute evil to a very active Devil who, for example, caused the 1995 bombing of the federal building in Oklahoma City.[12] The German theologian Hans Schwarz acknowledges that God may originally have been bipolar, but the intra-divine tension has since been dissolved. Evil was excluded from the Godhead because the Deity was in danger of being "perverted into a demonic power." While evil remains a potent force in the world, the Almighty, himself, has "set boundaries for evil that it cannot overstep."[13]

Without compromising either divine power or goodness, the philosopher John Hick swallows evil in the Grand Design. He envisions a series of post-mortem incarnations that move humankind progressively toward an eschatological community of "perfected" beings. In the Grand Plan, evil—defined as that which thwarts God's purposes—has no status, only "an interim and impermanent" role. In the pinched human view, evil is real enough. But in the eschatological perspective, the benevolent God included evil in this world "as a means to the creation of the infinite good" found in the Kingdom of Heaven. God looked down on the "utterly evil" Holocaust with "anger and grief." But its victims, Hick assures, will take their rightful place in the "final fulfillment" of the Plan. In Hick's theodicy—and the Christian tradition from which it draws its inspiration—evil is in the service of love, "divinely permitted" but ultimately "over-ruled."[14]

The third perspective is most congruent with the nature of the God of the Bible in that it recognizes that "woe" as well as "weal" may flow from the Godhead. In this rendering, God remains omnipotent and the ugly fact of evil challenges the claim of omni-benevolence. Robert Davidson has suggested that honest doubt regarding traditional views can prove to be "spiritually productive," leading to a more mature faith.[15] After reflecting on the human condition, the traditionalist Dennis Prager admits that "God isn't lovable."[16] James A. Sanders has urged repeatedly that Christians "monotheize," i.e., discard their "nice, good God" and face the full implications of a monistic Deity.[17] In response to the traditional Christian theodicy, the Russian novelist, Fyodor Dostoevsky, questioned why suffering children were needed in the divine economy to serve as "manure" to fertilize a "future harmony." He had no problem with retribution for adults; in fact, he insisted on it. But in what has become a classic formulation of the issue—and in anticipation of John Hick—he asked whether eternal, eschatological bliss for the righteous was worth the torture of "just one tiny creature."[18]

The philosopher Frederick Sontag has posed a number of heuristic questions relating to God's goodness. Since humankind has modified so much in the physical world, its interest in creation has naturally shifted from "necessity" (the immovable God) to "contingency" (divine possibilities). We need to have explained to us a world that appears less hospitable than is necessary. At creation, God had, and made, choices. His choices appear to include an excess of suffering and injustice—well beyond that needed to illustrate moral lessons. Do we really need tornadoes, congenital malformations and hereditary diseases—or so many of them? If humans can solve the problem of "instantaneous universal communication," Sontag asks, why did God choose to spread his Divine Word through the excruciatingly slow and painful process of cultural diffusion from a tiny group of "elect"?

Would a realistic appraisal of the human condition—independent of Christian dogma—lead one to conclude that the Creator is an impartial and just "democrat" whose love knows no bounds?[19]

In a penetrating and disturbing study of the suffering that stems from the Holocaust and child abuse, Rabbi David R. Blumenthal has taken a major step in confrontation of the bipolar God. Blumenthal falls squarely in the Jewish tradition of the "theology of protest" that has run continuously from Job to Elie Wiesel. Urging his fellow theologians to break the "conspiracy of silence," Blumenthal asks them to begin to "tell the truth" about the divine character. God makes mistakes; he can, and does, sin against the people! Both the canon and experience demand that "abusiveness" be added to the dimensions of the divine personality. Human beings certainly were implicated in the Holocaust, he argues, but the Sovereign of the Universe "allowed" it to happen. In his abusive mode, "God was involved, too; God was co-responsible."[20]

Blumenthal does not reject the abusing God in an atheistic pique; rather, he engages him defiantly in what for many can only be described as "heretical" prayers. He asks God to share with his children his "anguish" and "shame" at his "hateful actions." He calls on the Deity to "repent before us, in truth and with a whole heart." This is a God who is truly ambivalent: one who "injures, destroys, and harms beyond reason" but who also "loves graciously, and is compassionate, and cares."[21] In a final, cathartic "meditation"—reminiscent of Psalm 44—Blumenthal does not flinch as he places responsibility for massive injustice squarely on the shoulders of the God of Justice. But in full tension with that indictment, his abiding "hope" remains with the God of Israel:

> I do not deny You or Your Torah; You denied us, for we were innocent. You crushed us, yet we were guiltless. You were the Abuser; our sins were not commensurate with Your actions. The responsibility is Yours, not ours. . . . You must return to us, not we come to You.

In spite of all this, we will gather our strength and support one another. . . . We will love one another. We will defend our people and our land. We will believe in You, we will place our hope in You. We will yearn for You, we will wait for You, and we will anticipate the time when we will see Your Face again.

Amen.[22]

Notes

Abbreviations Used in the Notes

ABD	*Anchor Bible Dictionary*
Enc Jud	*Encyclopedia Judaica*
HBD	*Harper's Bible Dictionary*
IDB	*Interpreter's Dictionary of the Bible*

Preface

1. Robert Famighetti, *The World Almanac and Book of Facts 1996* (Mahwah, N.J.: Funk and Wagnalls, 1995), p. 652.
2. Lester G. McAllister and William E. Tucker, *Journey in Faith: A History of the Christian Church (Disciples of Christ)* (St. Louis: Bethany Press, 1975), p. 156.
3. G. Roger Schoenhals, editor, *John Wesley's Commentary on the Bible* (Grand Rapids, Mich.: Zondervan Publishing, 1990, first published in 1765), p. 19.
4. Brevard S. Childs, *Biblical Theology of the Old and New Testaments: Theological Reflection on the Christian Bible* (Minneapolis: Fortress Press, 1993), p. 369.
5. Lord Macaulay, *The History of England* (New York: Penguin Books, 1979, first published 1848–61), p. 96.

Chapter 1. Divine Election

1. Robert Redfield, *The Primitive World and Its Transformations* (Ithaca: Cornell University Press, 1953), pp. 6–13; Rodney Needham, *Primordial Characters* (Charlottesville: University Press of Virginia, 1978); Robert Smith Bader, *Hayseeds, Moralizers, and Methodists: The*

Twentieth-Century Image of Kansas (Lawrence: University Press of Kansas, 1988), pp. 185–87.

2. Mircea Eliade, *The Quest: History and Meaning in Religion* (Chicago: The University of Chicago Press, 1984), pp. 173–74.
3. William G. Sumner, *Folkways: A Study of the Sociological Importance of Usages, Manners, Customs, Mores, and Morals* (New York: Ginn, 1906), pp. 12–13. Jonathan Z. Smith, "What a Difference a Difference Makes," in *To See Ourselves As Others See Us: Christians, Jews, "Others" in Late Antiquity*, edited by Jacob Neusner and Ernest S. Frerichs (Chico, Ca.: Scholars Press, 1985), pp. 46–47.
4. Erik H. Erikson, *Identity: Youth and Crisis* (New York: W.W. Norton, 1968), p. 41.
5. Needham, Primordial, pp. 5–6.
6. Ralph Linton, *The Thunder Ceremony of the Pawnee,* Field Museum of Natural History, Dept. of Anthropology, Leaflet No. 5, 1922, p. 3; Sumner, *Folkways*, p. 14; John Friedl, *Cultural Anthropology* (New York: Harper and Row, 1976), p. 91; Daniel G. Freedman, *Human Sociobiology: A Holistic Approach* (New York: Free Press, 1979), pp. 136–37.
7. Edward O. Wilson, *On Human Nature* (Cambridge: Harvard University Press, 1978), p. 70; ABD, vol. 4, p. 1031; D. J. Wiseman, editor, *Peoples of Old Testament Times* (Oxford: Clarendon Press, 1973), p. XVIII; Friedl, *Anthropology*, p. 91; Huston Smith, *The Religions of Man* (New York: Harper and Row, 1958), p. 290.
8. James B. Pritchard, editor, *Ancient Near Eastern Texts Relating to the Old Testament* (Princeton: Princeton University Press, 1969), p. 164. Anum is the sky god, leader of the pantheon; Enlil is the storm god. Marduk is the god of the Babylonian Empire who has been delegated the functions of Enlil.
9. Pritchard, *Ancient,* p. 289.
10. Robert M. Good, "The Just War in Ancient Israel," *Journal of Biblical Literature* 104 (1985), p. 389.
11. Jerrold S. Cooper, *The Curse of Agade* (Baltimore: The Johns Hopkins University Press, 1983), pp. 5, 18, 31.
12. Morton Smith, "The Common Theology of the Ancient Near East." *Journal of Biblical Literature* 71 (1952), p. 145.
13. Pritchard, *Ancient*, p. 396; ABD, volume 3, p. 222.
14. J.A. Brinkman, "Through a Glass Darkly: Esarhaddon's Retrospects on the Downfall of Babylon," *Journal of the American Oriental Society* 103 (1983): 35–42; ABD, volume 4, p. 764.

15. Solomon Schechter, *Aspects of Rabbinic Theology* (Woodstock, Vt.: Jewish Lights, 1993, first published 1909), p. XII.
16. Dennis Prager and Joseph Telushkin, *Why the Jews? The Reason for Antisemitism* (New York: Simon and Schuster, 1985), pp. 40–45; Joseph Telushkin, *Jewish Wisdom: Ethical, Spiritual, and Historical Lessons from the Great Works and Thinkers* (New York: William Morrow, 1994), pp. 298–302; Harold S. Kushner, *To Life! A Celebration of Jewish Being and Thinking* (Boston: Little, Brown, 1993), pp. 29–35. For a contrary view, in which the concept of election is viewed as "pernicious," see Jeremy Cott, "The Biblical Problem of Election," *Journal of Ecumenical Studies* 21 (1984): 199–228.
17. Dale Patrick, "The Moral Logic of Election," *Encounter* 37 (1976): 198–210; ABD, volume 2, pp. 436–37; Telushkin, *Wisdom*, p. 300.
18. Louis Ginzberg, *The Legends of the Jews* (Philadelphia: Jewish Publication Society of America, 1937), volume 3, pp. 292–93; cf. Jer. 33:20–21.
19. Bruce M. Metzger and Roland E. Murphy, editors, *The New Oxford Annotated Bible* with the *Apocryphal / Deuterocanonical Books* (New Revised Standard Version) (New York: Oxford University Press, 1991), p. XIII; ABD, volume 3, p. 773; volume 6, p. 1011; Tryggve N.D. Mettinger, *In Search of God: The Meaning and Message of the Everlasting Names* (Philadelphia: Fortress, 1988), p. 16; George Howard, "The Tetragram and the New Testament." *Journal of Biblical Literature* 96 (1977): 63–83. Jehovah's Witnesses still insist that God's proper name is "Jehovah."
20. Mircea Eliade, *The Sacred and the Profane: The Nature of Religion* (New York: Harcourt Brace Jovanovich, 1959), pp. 20–42.
21. William G. Braude and Israel J. Kapstein, editors, *Pesikta de-Rab Kahana: R. Kahana's Compilation of Discourses for Sabbaths and Festal Days* (Philadelphia: Jewish Publication Society of America, 1975), p. XXIII; IDB, Supplementary volume, p. 622.
22. Richard S. Sarason, "The Significance of the Land of Israel in the Mishnah," in *The Land of Israel: Jewish Perspectives*, edited by Lawrence A. Hoffman (Notre Dame: University of Notre Dame Press, 1986), pp. 112–15; Scot McKnight, *A Light among the Gentiles* (Minneapolis: Fortress, 1991), pp. 22–23; Moshe Weinfeld, *The Promise of the Land: The Inheritance of the Land of Canaan by the Israelites* (Berkeley: University of California Press, 1993), pp. 219–20; E.P. Sanders, *Judaism: Practice and Belief 63* B.C.E.–66 C.E. (Philadelphia: Trinity Press International, 1992), pp. 308-13.

Chapter 2. Conquest of the Promised Land

1. A few references in which the moral dimension is briefly considered: W. Gunther Plaut, editor, *The Torah: A Modern Commentary* (New York: Union of American Hebrew Congregations, 1981), p. 1114; Patrick D. Miller, Jr., "The Gift of God: The Deuteronomic Theology of the Land," *Interpretation* 23 (1969): 451–65; Robert Polzin, "Deuteronomy," in *The Literary Guide to the Bible*, edited by Robert Alter and Frank Kermode (Cambridge: Harvard University Press, 1987), p. 99; Norman C. Habel, *The Land is Mine: Six Biblical Land Ideologies* (Minneapolis: Fortress, 1995); Lawrence A. Hoffman, editor, *The Land of Israel: Jewish Perspectives* (Notre Dame: University of Notre Dame Press, 1986).
2. William G. Dever, in Hershel Shanks, William G. Dever, Baruch Halpern and P. Kyle McCarter, Jr., *The Rise of Ancient Israel* (Washington, D.C.: Biblical Archaeology Society, 1992), p. 29.
3. NRSV, p. 69 OT; Shanks, Dever, Halpern and McCarter, *Rise*; Baruch Halpern, *The Emergence of Israel in Canaan* (Chico, Calif.: Scholars Press, 1983); J. Maxwell Miller, "Introduction to the History of Ancient Israel," in *The New Interpreter's Bible*, edited by Leander E. Keck (Nashville: Abingdon, 1994), volume 1, pp. 253–59; Norman K. Gottwald, *The Tribes of Yahweh: A Sociology of the Religion of Liberated Israel, 1250–1050* B.C. (Maryknoll, N.Y.: Orbis Books, 1979); idem, *The Hebrew Bible in Its Social World and in Ours* (Atlanta: Scholars Press, 1993), pp. 89–107.
4. M. Smith, "Common Theology," p. 140; Weinfeld, *Promise*, p. XVII.
5. See, e.g., among the many passages, Exod. 13:5; 32:13; 33:1; Num. 11:12; 14:23; 32:11; Deut. 1:35; 6:10, 18, 23; 8:1, etc.
6. In sequence: Deut. 9:1; 9:3; 11:23; 7:24; 12:2; 31:3; 7:16.
7. John Van Seters, "The Terms 'Amorite' and 'Hittite' in the Old Testament," *Vetus Testamentum* 22 (1972): 64–81.
8. Philip D. Stern, *The Biblical Herem: A Window on Israel's Religious Experience* (Atlanta: Scholars Press, 1991), p. IX; Susan Niditch, *War in the Hebrew Bible: A Study in the Ethics of Violence* (New York: Oxford University Press, 1993).
9. In Deut. 13:12–18, the ban is applied to an apostate Israelite town; all the inhabitants are killed and the spoil gathered in the town square and offered as "a whole burnt offering" to Yahweh.
10. In sequence: Deut. 3:22; 21:10; 7:24; Exod. 23:28, 27; Josh. 24:12; Deut. 9:3; 7:23; Josh. 11:20.

11. Miller, "Gift," p. 455; idem, *The Divine Warrior in Early Israel* (Cambridge: Harvard University Press, 1973).
12. *Harper's Bible Commentary*, p. 14; Edward Beecher, *History of Opinions on the Scriptural Doctrine of Retribution* (New York: D. Appleton, 1878), p. 7; ABD, volume 2, p. 700; Anthony R. Ceresko, *Introduction to the Old Testament: A Liberation Perspective* (Maryknoll, N.Y.: Orbis, 1992), p. 120; Joel Carmichael, *The Satanizing of the Jews: Origin and Development of Mystical Anti-Semitism* (New York: Fromm International, 1992), p.1.
13. Plaut, *Torah*, p. 1116; Rabbi Michael Zedek, Radio Station KCMO, February 18, 1996; Benjamin Netanyahu, *A Place among the Nations: Israel and the World* (New York: Bantam, 1993), p.23. Aside from this minor lapse, Netanyahu makes a very persuasive case for the state of Israel in its struggle with the Arabs.
14. Ceresko, *Introduction,* p. 121; Emanuel Rackman, "Judaism and Equality," in *Judaism and Human Rights*, edited by Milton R. Konvitz (New York: W.W. Norton, 1972), p. 54.
15. Marie Syrkin, editor, *Hayim Greenberg: Anthology* (Detroit: Wayne State University Press, 1968), pp. 25, 26, 31, 44.
16. NRSV, p. 270 OT.
17. Quoted in Niditch, *War*, p. 6.

    In his recent *Long Ago God Spoke: How Christians May Hear the Old Testament Today,* William L. Holladay wrestles bravely and at length with Conquest morality. The invasion of another's homeland "wasn't fair," he admits, but God evidently "couldn't figure out" a more pacific solution. However, we may be confident that he was "deeply sorry" for the resulting violence and injustice (Minneapolis: Fortress, 1995), p. 132.
18. Sara Japhet, "Conquest and Settlement in Chronicles," *Journal of Biblical Literature* 98 (1979): 205–18; David J.A. Clines, "Introduction to the Biblical Story: Genesis— Esther," in *Harper's Bible Commentary*, edited by James L. Mays (San Francisco: Harper and Row, 1988), pp. 74–80.
19. See 1 Chron. 16:18; 28:8; 2 Chron. 6:27.
20. Weinfeld, *Promise*, p. 208.
21. Ibid, pp. 207–13; Ginzberg, *Legends*, volume 1, p. 173; Plaut, *Torah*, p. 1519; Jubilees 10:27–34.
22. Lawrence H. Schiffman, *Reclaiming the Dead Sea Scrolls: The History*

of Judaism, the Background of Christianity, the Lost Library of Qumran (New York: Doubleday, 1995), pp. 376, 378.

23. Quoted in Michael Goldberg, *Why Should Jews Survive? Looking past the Holocaust toward a Jewish Future* (New York: Oxford University Press, 1995), p. 152.
24. Ginzberg, *Legends*, volume 1, p. 169.
25. Justo L. Gonzalez, "How the Bible has been Interpreted in Christian Tradition," in *The New Interpreter's Bible,* volume 1, pp. 88–90; ABD, volume 5, pp. 42–48.
26. Gedaliahu G. Stroumsa, "Old Wine and New Bottles: On Patristic Soteriology and Rabbinic Judaism," in *The Origins and Diversity of Axial Age Civilizations,* edited by S.N. Eisenstadt (Albany: State University of New York Press, 1986), pp. 258–60; Epistle of Barnabas 12:8. Origen was so concerned about his "guilty passions" that he mutilated his sexual organs.
27. Judg. 2:22; 3:1–2.
28. 1 Kings 18–19.
29. 1 Kings 19:17.
30. Joseph Telushkin, *Jewish Literacy* (New York: William Morrow, 1991), p. 86. Telushkin's characterization of Jehu as a "religious reformer" is accurate enough, but without further elaboration hardly does justice to the range and vigor of his activities.
31. 2 Kings 9–10.
32. Toward the end of the dynasty, after the damage had been done, the LORD seems to have revised his opinion of Jehu somewhat, declaring that he would "punish the house of Jehu" for the bloodshed at the outset of the dynasty and would "put an end" to the northern kingdom (Hos. 1:4). It appears unlikely that he had any misgivings about the duplicitous slaughter of the Baalists, nor are any indicated.

Chapter 3. The Neighbors

1. *Enc. Jud.*, volume 2, pp. 853–59; IDB, Volume 1, pp. 108–14; ABD, volume 1, pp. 194–96.
2. 2 Chron. 26:8; 27:5.
3. *Enc. Jud.*, volume 12, pp. 190–98; IDB, volume 3, pp. 409–19; ABD, volume 4, pp. 882–93.
4. Judg. 3:12–30. For an incisive analysis of Ehud's ability to murder the

king in his palace and escape with his life, see Baruch Halpern, *The First Historians: The Hebrew Bible and History* (San Francisco: Harper and Row, 1988), pp. 39–60.

5. 1 Sam. 22:3–4; 2 Sam. 8:2.
6. 1 Kings 16; 2 Kings 1:1; 3:4–27. Max Miller, "The Moabite Stone as a Memorial Stela," *Palestine Exploration Quarterly* 106 (1974): 9–18.
7. Translation by P. Kyle McCarter, Jr. in HBD, p. 645. For a thorough discussion of the religion of Moab and the Mesha Inscription, see Andrew Dearman, editor, *Studies in the Mesha Inscription and Moab* (Atlanta: Scholars Press, 1989) pp. 97–98 (inscription translation) and pp. 211–38 (Moabite religion).
8. In its several grammatical forms, *oppress* occurs 142 times in the Bible (NRSV including Apocrypha), almost all of these in the OT. In the overwhelming majority of instances, the word is used in connection with a social situation within Israel, e.g., a warning not to oppress the poor, widows, orphans, etc. In a dozen or so cases, a foreign nation is the subject and Israel the object. In one of the few NT instances, Jesus is said to heal "all who were oppressed by the devil" (Acts 10:38).
9. Deut. 2:5 (Edom); 2:9 (Moab); 2:19 (Ammon). A more general statement regarding the fixation of the "boundaries of the peoples" is found in Deut. 32:8; Plaut, *Torah*, p. 1336.
10. *Enc. Jud.*, volume 2, p. 860.
11. Zeph. 2:8–10. For other examples in the prophetic corpus, see, for Ammon: Jer. 49:1–6; Ezek. 25:1–7; Amos 1:13–15; for Moab: Isa. 15–16; Jer. 48:1–47; Ezek. 25:8–11; Amos 2:1–3.
12. Diana V. Edelman, editor, *You Shall Not Abhor an Edomite For He Is Your Brother: Edom and Seir in History and Tradition* (Atlanta: Scholars Press, 1995), pp. 96–99, 110; Bruce C. Cresson, "The Condemnation of Edom in Postexilic Judaism," in *The Use of the Old Testament in the New and Other Essays,* edited by James M. Efird (Durham: Duke University Press, 1972), p. 130.
13. 2 Sam. 8:13–14; 1 Kings 11:15–16.
14. John R. Bartlett, *Edom and the Edomites* (Sheffield: Sheffield Academic Press, 1989); ABD, volume 2, pp. 287–301; John Lindsay, "The Babylonian Kings and Edom, 605–550 B.C.," *Palestine Exploration Quarterly* 108 (1976): 23–39. Key biblical passages tracing the early history of Edom include: Num. 20:14–21; Deut. 2:1–8; 1 Kings 11:14–22; 22:47–48; 2 Kings 8:20–22; 14:7,22; 16:6; 2 Chron. 25:11–12; 26:1–2; 28:16–17.

15. J.R. Bartlett, "The Brotherhood of Edom," *Journal for the Study of the Old Testament* 4 (1977), pp. 20–21.
16. Gen. 26:34; 28:8–9; 36:1–2.
17. The Esau-Jacob story line may be followed in Gen. 25:19–34; 26:34–35; 27–33; 35:1–8; 36. Esau does receive a "blessing" of sorts in Gen. 27:39–40.
18. "Quas" appears in a number of theophoric names that convey a message similar to those utilizing "Yahweh" in Israel: "Quas is judge"; "Quas is powerful"; "Quas has blessed"; "Quas has created"; "son of Quas"; Bartlett, *Edom,* pp. 203–07.
19. Bartlett, "Brotherhood"; idem, "Yahweh and Quas: A Response to Martin Rose (*JSOT* 4 (1977) 28–34)," *Journal for the Study of the Old Testament* 5 (1978):29–38; M. Rose, "Yahweh in Israel—Quas in Edom?", *Journal for the Study of the Old Testament* 4 (1977): 28–34. In the secondary history, King Amaziah of Judah is condemned for worshiping the gods of Edom (2 Chron. 25:14–20). Additional references locating Yahweh initially in the region southeast of Israel include Deut. 33:2; Isa. 63:1; Hab. 3:3.
20. Deut. 2:1–22; 23:8. The account of peaceful passage through Edom in Deuteronomy is contradicted in Num. 20:14–21 where the Edomites refuse entry into their land.
21. The phrase "Damn-Edom" in this context is credited to Professor William F. Stinespring: Cresson, "Condemnation," p. 125.
22. Philip J. King, *Jeremiah: An Archaeological Companion* (Louisville: Westminster/John Knox, 1993), pp. 45–47; Rudolf Cohen and Yigal Yisrael, "Smashing the Idols: Piecing Together an Edomite Shrine in Judah," *Biblical Archaeology Review* 22, no. 4 (1996): 40–51; Itzhaq Beit-Arieh, "Edomites Advance into Judah—Israelite Defensive Fortresses Inadequate," *Biblical Archaeology Review* 22, no. 6 (1996): 28–36.
23. 2 Kings 24:2 lists the nations that helped Babylon subdue the rebellion; some ancient manuscripts list Edom in place of Aram. The plot against Babylon is found in Jer. 27:3; the refugee report in Jer. 40:11.
24. Obad. 13; Ezek. 25:12; Joel 3:19; Ezek. 35:5.
25. Obad. 11–12; Ezek. 35:5; Ps. 137:7.
26. John Bright, cited in Bartlett, "Brotherhood," p. 22; Keith N. Schoville, *Biblical Archaeology Review* 20, no. 3 (1994), p. 4; Cresson, "Condemnation," pp. 143, 148; Leslie F. Church, editor, *Commentary on the Whole Bible by Matthew Henry* (Grand Rapids: Zondervan, 1961), p. 1016.

27. Bartlett, *Edom*, pp. 156–57; idem, "Edom and the Fall of Jerusalem, 587 B.C.," *Palestine Exploration Quarterly* 114 (1982), p. 23.
28. Beth Glazier-McDonald, "Edom in the Prophetical Corpus," in Edelman, *You*, pp. 23–32.
29. Jer. 49:13,18,20.
30. Glazier-McDonald, "Edom," pp. 31–32; Bert Dicou, *Edom, Israel's Brother and Antagonist: The Role of Edom in Biblical Prophecy and Story* (Sheffield: Sheffield Academic Press, 1994), pp. 198–204; Peter R. Ackroyd, *Exile and Restoration: A Study of Hebrew Thought of the Sixth Century* B.C. (Philadelphia: Westminster, 1968), p. 224.
31. Isa. 34:1,2,5,6,8; See also Isa. 63:1–6.
32. Florentino G. Martinez, *The Dead Sea Scrolls Translated: The Qumran Texts in English* (New York: E.J. Brill, 1996), p. 95.
33. Ginzberg, *Legends*, volume 5, p. 273, volume 1, p. 315.
34. Ginzberg, *Legends*, volume 1, p. 105, volume 5, pp. 310–11 (Satan); volume 5, p. 320 (land rights); volume 2, p. 231 (wicked plans); volume 5, p. 272 (Edom = Rome); Braude and Kapstein, *Pesikta*, pp. 43–44 (Esau's crimes), p. 482 (requited Edom).
35. Mal. 1:1–4. In the Maccabean period, Judas attacked the "descendants of Esau" in Idumea (1 Macc. 5:3,65).
36. ABD, volume 1, pp. 169–71; Plaut, *Torah*, pp. 511–12. Regarding the presence of Amalek in Samaria, see Diana Edelman, "Saul's Battle Against Amaleq (1 Sam. 15)," *Journal for the Study of the Old Testament* 35 (1986): 71–84. The secondary history (1 Chron. 4:43) suggests that a "remnant" of Amalek escaped extinction until the time of King Hezekiah (727–698 B.C.E.).
37. ABD, volume 1, p. 170; Walter A. Elwell, editor, *Evangelical Commentary on the Bible* (Grand Rapids, Mich.: Baker Book House, 1989), p. 202.
38. Epistle of Barnabas 12:2–3.
39. Braude and Kapstein, *Pesikta*, p. XI; *Enc. Jud.*, volume 5, pp. 773–74; volume 13, p. 1392; volume 14, p. 573.
40. Num. 13: 17–29; 14:39–45.
41. Robert G. Hoerber, editor, *Concordia Self-Study Bible: New International Version* (St. Louis: Concordia Publishing House, 1986), p. 395.
42. 1 Sam. 15:23,33,11,28,29.
43. *Enc. Jud.*, volume 2, p. 341; Plaut, *Torah*, p. 514 (Antiochus, Titus, Hadrian, Hitler); Telushkin, *Wisdom*, pp. 550–51 (A. Eichmann);

Ginzberg, *Legends*, volume 5, p. 272 (Rome); Goldberg, *Why?*, p. 152 (Arabs); Niditch, *War*, pp. 3–4 (Native Americans).

44. Braude and Kapstein, *Pesikta*, pp. XXI, 37–56.
45. Quoted in Plaut, *Torah*, p. 512.
46. Irving Greenberg, "Cloud of Smoke, Pillar of Fire: Judaism, Christianity, and Modernity after the Holocaust," in *Auschwitz: Beginning of a New Era? Reflections on the Holocaust,* edited by Eva Fleischner (New York: K TAVPublishing, 1977), p. 23. Passages in which children are at risk include inter alia Exod. 11:5; Num. 31:17; Deut. 2:34; Josh. 6:21; 2 Kings 8:12; Job 1:19; Ps. 137:9; Isa. 13:16,18; Jer. 49:20; 51:22.
47. Roland H. Bainton, *Christian Attitudes toward War and Peace* (Nashville: Abingdon Press, 1960), pp. 167–69.
48. Schoenhals, *Wesley's*, p. 187.

Chapter 4. Nationalism and Universalism

1. The 25 chapters include 617 verses, of which 77 pertain directly to Israel.
2. Although the OAN loom large in the prophets, the genre is unattractive to many theologians because of its harsh, uncompromising tone. In addition to the standard commentaries and dictionaries, see: John H. Hayes, "The Usage of Oracles Against Foreign Nations in Ancient Israel," *Journal of Biblical Literature* 87 (1968): 81–92; Yair Hoffmann, *The Prophecies against Foreign Nations in the Bible* (Tel-Aviv: Tel-Aviv University, 1977, in Hebrew with English summary); G.R. Hamborg, "Reasons for Judgement in the Oracles Against the Nations of the Prophet Isaiah," *Vetus Testamentum* XXXI (1981): 145–59; John B. Geyer, "Mythology and Culture in the Oracles against the Nations," Vetus Testamentum XXXVI (1986): 129–45; James M. Ward, *Thus Says The* LORD: *The Message of the Prophets* (Nashville: Abingdon Press, 1991).
3. John Barton, *Amos's Oracles against the Nations: A Study of Amos 1.3–2.5* (Cambridge: Cambridge University Press, 1980); Geyer, "Mythology."
4. The Hagrites were a tribe in the Transjordan east of the Israelite territory of Gilead. Gebal is probably an Edomite region known also as Teman.
5. Ward, *Thus Says*, pp. 40–41, 60–61; Hayes, "Usage," p. 92; Walther

Zimmerli, *Ezekiel 2: A Commentary on the Book of the Prophet Ezekiel chapters 25–48* (Philadelphia: Fortress Press, 1983), pp. 3, 5, 324; Norman K. Gottwald, *The Hebrew Bible: A Socio-Literary Introduction* (Philadelphia: Fortress Press, 1987), p. 466; *Harper's Bible Commentary*, p. 684. Though the OAN in Jeremiah now appear at the end of the book, they originally followed 25:13a.

6. HBD, p. 787 (Philistines); NRSV, p. 92 note (Amalekites); Niditch, *War*, p. 54 (Mesha); Cynthia Ozick, "Ruth," in *Congregation: Contemporary Writers Read the Jewish Bible*, edited by David Rosenberg (New York: Harcourt Brace Jovanovich, 1987), p. 365 ("callous, pitiless"); Halpern, *First*, p. 44 ("bovine"); Church, *Matthew Henry*, p. 276 ("bad place," "wicked people").
7. Telushkin, *Literacy*, pp. 75, 86; idem, *Wisdom*, pp. 194, 551.
8. Paul D. Hanson, "War and Peace in the Hebrew Bible," *Interpretation* 38 (1984), p. 351 ("greedy," "hostile and envious"); Church, *Matthew Henry*, p. 1061 ("ill-natured"); William M. Ramsay, *The Westminster Guide to the Books of the Bible* (Louisville: Westminster/John Knox, 1994), p. 216 ("surely deserved").
9. Barton, *Oracles*, pp. 26–31; Barton is a highly regarded scholar and by no means the greatest sinner in this regard. In his recent best-seller, *The Gifts of the Jews* (New York: Doubleday 1998), Thomas Cahill writes engagingly of the contributions of the Israelites to modern culture. Unfortunately, he appears trapped in the ancient "us-them" dichotomy, routinely disparaging the role of the ANE "other." This attitude is captured in his characterization of Yahweh's command to exterminate the Amalekites as one of his "less pretty" directives (p. 176).
10. Greenberg, "Cloud," p. 47 ("fearing God"); Deut. 25:18; Rosemary R. Ruether, "The Faith and Fratricide Discussion: Old Problems and New Dimensions," in *Antisemitism and the Foundations of Christianity*, edited by Alan Davies (New York: Paulist Press, 1979), p. 255.
11. John H. Walton, *Chronological and Background Charts of the Old Testament*, Revised Edition (Grand Rapids: Zondervan, 1994), p. 84. For a more balanced treatment of the ANE peoples and religions, see Jon D. Levenson, "Is There a Counterpart in the Hebrew Bible to New Testament Antisemitism?" *Journal of Ecumenical Studies* 22 (1985): 242–60.
12. Telushkin, *Wisdom*, p. 551; Plaut, *Torah*, p. 514; Alan M. Dershowitz, *Chutzpah* (Boston: Little, Brown, 1991), p. 207; Goldberg, *Why?*, p. 145.
13. Jon 4:11. Useful analyses of the ANE religions may be found in M. Smith, "Common Theology"; Thorkild Jacobsen, *The Treasures of Dark-*

ness: A History of Mesopotamian Religion (New Haven: Yale University Press, 1976); H.W.F. Saggs, *The Encounter with the Divine in Mesopotamia and Israel* (London: Athlone Press, 1978); Bertil Albrektson, *History and the Gods* (Lund, Sweden: Coniectanea Biblica, OT Series 1, 1967).

14. Walter C. Kaiser, Jr., *Toward an Old Testament Theology* (Grand Rapids: Zondervan, 1991), p. 14; Albrektson, *History,* pp.78–81; Walter Brueggemann and Hans W. Wolff, *The Vitality of Old Testament Traditions*, Second Edition, (Atlanta: John Knox, 1982), pp. 46–59; H.H. Rowley, *The Biblical Doctrine of Election* (London: Lutterworth Press, 1950), pp. 65–66.
15. Bruce M. Metzger and Michael D. Coogan, editors, *The Oxford Companion to the Bible* (New York: Oxford University Press, 1993), p. 84–85.
16. Moshe Weinfeld, "The Protest against Imperialism in Ancient Israelite Prophecy," in *The Origins and Diversity of Axial Age Civilizations,* edited by S.N. Eisenstadt (Albany: State University of New York Press, 1986), pp. 176–78.
17. Isa. 7:18; 10:6, 12–13, 15, 18.
18. Ezek. 26:7–14, 20–21; 29:17–20.
19. Compare with Deut. 32:31: "Indeed their rock is not like our Rock."
20. Isa. 46:9; 51:1–2; 40:3.
21. Isa. 41:23; 48:3.
22. Isa. 54:7; 49:15; 41:11.
23. Isa. 40:17 in the pericope 40:12–31; Stephen L. Harris, *Understanding the Bible*, Third Edition (London: Mayfield Publishing, 1992), p. 135.
24. Isa. 43:4.
25. Levenson, "Counterpart," pp. 253–54. Note the form of the divine name "YHWH"; some Jewish scholars fully capitalize the tetragram and do not vocalize it.
26. This verse is quoted favorably in Rom. 14:11 and identified with Jesus in Phil. 2:10–11.
27. Joseph Blenkinsopp, "Second Isaia—hProphet of Universalism," *Journal for the Study of the Old Testament* 41 (1988), p. 89.
28. Sanders, *Judaism*, p. 291.
29. *Harper's Bible Commentary*, p. 561.
30. Herbert G. May, "Theological Universalism in the Old Testament," *Journal of Bible and Religion* 16 (1948), p. 100. For a more realistic appraisal, see John H. Hayes and Stuart A. Irvine, *Isaiah, The Eighth-*

century Prophet: His Times and Preaching (Nashville: Abingdon Press, 1987), pp. 263–66.

31. Alice K. Turner, *The History of Hell* (New York: Harcourt Brace, 1993), p. 4.
32. The tone of the final verse so disturbed some rabbis that they directed that in synagogue readings the preceding verse (v. 23) was to be repeated so that the Book of Isaiah would end on a more uplifting note; *Harper's Bible Commentary*, p. 596.
33. Ezra 9:1–15; 10:1–15; Neh. 13:23–31.
34. HBD, p. 886.
35. Jack Miles, *God: A Biography* (New York: Alfred A. Knopf, 1995), pp.340, 342.
36. Jon. 1:5, 14, 16.
37. Jon. 3:4–9; 4:11.
38. These several arguments are summarized in D.E. Hollenberg, "Nationalism and 'The Nations' in Isaiah XL–LV," *Vetus Testamentum* 19 (1969), pp. 23–25.
39. Norman H. Snaith, "Isaiah 40–66: A Study of the Teaching of the Second Isaiah and Its Consequences" in *Studies on the Second Part of the Book of Isaiah* (Leiden: E.J. Brill, 1977), p. 175; Joseph Blenkinsopp, "Second Isaiah," pp. 88–89.
40. Harry M. Orlinsky, "Nationalism-Universalism and Internationalism in Ancient Israel," in *Translating and Understanding the Old Testament*, edited by Harry T. Frank and William L. Reed (Nashville: Abingdon Press, 1970), pp. 206–07. See also: idem, "Nationalism-Universalism in the Book of Jeremiah," in *Essays in Biblical Culture and Bible Translation* (New York: KTAV Publishing House, 1974); idem, "The So-called 'Servant of the LORD' and 'Suffering Servant' in Second Isaiah," in *Studies on the Second Part of the Book of Isaiah* (Leiden: E.J. Brill, 1977).
41. Orlinsky, "Internationalism," p. 213. Other recent studies utilizing the "us-them" approach include Gary G. Porton, *GOYIM: Gentiles and Israelites in Mishnah-Tosefta* (Atlanta: Scholars Press, 1988) and William R. Hutchison and Hartmut Lehmann, editors, *Many Are Chosen: Divine Election and Western Nationalism* (Minneapolis: Fortress Press, 1994).
42. Orlinsky, "Internationalism," p. 219.
43. Snaith, "Isaiah," p. 159.

The Deuteronomic Hypothesis

1. Gen. 18:25.
2. Lev. 26:12.
3. The sources and age of the covenantal idea in Israel are much debated among scholars; ABD, volume 1, pp. 1179–1202; Harris, *Understanding,* pp. 70–71, 106–07; Ernest W. Nicholson, *God and His People: Covenant and Theology in the Old Testament* (Oxford: Clarendon Press, 1986).
4. Jer. 31:31–34; Ezek. 44:7; Isa 54:7.
5. *Enc. Jud.,* volume 5, pp. 760–82.
6. Deut. 5:9–10; identical language is found in Exod. 20:5–6. In what are considered the "original" versions (Exod. 34:6–7 and Num. 14:18), the qualifications of "reject" and "love" are absent; Joseph Blenkinsopp, "Abraham and the Righteous of Sodom," *Journal of Jewish Studies* 33 (1982), p. 124.
7. The next most detailed exposition of blessings and curses is located in Lev. 26; Deut. 27:15–26 lists curses only.
8. Deut. 28:15. The count of 98 curses is from a rabbinic source cited in Plaut, *Torah*, p. 1523.
9. In the annual cycle of *Torah* readings, some synagogues have arranged for their sextons to read Deut. 28 as part of their official duties. It is read in a lower than normal voice, reflecting an ancient belief that speaking too loudly of misfortune may bring it about; Plaut, *Torah*, p. 1529.
10. Blenkinsopp, "Abraham," pp. 119–32.
11. Gen. 6–8. For a very readable account of the "twice-told" tale of Noah and the Flood, see Richard E. Friedman, *Who Wrote the Bible?* (New York: Summit Books, 1987), pp. 53–60.
12. Exod. 31:18; 32. As an abstract proposition, fashioning "golden calves" as the ultimate in sinfulness seems most unlikely. How these icons were linked to priesthood rivalries between the northern and southern kingdoms is discussed in Friedman, *Who?,* pp. 29–30, 70–76.

    With regard to the change of the divine mind in Exod. 32:14, an NRSV footnote bravely attempts to explain the changeability of an unchangeable God. It declares that God is "not bound inflexibly" to a fixed plan but is "free" to change his mind so long as it is "consistent with the divine purpose" (p. 112).
13. Klaus Koch, "Is There a Doctrine of Retribution in the Old Testament?," in *Theodicy in the Old Testament,* edited by James L. Crenshaw (Phila-

delphia: *Fortress Press,* 1983), pp. 57–87; John G. Gammie, "The Theology of Retribution in the Book of Deuteronomy, " *Catholic Biblical Quarterly* 32 (1970): 1–12.

The "automatic" sequence resembles "magic" in that it runs its course independent of, or in spite of, the controlling supernatural power.

14. Patrick D. Miller, Jr., *Sin and Judgment in the Prophets: A Stylistic and Theological Analysis* (Chico, Calif.: Scholars Press, 1982).
15. Joel S. Kaminsky, "Joshua 7: A Reassessment of Israelite Conceptions of Corporate Punishment," in *The Pitcher Is Broken: Memorial Essays for Gosta W. Ahlstrom,* edited by Steven W. Holloway and Lowell K. Handy (Sheffield: Sheffield Academic Press, 1995), pp. 315–46.
16. Kaminsky, "Joshua 7," p. 324.
17. Quoted in John Hick, *Evil and the God of Love* (New York: Harper and Row, 1966), p. 93.
18. David Birnbaum, *God and Evil: A United Theodicy / Theology / Philosophy* (Hoboken, J.J.: Ktav, 1989); Samuel Terrien, *The Elusive Presence: Toward a New Biblical Theology* (New York: Harper and Row, 1978); Andre Neher, *The Exile of the Word: From the Silence of the Bible to the Silence of Auschwitz* (Philadelphia: Jewish Publication Society of America, 1981); Miles, *God.*
19. Eliade, *Sacred,* pp. 121–22.
20. Richard E. Friedman, *The Disappearance of God: A Divine Mystery* (Boston: Little, Brown, 1995).
21. 1 Kings 11:31–32. The tribe of Benjamin became incorporated into Judah, accounting for the twelve original tribes.
22. 1 Kings 12:28–30; 14:15. Scholars are divided over whether the calves offended Yahweh primarily because they represented other gods, because they violated the second commandment that prohibits the making of idols, or because they defied the Deuteronomist's command to centralize worship in Jerusalem. The northern community undoubtedly viewed the situation differently than did the southern; E. Theodore Mullen, Jr., "The Sins of Jeroboam: A Redactional Assessment," *Catholic Biblical Quarterly* 49 (1987): 212–32; Halpern, *First,* pp. 220–28; Frank M. Cross, *Canaanite Myth and Hebrew Epic: Essays in the History of the Religion of Israel* (Cambridge: Harvard University Press, 1973), p. 75; *Harper's Bible Commentary,* pp. 315–16.
23. Those not tied specifically to the sins of Jeroboam include Elah (883–882), Shallum (747), and Hoshea (732–724).

24. 1 Kings 15:25 (Jeroboam); 1 Kings 16:19 (Zimri); 1 Kings 16:25–26 (Omri); 2 Kings 17:2 (Hoshea).
25. Mullen, "Sins"; Halpern, *First,* pp. 220–28. The total of twenty "kings" includes Athaliah (842–836), the daughter of Ahab, and wife of Jehoram of Judah, who ruled Judah as an unanointed queen.
26. 2 Kings 8:19 (Jehoram); 2 Kings 20:6 (Hezekiah); James A. Wharton, "The Unanswerable Answer: An Interpretation of Job," in *Texts and Testaments: Critical Essays on the Bible and Early Church Fathers*, edited by W. Eugene March (San Antonio: Trinity University Press, 1980), pp. 42–45.
27. 2 Kings 22:20; 23:1–25.
28. 2 Kings 21:11–12; Jer. 15:1–4.
29. Jer. 5:1,9; 11:13; 14:11–12; Ezek. 14:21. Wild animals also appear as instruments in Jer. 5:6; 15:3.
30. Jer. 16:11–12; 32:30–32; 2 Kings 24:20.
31. Ezek. 18:2–4, 20–24, 30; Gordon H. Matties, *Ezekiel 18 and the Rhetoric of Moral Discourse* (Atlanta: Scholars Press, 1990). The "sour grapes" adage is also taken up briefly in Jer. 31:28–30; in Ezek. 14:12–20, it is suggested that even the righteousness of Noah, Daniel, and Job is not transferable. See also: Deut. 24:16; 2 Kings 14:6; 2 Chron. 25:4.
32. Joel S. Kaminsky, *Corporate Responsibility in the Hebrew Bible* (Sheffield: Sheffield Academic Press, 1995); John W. Rogerson, "The Hebrew Conception of Corporate Personality: A Reexamination," in *Anthropological Approaches to the Old Testament*, edited by Bernhard Lang (Philadelphia: Fortress Press, 1985); J. R. Porter, "The Legal Aspects of the Concept of 'Corporate Personality' in the Old Testament," *Vetus Testamentum* 15 (1965), pp. 361–80.
33. William F. Lanahan, "The Speaking Voice in the Book of Lamentations," *Journal of Biblical Literature* 93 (1974): 41–49.
34. Jer. 31:31–34; Ezek. 11:19; 18:31.
35. Jer. 44:15–19.

Chapter 6. Dissent and Its Aftermath

1. The celebrated jurist Alan M. Dershowitz recalls being required as a child to recite Psalm 37:25 several times a day; as an adult he pronounced it "pretty poetry but ugly philosophy"; Alan M. Dershowitz, *Chutzpah* (Boston: Little, Brown, 1991), pp. 131–32.

2. Robert Davidson, *The Courage to Doubt: Exploring an Old Testament Theme* (London: SCM Press, 1983), pp. 31–32.
3. Kushner, *Life!,* p. 209. See also: William Neil, *Can We Trust the Old Testament?* (New York: Seabury Press, 1979), p. 90.
4. David R. Blumenthal, *Facing the Abusing God* (Louisville: Westminster/John Knox Press, 1993), p. 94.
5. William Safire, *The First Dissident: The Book of Job in Today's Politics* (New York: Random House, 1992), pp. XVI, 41; Mettinger, *Search,* p. 175.
6. Marvin H. Pope, *The Anchor Bible: Job* (New York: Doubleday, 1973), pp. LVI–LXXI; Pritchard, *Ancient*, pp. 405–10, 589–91, 596–604. The well–known journalist William Safire has written a provocative book relating Job to the current political scene. Unfortunately, he entitled it *The First Dissident* (see note 5).
7. James 5:11 speaks of the "patience" of Job in the KJV; it becomes "steadfastness" in the RSV and "endurance" in the NRSV.
8. Job 5:17; 11:16. "Discipline" may be distinguished from "punishment" in that the former anticipates reform while the latter implies indifference to change.
9. James L. Crenshaw, *Trembling at the Threshold of a Biblical Text* (Grand Rapids: William B. Eerdmans, 1994), p. 85.
10. Gottwald, *Bible*, p. 576.
11. Leslie Fiedler, "Job," in *Congregation: Contemporary Writers Read the Jewish Bible,* edited by David Rosenberg (New York: Harcourt Brace Jovanovich, 1987), p. 340 ("lies"), p. 334 ("platitudes"); Pope, *Job*, p. XXIX ("sycophany," "clichés").
12. Quoted in Timothy J. Gorringer, "Job and the Pharisees," *Interpretation* 40 (1986), p. 25.
13. HBD, p. 493.
14. Mettinger, *Search*, pp. 178, 180, 198.
15. ABD, volume 3, p. 862; Crenshaw, *Trembling*, pp. 83–87. The phrase "magical assumption" was coined by E. M. Good: J. L. Crenshaw, "Popular Questioning of the Justice of God in Ancient Israel," *Zeitschrift für die alttestamentliche Wissenschaft* 82 (1970), p. 393.
16. Roger Schmidt, *Exploring Religion*, Second Edition (Belmont, Cal.: Wadsworth Publishing, 1988), pp. 106–07.
17. Pope, *Job,* p. LXXXI.
18. HBD, p. 493.
19. Pope, *Job,* p. LXXX ("discredited"); Margaret B. Crook, *The Cruel God:*

Job's Search for the Meaning of Suffering (Boston: Beacon Press, 1959), p. 197 ("adolescence").

20. Bruce C. Birch, *Let Justice Roll Down: The Old Testament, Ethics, and Christian Life* (Louisville: Westminster/John Knox Press, 1991), p. 343 ("bankruptcy"); Harris, *Understanding,* p. 174 ("intellectual"); Pope, *Job,* p. LXXVII ("once").
21. Safire, *First*, pp. 65, 73.
22. Crenshaw, *Trembling*, p. 86.
23. Friedman, *Disappearance*, pp. 173, 193, 209–10; Moises Silva, "Contemporary Theories of Biblical Interpretation" in *The New Interpreter's Bible*, Volume 1, p. 117.
24. Cross, *Canaanite Myth*, pp. 343–46; Friedman, *Disappearance*; Miles, *God.*
25. David Penchansky, *The Betrayal of God: Ideological Conflict in Job* (Louisville: Westminster/John Knox Press, 1990), pp. 83–84.
26. Quoted in Sara Japhet, *The Ideology of the Book of Chronicles and Its Place in Biblical Thought* (Frankfurt: Peter Lang, 1989), p. 150.
27. Japhet, *Ideology*, pp. 162–67.
28. Eccles. 7:18; 8:12–13; 12:13.
29. Eccles. 3:16–22; 7:15–18; 8:14; 11:9.
30. Eccles. 1:2; 8:15 (KJV).
31. Sir. 2:10; 39:28–34; James L. Crenshaw, "The Problem of Theodicy in Sirach: On Human Bondage," in *Theodicy in the Old Testament,* edited by idem (Philadelphia: Fortress Press, 1983), pp. 119–40.
32. Schiffman, *Reclaiming,* pp. 85, 148, 263, 296 (past); 119, 153–57, 250, 270 (present); 153–57, 317, 329–33, 380–82 (future); 163 (Job).
33. NRSV, p. 865.
34. Raymund Schwager, *Must There Be Scapegoats? Violence and Redemption in the Bible* (San Francisco: Harper and Row, 1987), p. 55.
35. RSV, p. 263; the statement does not appear in the NRSV.

    In a similar vein, former President Jimmy Carter, a devout Christian, recently admitted that he found it "impossible to imagine" Jesus issuing the orders to Saul to exterminate the Amalekites (1 Sam. 15); *Sources of Strength* (New York: Times Books, 1997), p. 227.
36. Hermann Gunkel, *What Remains of the Old Testament and Other Essays* (New York: MacMillan, 1928, originally published in 1914), pp. 44–45.
37. ABD, volume 2, pp. 1041–48; Childs, *Biblical*, 1993), p. 373; Phyllis Tri-

ble, *Texts of Terror* (Minneapolis: Fortress Press, 1984), p. 2; Niditch, *War*, p. 5. See also: Ramsay, *Westminster,* pp. 10–11.

38. In the NT, outside the Book of Revelation, God speaks without intermediary only at Jesus' baptism and transfiguration.
39. The United Presbyterian Confession of 1967, quoted in W. Sibley Towner, *How God Deals with Evil* (Philadelphia: Westminster Press, 1976), p. 88.
40. Pope, *Job,* p. LXXVII.
41. Additional passages conveying the same message include: Exod. 4:11; Josh. 23:15; 1 Sam. 2:25; 2 Kings 5:7; Job 1:21; 2:10; 5:18; Prov. 16:4; Isa. 1:19–20; 41:23; Jer. 1:10; Hos. 6:1; Amos 3:6; Hab. 3:5; Wisdom 18:15–19.
42. Matt. 24:1–3; Mark 13:2; Luke 21:5–7, etc.

Chapter 7. The Afterlife Solution

1. If Malachi were written in the fifth century B.C.E. as generally assumed, the chronological gap would be about five hundred years. Other OT books, such as Esther, Ecclesiastes and Daniel, were written after Malachi. In the Roman Catholic canon 1 and 2 Maccabees follow Malachi.
2. ABD, volume 5, p. 680.
3. Davidson, *Courage*, p. 27.
4. Telushkin, *Wisdom*, pp. 276–77; Dennis Prager, talk-show host, KABC, Los Angeles, December 19, 1994.
5. Lloyd R. Bailey, Sr., *Biblical Perspectives on Death* (Philadelphia: Fortress Press, 1979), pp. 48–61; Bruce Vawter, "Intimations of Immortality and the Old Testament," *Journal of Biblical Literature* 91 (1972): 158–71; ABD, volume 2, pp.108–10; volume 5, p. 680.
6. Bailey, *Perspectives*, pp. 28–36; ABD, volume 2, pp. 105–08.
7. ABD, volume 2, pp. 102–05; volume 3, pp.14–15; volume 5, pp.680–81.
8. ABD, volume 2, p. 102.
9. Bailey, *Perspectives,* p. 6; ABD, volume 1, p. 834; S.G.F. Brandon, *The Judgment of the Dead: The Idea of Life after Death in the Major Religions* (New York: Charles Scribner's Sons, 1967), pp. 49–55.
10. Brandon, *Judgment*, pp.20–28.
11. ABD, volume 1, pp. 279–88; Paul D. Hanson, *The Dawn of the Apocalyptic: The Historical and Sociological Roots of Jewish Apocalyptic Escha-*

tology (Philadelphia: Fortress Press, 1979); idem, *Old Testament Apocalyptic* (Nashville: Abingdon Press, 1987); John J. Collins, *The Apocalyptic Imagination: An Introduction to the Jewish Matrix of Christianity* (New York: Crossroad, 1984), pp. 1–32.

12. 1 En. 18:2,3,5; 19:3; 22:6–8; Collins, *Imagination,* pp. 38–46; George W.E. Nickelsburg, Jr., *Resurrection, Immortality, and Eternal Life in Intertestamental Judaism* (Cambridge: Harvard University Press, 1972), pp. 134–37.
13. Nickelsburg, *Resurrection,* pp. 124–26; idem, "Riches, the Rich, and God's Judgment in 1 Enoch 92–105 and the Gospel According to Luke," *New Testament Studies* 25 (1979):324–44.
14. Daniel 11:31; ABD, volume 5, pp. 682–83.
15. Nickelsburg, *Resurrection,* pp. 18–19.
16. Quoted in ABD, volume 5, p. 683.
17. Nickelsburg, *Resurrection,* pp. 173–74.
18. Hans C.C. Cavallin, *Life after Death: Paul's Argument for the Resurrection of the Dead in 1 Cor. 15,* Part I (Lund, Sweden: CWK Gleerup, 1974), p. 126.
19. Nickelsburg, *Resurrection,* pp. 166–67.
20. Cavallin, *Life,* p. 88.
21. Ibid., p. 201.
22. George W.E. Nickelsburg, *Jewish Literature between the Bible and the Mishnah: A Historical and Literary Introduction* (Philadelphia: Fortress Press, 1981), p. 290.
23. Ibid., pp. 293–94.
24. The other two passages are Job 1–2 and Zech. 3:1–2. In Num. 22:21–35, the angel of the LORD confronts the seer Balaam as his "adversary" (vv. 22,32).
25. Harry E. Gaylord, "How Satanael lost his '-el'," *Journal of Jewish Studies* 33 (1982): 303–09; Life of Adam and Eve 14:3; ABD, volume 5, p. 987.
26. ABD, volume 5, pp. 987–88. Elaine Pagels makes a persuasive case that Satan came to represent especially conflict within Israel—and by inference within its God—as the "intimate" enemy: "The Social History of Satan, the 'Intimate Enemy': A Preliminary Sketch," *Harvard Theological Review* 84 (1991): 105–28; idem, *The Origin of Satan* (New York: Random House, 1995).
27. Ginzberg, *Legends,* volume 5, p. 311; *Enc. Jud.,* volume 8, pp. 1318–19.
28. Jacob Neusner, *What Is Midrash?* (Philadelphia: Fortress Press, 1987), pp. 95–101.

29. E.P. Sanders, "The Covenant as a Soteriological Category and the Nature of Salvation in Palestinian and Hellenistic Judaism," in *Jews, Greeks and Christians: Religious Cultures in Late Antiquity,* edited by Robert Hamerton-Kelly and Robin Scroggs (Leiden: E.J. Brill, 1976), p. 41.
30. Ibid., pp.40–41.
31. Ibid., p. 42.
32. David Novak, *The Image of the Non-Jew in Judaism: An Historical and Constructive Study of the Noahide Laws* (New York: Edwin Mellen Press, 1983); idem, *Jewish-Christian Dialogue: A Jewish Justification* (New York: Oxford University Press, 1989), pp. 26–41.
33. Novak, *Image*; *Enc. Jud.,* volume 12, pp. 1189–91; Plaut, *Torah,* p. 1519. A truncated form of the Laws appears in Acts 15:19–20 as the "apostolic decree."
34. Aaron Lichtenstein, *The Seven Laws of Noah,* Second Edition (New York: Z. Berman Books, 1986), pp. 89–91.
35. Elliot N. Dorff, "A Jewish Theology of Jewish Relations to Other Peoples," in *People of God, Peoples of God: A Jewish- Christian Conversation in Asia,* edited by Hans Ucko (Geneva: WCC Publications, 1996), p. 56.
36. Steven S. Schwarzschild, "Do Noachites Have to Believe in Revelation?" *Jewish Quarterly Review* 52 (1961–62), p. 297.
37. *Enc. Jud.,* volume 11, p. 754.
38. Isadore Twersky, editor, *A Maimonides Reader* (West Orange, N.J.: Behrman House, 1972), p. 221; Schwarzschild, "Noachites," pp. 299–301.
39. Steven S. Schwarzschild, "Do Noachites Have to Believe in Revelation?", *Jewish Quarterly Review* 53 (1961–62), pp. 64–65.
40. Wilhelm Vischer, *The Witness of the Old Testament to Christ* (London: Lutterworth Press, 1949), p. 99.
41. Rosemary R. Ruether, *Faith and Fratricide: The Theological Roots of Anti-Semitism* (New York: Seabury Press, 1974), p. 236.
42. Norman Solomon, "Faith in the Midst of Faiths: Traditional Jewish Attitudes," in Ucko, *People,* p. 89.
43. Jacob Neusner, *Jews and Christians: The Myth of a Common Tradition* (Philadelphia: Trinity Press International, 1991), pp. 110–11.
44. In modern scholarship, the eschatological and judgmental dimensions of the text are often downplayed or ignored; see Richards H. Hiers, *Jesus and the Future: Unresolved Questions for Understanding and Faith*

(Atlanta: John Knox Press, 1981); ABD, volume 2, pp. 79–82. Pope John Paul II laments the insensitivity of the modern believer to "Last Things" and reaffirms the belief of the Roman Catholic Church in the traditional judgmental afterlife, in *Crossing the Threshold of Hope* (New York: Alfred A. Knopf, 1994), pp. 178–87.

45. D. Moody Smith, Jr., "The Use of the Old Testament in the New," in *The Use of the Old Testament in the New and Other Essays*, edited by James M. Efird (Durham, N.C.: Duke University Press, 1972), p. 61.
46. Brandon, *Judgment,* pp. 98–135; Simon Tugwell, *Human Immortality and the Redemption of Death* (London: Darton, Longman and Todd, 1990); James Barr, *The Garden of Eden and the Hope of Immortality* (Minneapolis: Fortress Press, 1993).
47. Tugwell, *Immortality*, pp. 125–155.
48. Ibid., p. 131.
49. Schechter, *Aspects*, p. 307.
50. Idem, *Studies in Judaism* (New York: Macmillan, 1920, first published 1896), p. 220.
51. Ibid., p. 226.
52. Jacob Neusner, "Four Responses to Catastrophe in Formative Judaism," in *Faith Renewed: The Judaic Affirmation Beyond the Holocaust*, edited by Jacob Neusner (Macon, Ga.: Mercer University Press, 1994), p. 19.
53. Norman Lamm, *The Face of God: Thoughts on the Holocaust* (New York: Yeshiva University, 1986), p. 2.
54. James H. Charlesworth, "The Triumphant Majority as Seen by a Dwindled Minority: The Outsider according to the Insider of the Jewish Apocalypses, 70–130," in *"To See Ourselves As Others See Us": Christians, Jews, "Others" in Late Antiquity,* edited by Jacob Neusner and Ernest S. Frerichs (Chico, Cal,: Scholars Press, 1985), p. 314.
55. Matt. 23:37–39; 24:1–2; etc.
56. John C. Fitzpatrick, editor, *The Writings of George Washington,* volume 35 (Washington: United States Government, 1940), p. 231.
57. Ruether, *Faith,* see especially pp. 95, 134, 185–86, 196, 205.
58. Jonathan Sacks, "The Holocaust in the Context of Judaism" in Neuser, *Faith,* p. 40.
59. World Council of Churches, *The Theology of the Churches and the Jewish People: Statements by the World Council of Churches and Its Member Churches* (Geneva: WCC Publications, 1988); James Limburg, *Judaism: An Introduction for Christians* (Minneapolis: Augsburg,

1987), pp. 235–55; W. Eugene March, editor, *A Theological Understanding of the Relationship Between Christians and Jews* (Louisville: Presbyterian Church, 1987).

60. Lamm, *Face*, pp. 2–4; Dershowitz, *Chutzpah,* p. 132 note; Sacks "Holocaust," p. 40.
61. Ibid., p. 40.
62. Lamm, *Face,* pp. 4–5.
63. A. Roy Eckardt, "The Recantation of the Covenant?" in *Confronting the Holocaust: The Impact of Elie Wiesel,* edited by Alvin H. Rosenfeld and Irving Greenberg (Bloomington: Indiana University Press, 1978), p. 161; idem, "Salient Christian-Jewish Issues of Today: A Christian Exploration," in *Jews and Christians: Exploring the Past, Present, and Future,* edited by James H. Charlesworth (New York: Crossroad, 1990), pp. 151–84.
64. For the record, I personally do not believe for a millisecond that Jewish sin caused so much as one death among the Holocaust's six million victims. The argument is made entirely as a deduction—actually the most reasonable deduction—from the principles enunciated in the biblical text.

Chapter 8. The Ghost of Marcion

1. R. Joseph Hoffmann, *Marcion: On the Restitution of Christianity* (Chico, Cal.: Scholars Press, 1984); E.C. Blackman, *Marcion and His Influence* (London: SPCK, 1948); John Knox, *Marcion and the New Testament: An Essay in the Early History of the Canon* (Chicago: University of Chicago Press, 1942); Gonzalez, "How the Bible," in *The New Interpreter's Bible,* Volume 1, pp. 84–86; ABD, volume 4, pp. 514–16.
2. David P. Efroymson, "The Patristic Connection," in *Antisemitism and the Foundations of Christianity,* edited by Alan Davies (New York: Paulist Press, 1979), pp. 98–117.
3. Blackman, *Marcion,* pp. 48, 102.
4. ABD, volume 4, p. 515.
5. Willis Barnstone, editor, *The Other Bible* (San Francisco: Harper and Row, 1984), p. 645.
6. Hoffmann, *Marcion,* p. XI.
7. Hoffmann, *Marcion,* p. 1.
8. Quoted in Efroymson, "Patristic," p. 110.

9. Ibid., p. 112.
10. Ruether, *Faith,* p. 133.
11. Stephen G. Wilson, "Marcion and the Jews," in *Anti-Judaism in Early Christianity,* edited by Stephen G. Wilson (Waterloo, Ontario: Canadian Corporation for Studies in Religion, 1986), pp. 45–58.
12. KJV; "young woman" in NRSV.
13. Quoted in Ben Zion Bokser, *Judaism and the Christian Predicament* (New York: Alfred A. Knopf, 1967), p. 34.
14. ABD, volume 2, p. 434. For a recent study on "Biblical Theology" by a leading proponent, see Childs, *Biblical*; a more critical position is taken by John J. Collins in "Is a Critical Biblical Theology Possible?" in *The Hebrew Bible and Its Interpreters,* edited by William H. Propp, Baruch Halpern, and David N. Freedman (Winona Lake, Ind.: Eisenbrauns, 1990), pp. 1–17.
15. ABD, volume 6, p. 471.
16. Carl Michalson, "Bultmann against Marcion" in *The Old Testament and Christian Faith: A Theological Discussion,* edited by Bernhard W. Anderson (New York: Harper and Row, 1963), p. 62.
17. Birch, *Justice,* p. 17.
18. World Council of Churches, *Theology*, p. 157.
19. ABD, volume 4, p. 516.
20. Lawrence E. Toombs, "The Problematic of Preaching from the Old Testament," *Interpretation* 23 (1969), p. 302.
21. Gonzalez, "Bible," p. 84.
22. Neil, *Trust?,* p. 123.
23. Toombs, "Problematic," p. 303.
24. Elizabeth Achtemeier, *Preaching from the Old Testament* (Louisville: Westminster/John Knox Press, 1989), pp. 11–22.
25. Achtemeier, *Preaching,* p. 25.
26. Quoted in Vischer, *Witness,* p. 34.
27. Tanakh is an acronym derived from the three divisions of the Hebrew Bible: Torah (law or instruction), Nevi'im (prophets), and Kethuvim (writings).
28. Rudolf Bultmann, "The Significance of the Old Testament for the Christian Faith," orig. publ. 1933, in Anderson, *Old Testament,* p. 32; Neil, *Trust?,* pp. 104–06.
29. Plaut, *Torah,* p. XXIX. In his *What Is Scripture? A Comparative Approach* (Minneapolis: Fortress, 1993) Wilfred Cantwell Smith ana-

lyzes the relative historical roles of Torah, Bible, Mishnah, Talmud, and Scripture in Judaism (see esp. pp.92–123).

30. Isaac Unterman, *The Jewish Holidays,* Second Edition (New York: Bloch Publishing, 1950), pp. 197–98.
31. Plaut, *Torah,* p. XVIII.
32. Kushner, *Life!,* p. 39.
33. Clark M. Williamson, *A Guest in the House of Israel: Post-Holocaust Church Theology* (Louisville: Westminster/John Knox Press, 1993).
34. Gerhard von Rad, "Typological Interpretation of the Old Testament," *Interpretation* 15 (1961), p. 189.
35. Ibid., pp. 189–90.
36. World Council of Churches, *Theology.*

    In his recent monumental *Theology of the Old Testament: Testimony, Dispute, Advocacy,* the Christian theologian Walter Brueggemann declares forthrightly that the OT is "not a witness to Jesus Christ, in any primary or direct sense" nor does it "narrowly or resolutely" point to Jesus; (Minneapolis: Fortress, 1997), pp. 107, 109.
37. Bokser, *Predicament,* pp. 25–35; Neusner, *Myth,* pp. 23, 28. The issue of Jewish conversion continues to receive a mixed response among mainline Protestant denominations. In 1996, the largest Protestant denomination in the United States, the Southern Baptists, issued a renewed call to convert Jews. But in the same year, the United Methodists affirmed in general conference their policy of emphasizing dialogue and understanding rather than conversion.
38. Limburg, *Judaism*, pp. 246–47.
39. John Paul II, *Crossing the Threshold of Hope* (New York: Alfred A. Knopf, 1994), pp. 99–100.
40. Achtemeier, *Preaching,* p. 26.
41. Jon D. Levenson, "Ezekiel in the Perspective of Two Commentators," *Interpretation* 38 (1984), p. 211.
42. Ibid.
43. Michael Goldberg, "God, Action, and Narrative: *Which* Narrative? *Which* Action? Which God?," *Journal of Religion* 68 (1988), p. 40.
44. Ibid., p. 48. See also idem, *Jews and Christians, Getting Our Stories Straight: The Exodus and the Passion-Resurrection* (Nashville: Abingdon Press, 1985).
45. Norman Perrin, *The Promise of Bultmann* (Philadelphia: J.B. Lippincott, 1969), p. 10.
46. Bultmann, "Significance," p. 33.

47. Ibid., pp. 17, 29–32.
48. Terence E. Fretheim, *The Suffering of God* (Philadelphia: Fortress Press, 1984), p. 1.
49. Ibid., p. 2.
50. Robin Scroggs, "The Bible as Foundational Document," *Interpretation* 49 (1995): 17–30.

Appendix B. Theodicy

1. *Topeka Capital-Journal,* March 29, 1994; CBS-TV Morning News, February 27, 1995.
2. In this study, the attributes of "omniscience" and "omnipresence" are subsumed under "omnipotence."

   In Archibald MacLeish's play, *J.B.,* the problem is posed as follows:

   If God is God [omnipotent] He is not good.
   If God Is good He is not God [omnipotent].

   Quoted in Miles, *God,* p. 321.
3. Harold S. Kushner, *When Bad Things Happen to Good People* (New York: Schocken Books, 1981), p. 7. See also: Towner, *God,* p. 12.
4. Fretheim, *Suffering.*
5. Crenshaw, *Trembling,* pp. 26–27.
6. Jon D. Levenson, *Creation and the Persistence of Evil: The Jewish Drama of Divine Omnipotence* (San Francisco: Harper and Row, 1988).
7. Birnbaum, *God and Evil.* See also: Friedman, *Disappearance.*
8. Lamm, *Face.*
9. A. van de Beek, *Why? On Suffering, Guilt, and God* (Grand Rapids: William B. Eerdmans Publishing, 1990), pp. 263, 265.
10. Gonzalez, "Bible," p. 90.
11. Quoted in John H. Hick, *Philosophy of Religion,* Fourth Edition (Englewood Cliffs, N.J.: Prentice Hall, 1990), p. 42.
12. *Larry King Live,* CNN-TV, June 29, 1995.
13. Hans Schwarz, *Evil: A Historical and Theological Perspective* (Minneapolis: Fortress Press, 1995), pp. 207, 211.
14. John Hick, *Evil and the God of Love* (New York: Harper and Row, 1966), pp. 395, 397, 399; idem, *Death and Eternal Life* (New York: Harper and Row, 1976). Useful critiques of Hick's theodicy are found in: C. Robert

Mesle, *John Hick's Theodicy: A Process Humanist Critique* (New York: St. Martin's Press, 1991) and Harold Hewitt, Jr., editor, *Problems in the Philosophy of Religion: Critical Studies of the Work of John Hick* (New York: St. Martin's Press, 1991). See also: Al Truesdale, *If God is God, Then Why? Letters from Oklahoma City* (Kansas City, MO: Beacon Hill Press of Kansas City, 1997.

15. Davidson, *Courage,* pp. 17, 36.
16. Dennis Prager, *Think a Second Time* (New York: Harper Collins, 1995), pp. 244–46.
17. James A. Sanders, *Canon and Community: A Guide to Canonical Criticism* (Philadelphia: Fortress Press, 1984), pp. 57–60.
18. Fyodor Dostoevsky, *The Brothers Karamazov* (San Francisco: North Point Press, 1990), pp. 244–245.
19. Frederick Sontag, *God, Why Did You Do That?* (Philadelphia: Westminster Press, 1970), pp. 19, 34, 44, 165; idem, *The God of Evil: An Argument from the Existence of the Devil* (New York: Harper and Row, 1970), p. 94.
20. Blumenthal, *Facing,* pp. 247, 249, 251, 262, 263.
21. Ibid., pp. 285, 291.
22. Ibid., p. 299.

Index